American Cinema of the 2000s

SCREEN
DECADES

AMERICAN CULTURE / AMERICAN CINEMA

Each volume in the Screen Decades: American Culture/American Cinema series presents a group of original essays analyzing the impact of cultural issues on the cinema and the impact of the cinema in American society. Because every chapter explores a spectrum of particularly significant motion pictures and the broad range of historical events in one year, readers will gain a continuing sense of the decade as it came to be depicted on movie screens across the continent. The integration of historical and cultural events with the sprawling progression of American cinema illuminates the pervasive themes and the essential movies that define an era. Our series represents one among many possible ways of confronting the past; we hope that these books will offer a better understanding of the connections between American culture and film history.

LESTER D. FRIEDMAN AND MURRAY POMERANCE
SERIES EDITORS

André Gaudreault, editor, *American Cinema, 1890–1909: Themes and Variations*

Charlie Keil and Ben Singer, editors, *American Cinema of the 1910s: Themes and Variations*

Lucy Fischer, editor, *American Cinema of the 1920s: Themes and Variations*

Ina Rae Hark, editor, *American Cinema of the 1930s: Themes and Variations*

Wheeler Winston Dixon, editor, *American Cinema of the 1940s: Themes and Variations*

Murray Pomerance, editor, *American Cinema of the 1950s: Themes and Variations*

Barry Keith Grant, editor, *American Cinema of the 1960s: Themes and Variations*

Lester D. Friedman, editor, *American Cinema of the 1970s: Themes and Variations*

Stephen Prince, editor, *American Cinema of the 1980s: Themes and Variations*

Chris Holmlund, editor, *American Cinema of the 1990s: Themes and Variations*

Timothy Corrigan, editor, *American Cinema of the 2000s: Themes and Variations*

American Cinema of the
2000s

Themes and Variations

EDITED BY

TIMOTHY CORRIGAN

RUTGERS UNIVERSITY PRESS
NEW BRUNSWICK, NEW JERSEY, AND LONDON

LIBRARY OF CONGRESS CATALOGING-IN-PUBLICATION DATA

American cinema of the 2000s : themes and variations / edited by Timothy Corrigan.
    p.   cm. — (Screen decades)
  Includes bibliographical references and index.
  ISBN   978–0–8135–5281–1   (hardcover : alk. paper)
  ISBN   978–0–8135–5282–8   (pbk. : alk. paper)
  ISBN   978–0–8135–5323–8   (e-book)
  1. Motion pictures—United States—History—21st century.   2. Motion pictures—
United States—Plots, themes, etc.   I. Corrigan, Timothy.
  PN1993.5.U6A85795   2012
    791.43097309'05—dc23

                                                            2011033051

A British Cataloging-in-Publication record for this book is available from the British
Library.

Visit our Web site: http://rutgerspress.rutgers.edu

Manufactured in the United States of America

CONTENTS

ACKNOWLEDGMENTS

I would like to thank the ten contributors to this volume for their patience, care, and intelligence in preparing this book. I am also grateful for the support of Lester Friedman, Murray Pomerance, Leslie Mitchner, and all the professionals at Rutgers University Press, particularly Eric Schramm for his superb copyediting. My colleagues and students at Penn have been the foundation for my research and the writing of this book, while my immediate and extended families have made the last decade as rich as it was complex.

T I M E L I N E

The 2000s

■ 2000

22 APRIL   In a predawn raid, federal agents seize six-year-old Elián González from his relatives' home in Miami, Florida, and fly him to his Cuban father in Washington, D.C., ending one of the most publicized custody battles in U.S. history.

5 JUNE   *405 The Movie*, the first short film widely distributed on the Internet, is released.

6–8 SEPTEMBER   World leaders attend the Millennium Summit at the United Nations.

7 NOVEMBER   Hillary Rodham Clinton is elected to the U.S. Senate, becoming the first First Lady of the United States to win public office.

13 DECEMBER   *Bush v. Gore*: The U.S. Supreme Court stops the Florida recount, effectively giving the state, and the presidency, to George W. Bush.

■ 2001

1 JANUARY   A black monolith measuring approximately nine feet tall appears in Seattle's Magnuson Park, placed by an anonymous artist in reference to the movie *2001: A Space Odyssey*.

11 JANUARY   The U.S. Federal Trade Commission approves the merger of America Online and TimeWarner to form AOL TimeWarner.

20 JANUARY   George W. Bush succeeds Bill Clinton, becoming the 43rd president of the United States.

11 JUNE   In Terre Haute, Indiana, Timothy McVeigh is executed for the Oklahoma City bombing of 1995.

2 JULY   The world's first self-contained artificial heart is implanted in Robert Tools at Jewish Hospital in Louisville.

11 SEPTEMBER   Almost 3,000 are killed in attacks at the World Trade Center in New York City, the Pentagon in Arlington, Virginia, and in rural Shanksville, Pennsylvania, after American Airlines Flight 11 and United Airlines Flight 175 crash into the World Trade Center's Twin Towers, American Airlines Flight 77 crashes into the Pentagon, and United Airlines Flight 93 crashes into a grassland in Shanksville.

18 SEPTEMBER	The 2001 anthrax attacks commence as letters containing anthrax spores are mailed from Princeton, New Jersey, to ABC News, CBS News, NBC News, the *New York Post*, and the *National Enquirer*. Twenty-two people are exposed; five die.
23 OCTOBER	Apple Inc. launches the iPod.
26 OCTOBER	In response to threats of terrorism, President Bush signs the Patriot Act into law, increasing the powers of law enforcement to search private records and monitor communication networks.

2002

8 JANUARY	The No Child Left Behind Act, which mandates standards and testing as part of educational reform, becomes federal law.
1 FEBRUARY	Kidnapped *Wall Street Journal* reporter Daniel Pearl is murdered in Karachi, Pakistan.
1 MARCH	The U.S. invasion of Afghanistan begins in the eastern part of the country with Operation Anaconda.
7 MAY	Gay Canadian teenager Marc Hall is granted a court injunction ordering that he be allowed to attend his high school prom with his boyfriend.
22 MAY	A jury in Birmingham, Alabama, convicts former Ku Klux Klan member Bobby Frank Cherry of the 1963 murders of four girls in the 16th Street Baptist Church bombing.
1 JULY	The International Criminal Court is established to prosecute individuals for genocide, crimes against humanity, war crimes, and the crime of aggression. Crimes committed on or after this date may be prosecuted by the court.

2003

1 FEBRUARY	At the conclusion of the STS-107 mission, the space shuttle *Columbia* disintegrates during reentry over Texas, killing all seven astronauts on board.
12 MARCH	The World Health Organization (WHO) issues a global alert on severe acute respiratory syndrome.
20 MARCH	Land troops from the United States, United Kingdom, Australia, and Poland invade Iraq.
9 APRIL	U.S. forces seize control of Baghdad, ending the regime of Saddam Hussein.
24 OCTOBER	The Concorde makes its last commercial flight, bringing the era of airliner supersonic travel to a close, at least for the time being.

17 NOVEMBER	Actor Arnold Schwarzenegger is sworn in as governor of California following the recall of the incumbent governor.
13 DECEMBER	Saddam Hussein is captured in Tikrit by the U.S. 4th Infantry Division.

2004

3 FEBRUARY	The CIA admits that there was no imminent threat from weapons of mass destruction before the 2003 invasion of Iraq.
4 FEBRUARY	Facebook is founded in Cambridge, Massachusetts.
12 MAY	An American civilian contractor in Iraq, Nick Berg, is shown on a web-distributed video being decapitated by a group allegedly linked to al-Qaeda.
17 MAY	Massachusetts legalizes same-sex marriage in compliance with a ruling from the state's Supreme Judicial Court.
2 NOVEMBER	President George W. Bush defeats Senator John Kerry to win a second term as president. Republicans make gains in the House and Senate.

2005

15 FEBRUARY	YouTube goes online.
2 APRIL	Pope John Paul II dies; over 4 million people travel to the Vatican to mourn him. Pope Benedict XVI succeeds him the next month.
31 MAY	W. Mark Felt is confirmed to be "Deep Throat," the *Washington Post*'s secret source whose information led to the downfall of the Nixon administration.
2 JULY	Live 8, a set of ten simultaneous concerts, takes place throughout the world, raising interest in the Make Poverty History campaign.
30 AUGUST	Hurricane Katrina leaves thousands dead and many others without homes in the Mississippi delta region.

2006

16 MARCH	The Blu-ray disc format is released in the United States.
1 MAY	The Great American Boycott takes place across the United States as marchers protest for immigration rights.
31 JULY	Cuban president Fidel Castro temporarily relinquishes power to his brother Raúl before surgery.
17 NOVEMBER	PlayStation 3 is released in North America.
30 DECEMBER	Saddam Hussein is executed in Baghdad.

2007

4 JANUARY Nancy Pelosi becomes the first female Speaker of the U.S. House of Representatives.

9 JANUARY Apple Inc. announces and introduces the iPhone at the Macworld Conference & Expo.

16 APRIL Thirty-two people are killed in a massacre on the campus of Virginia Tech in Blacksburg, Virginia.

3 MAY The U.S. House of Representatives passes the Matthew Shepard Act. It is the first time that the House brings a gay rights bill to the floor for a vote.

21 JULY The final book of the Harry Potter series, *Harry Potter and the Deathly Hallows*, is released and sells over 11 million copies in the first twenty-four hours, becoming the fastest-selling book in history.

5 NOVEMBER The Writers Guild of America goes on a strike that lasts until 12 February 2008.

2008

2 JANUARY The price of petroleum hits $100 per barrel for the first time.

15 SEPTEMBER The investment bank Lehman Brothers files for Chapter 11 bankruptcy protection.

3 OCTOBER Global financial crisis: President George W. Bush signs the revised Emergency Economic Stabilization Act into law, creating a $700 billion Treasury fund to purchase failing bank assets.

4 NOVEMBER Senator Barack Obama is elected president, defeating Senator John McCain.

2009

20 JANUARY Barack Obama is inaugurated as the 44th president of the United States, the first African American to hold the office.

22 JANUARY President Obama signs an order to close the Guantanamo Bay detention camp within one year.

1 JUNE Air France Flight 447 from Rio de Janeiro to Paris disappears from radar over the Atlantic Ocean.

1 JUNE General Motors files for government-assisted Chapter 11 bankruptcy protection.

1 JUNE Conan O'Brien becomes the fifth host of *The Tonight Show*; Will Ferrell is his first guest.

American Cinema of the 2000s

In *The Matrix Reloaded* (Andy and Lana Wachowski, Warner Bros., 2003), a decade expands its frontiers to explore not only outer space but also cyberspace and inner space. Digital frame enlargement.

INTRODUCTION

Movies and the 2000s

TIMOTHY CORRIGAN

In 1968, Stanley Kubrick's film *2001: A Space Odyssey* eerily envisioned a new millennium obsessively driven by technology and violence. Before the arrival of that millennium, Kubrick's film described an epic space journey that begins with the prehistoric discovery of crude weapons that would develop and drive human history through many centuries of exploration and conquest. Linking the past and future with a famous match-on-action edit that transforms a prehistoric club into a sleek twenty-first-century space ship, the film tells the tale of an intergalactic quest for a mysterious monolith, a quest that concludes when the ship and its astronauts become waylaid by an animated computer gone bad and bent on destroying the human crew. *2001* concludes with the image of an embryo floating in space, announcing an ambiguous new age about to be born out of cycles of intellectual discovery and human brutality.

When that year 2001 actually arrived, a different apocalyptic violence stunned the world as al-Qaeda terrorists crashed two hijacked jet airliners into the Twin Towers in New York City. As a darkly ironic reminder of Kubrick's film, witnesses of those shocking images, either on the streets of Lower Manhattan or as television viewers around the world, stated that the crash of the airliners and the crumbling of the towers was "like a movie." Reflecting this uneasy and uncanny merging of film history and historical catastrophe, the first decade of the 2000s became defined by revolutions of seen and unseen violence, of astonishing and threatening technologies, of cultural and political conquests and reversals, and of a wavering humanity within inhumane worlds. In this decade, new communicative technologies, from Internet news to cell phone tweets, moved more rapidly than ever, almost with a life of their own. In this decade, new speeds drove a cultural and political impatience that continually demands cycles of change that hardly progress. In this decade, American films and film genres, like *2001* as 2001, cyclically and centrifugally intersected with social and political worlds, giving birth to new visions, invariably stretching the terms and borders of reality, realism, and the definition of the human.

In virtually every cultural and social arena, the decade appeared as a turbulent series of rapid movements and turnabouts. The population of the United States reached 300 million, taking only forty-two years to gain 100 million people since reaching a population of 200 million in 1964. In the wake of the 9/11 attacks, the United States quickly became embroiled in two wars that spanned the remainder of the decade—one in Iraq and another in Afghanistan. Even the natural world erupted on 29 August 2005, when Hurricane Katrina inundated New Orleans and the Gulf Coast and exposed the failures of the U.S. government to protect its own natural borders with the speed with which it cavalierly entered those two wars. As a result, over 1,300 people perished from Alabama to Louisiana, sparking heated debates about the shadow of racism in that slow federal response. Meanwhile, an escalating and often bitter debate about another kind of putative racism swept across the nation as it confronted a tide of illegal immigration and a troubled immigration policy. In 2008–2009 a massive global recession, generated by unregulated banking practices, brought the U.S. economy to its knees, while a "Green Revolution," promoting conservation practices in daily life and public policies to wean America from the soaring costs of oil extracted from the war-torn Middle East, gained momentum.

Responding to the ubiquity of the Internet and the apparent triumph of the digital revolution, media culture embraced a widespread fascination with YouTube, 3D movies, Blu-ray discs, and video-on-demand via the Internet. In the midst of fast-paced turbulence and change, the election of the first African American president in November 2008 stood out for many as the most remarkable and dramatic event of a new millennium, inspiring many with an exuberant energy that a year later would stagnate in old political cycles. If the first decade of the twenty-first century seemed continually and quickly to expand through the promise of the virtual, those virtualities again and again ran hard up against the resistant realities they often seemed to control and reshape. Indeed, a tragic emblem of the decade might be the shocking disaster of the space shuttle *Columbia* on 1 February 2003 during the 113th mission in a visionary program to explore outer space: it ended with the disintegration of the shuttle as it reentered the Earth's atmosphere, resulting in the deaths of all seven crew members.

Politics and Culture

Few decades in the twentieth century match the cultural turbulence and tensions of the first decade of the twenty-first, a decade that was alternately sensationally progressive and sensationally regressive. Media communications proliferated rapidly and broadly through a cultural landscape that seemed to become at once more public and more private, with television programming adapting to these new technologies in a manner that movies seemed slow to respond to. Media sports figures became a key barometer and metaphor for a decade that fluctuated between heroic rises and ignominious falls. And a political stage, framed by two wars in the Middle East, appeared at once invigorated by new promises and possibilities and frustrated by fears and confusions. As new realities (often through new media) opened in all these cultural arenas, the decade became one of surprise, scandal, and shock. If one individual epitomized this decade of cultural backlash, it might be Michael Jackson and his sudden death on 25 June 2009, just as the notoriously public private pop star appeared on the verge of a comeback tour that ended mysteriously in a drug-related death.

At the peak of popularity, professional sports likewise discovered that remarkable achievements can be darkly overshadowed by scandals. American Lance Armstrong dominated world cycling, winning the Tour de France for the seventh consecutive time in 2005 while responding to suspicion of drug use or "doping," charges that are proven in another case when American Floyd Landis is stripped of his victory in 2006. Steroids also stained the glamour and myths of professional baseball. On 13 December 2007, the Mitchell Report on the Steroids Scandal appeared, detailing a year-long investigation into the use of performance-enhancing drugs over a two-decade period. The report named nearly ninety professional baseball players and urged more careful and regular testing to correct a problem that threatened the integrity of the national pastime and cast suspicion on superstar Barry Bonds's surpassing of Hank Aaron's home run record the year before. Perhaps the most renowned and accomplished sports figure of the 2000s, Tiger Woods, became the first golfer to win all four major golf titles in a calendar year when he claimed the Masters Tournament in Augusta, Georgia, in April 2001; during the decade he would win fourteen major golf championships and be named PGA Player of the Year an unprecedented ten times. By the end of the decade *Forbes* magazine had designated him the richest sportsman in the world. Then, in December 2009, Woods suddenly announced that he would take an indefinite leave from professional golf in the wake of scandalous revelations about his sexual infidelity and promiscuity.

Media and digital coverage and cultures moved faster than ever through these public and private domains, offering a technological interactivity with the public and transforming especially the worlds of video games, music, and the broader social networks. With a significant impact on film topics and forms, video games offered tactile and bodily participation for a growing culture of gamers: *Halo*, released in 2001, promoted its dramatic format of "first-person shooters"; *Guitar Hero*, released in 2005, allowed players to physically simulate musical performances; and Wii, released in 2006, introduced 3D interaction between player and screen. Similar revolutions markedthe music industry. In February 2006, the one billionth song was downloaded from iTunes, Apple's Internet music store, as part of a pronounced shift of the industry toward new platforms and away from brick-and-mortar chain stores. Between June 1999 and July 2001, Shawn Fanning's Napster site allowed individuals to share MP3 music files without fees and without regard to traditional copyright laws. In October 2007 the alternative rock band Radiohead rattled the music industry by releasing their latest CD, *In Rainbows*, on their website, with customers paying only what they felt was appropriate. Informing all these changes, cell phones and the spread of wireless Internet provided ubiquitous activities for almost all age groups and economic backgrounds; Blackberries, iPhones, and their imitators offered constant access to games, information, and conversations so that private life seemed fully wired into a dynamic public sphere. These new satellite networks became platforms for, perhaps most famously, two new social networks: Facebook, launched in 2004 and by the end of the decade supporting over 500 million subscribers sharing photos, information, and chat online; and Twitter, introduced in July 2006, which opened individual lives to a vast public circuit of interactive communication.

More so than movies, television programs during the decade responded to this rapidly changing media landscape with metaphoric and real interactivities that engaged viewers in complex serializations of contemporary realities and reality contests that nervously and dangerously muddled private and public lives. Fast-paced dramas dominated the decade, alongside gritty soap operas stretched to include more violence and sex as part of their family melodramas. One of the most popular of these series, "CSI" (Crime Scene Investigation), spanned the entire decade and became a flexible formula for spinoffs of other crime scene investigation shows, such as "CSI: Miami." In 2002, "Sex and the City" began chronicling the urban adventures of a group of professional women whose lives are entwined with simultaneously intimate and open sexual activity. Debuting in 2001, "24" followed its hero, Jack Bauer, through the minute-by-minute suspense and danger of a government counterterrorism unit, in which the contemporary anxiety of different terrorist threats leads to testing the moral and juridical limits of Bauer's (and the U.S. government's) interrogation and retaliation tactics. "The Sopranos," one of most critically acclaimed television series of the decade, running from 1999 to 2007, might be described as an allegory for the intriguingly dangerous seepages between private and public life, as mobster Tony Soprano struggles to balance the two worlds of criminal and domestic living. Equally popular through the decade, two reality shows turned this troubling interface into games in which audiences actively participated as viewers and voters: based on foreign versions of the show, "Survivor" transported groups of individuals to exotic locations around the world where they competed as "tribes" facing various physical challenges, while "American Idol" made that test of survival explicitly an entertainment challenge to discover which man or woman from the streets can win enough votes from audiences and judges to be declared the latest singing star of the media.

The central cultural drama of this decade, however, was decidedly political, full of cycles and reversals that blurred the lines between global, national, and local politics. Politically, local politics became, more often than not, inseparable from world politics in an age of ubiquitous satellite communication and continual Internet chat. The results were seen in the rapid notoriety of, among other events, the U.S. soldiers who tortured prisoners at Abu Ghraib in Iraq, the war and genocide in Darfur, the terrorist bombings in Madrid and London, and the viral emergence of a Tea Party revolution. Perhaps no film better sketches these swift political movements and global overlappings than *Syriana* (2005), in which a CIA agent wanders through violence and subterfuge spread from Iran, China, Kazakhstan, the United Arab Emirates, and the United States, a dizzying network of greed and betrayal connected primarily by oil and its pipelines. In this decade, the dominant drama revolved around the violence of territorial invasion and conquest, propelled by the "shock and awe" strategies associated with the U.S. invasion of Iraq and glamorized through the new technologies of that war.

The single event that would resonate throughout the decade and beyond was of course the al-Qaeda attacks on 11 September 2001, when fundamentalist terrorists, under the command of Osama bin Laden, hijacked four U.S. airliners and crashed two of them into the World Trade Center in New York City and one into the Pentagon in Arlington, Virginia. A fourth plane was brought down by a passenger rebellion and plunged into a cornfield in Pennsylvania, presumably preventing the destruction of the White House or the U.S. Capitol. In all, nearly 3,000 people were killed.

In response to the tragic attack, a month later the United States invaded Afghanistan and the strongholds of the Taliban and al-Qaeda, the start of a war that would continue through the decade and depend increasingly on futuristic unmanned drone attacks.

At the same time, President George W. Bush turned most of his attention to Iraq and that country's resistance to United Nation teams inspecting sites that were presumed to be hiding chemical and biological "weapons of mass destruction." On 19 March 2003, the U.S.-led invasion of Iraq began, featuring a coalition of international forces whose attacks as they appeared on television screens seemed to transform the carnage into an eerie video game. This was the second U.S. war in Iraq in as many decades, in this case leading to the capture and execution of Iraqi leader Saddam Hussein, yet never discovering the supposed weapons of mass destruction that were used to justify the invasion. On 3 February 2004, the Central Intelligence Agency acknowledged that the imminent threat from weapons of mass destruction had never been actually verified.

National politics framed these violent upheavals with three presidential elections in the decade, permeated with political intrigue, social polarization, and quick power shifts. In one of the most controversial elections in American history, Texas governor George W. Bush and Vice President Al Gore remained in a virtual dead-heat for the presidency more than a month following Election Day. A disputed vote in Florida—made more controversial because of poorly constructed punch ballots—was the key to victory, with Bush leading by a few hundred votes as a recount progressed until a sharply divided Supreme Court halted the recount in favor of Bush. Four years later, Bush won reelection over Massachusetts senator John Kerry with only 50.7 percent of the popular vote and 286 votes in the Electoral College. In the third presidential election of the decade, in 2008, Democratic senator Barack Obama of Illinois easily defeated Republican senator John McCain of Arizona to become the nation's first African American president, carried into office by his message to enact major cultural and political changes and the promise of national health care reform. Most notable among political newcomers of the year was McCain's running mate, Alaska governor Sarah Palin. Though she would resign as governor in 2009 midway through her first term, she would become a national leader of the grassroots Tea Party, a loose coalition of conservatives intent on shrinking the size of government. Among other political breakthroughs for individual women in the decade, Hillary Rodham Clinton was elected to the U.S. Senate from New York in 2000, the first time a First Lady had won public office; after a hard-fought run for the Democratic nomination against Obama in

2008, she became the new president's secretary of state. And following the Democrats' takeover of Congress in 2006, Nancy Pelosi became the first woman to serve as Speaker of the House.

By the end of 2009 this turbulent back and forth had become concentrated on the American economy. Entering the decade with a large economic surplus, the U.S. government ten years later was mired in a crippling recession, triggered by a massive bank and housing crisis and two ongoing wars. Besides the extraordinary military costs, two related events created the economic crisis: the subprime mortgage collapse of 2007–08, in which excessive and unregulated lending by banks resulted in a shortage of monetary funds and a wave of home foreclosures, and the subsequent government bailout of large banks and other large corporations labeled "too big to fail." On 3 October 2008, the Congress and President Bush passed the Emergency Economic Stabilization Act, which provideda $700 billion bailout for Wall Street firms. As oil prices rose above $140 per barrel, this financial turmoil expanded into a global economic recession that many would compare to the Great Depression of the 1930s. By 2009, China would replace the United States as the world's largest economic power, and the U.S. jobless rate hovered near 10 percent, with a $10 trillion deficit projected over the next decade.

The Movie Industry in the 2000s: Distribution, Revenues, and VOD

Like other areas of popular culture, the movies would act out their own rapid shifts and changes of directions. As the movie industry entered its third century, movements between old and new realities and between consistency and change informed especially the institutional forces behind the movies as they adjusted to increasingly expanding markets and more actively discriminating viewers. Just as it had continually evolved since the 1920s, the Hollywood studio system—specifically the reconfigured Big Six of Warner Bros., Paramount, Twentieth Century–Fox, Universal, Columbia, and Disney—remained more or less intact, yet structural changes and mergers reshaped those studios as they shifted focus from in-house production of movies to distribution.[1] With MGM now considered a "mini-major" supported in part by the Sony Corporation, the large studios for the most part became backers and distributors of films with independent companies actually handling production. Most traditional studios continued to do a modicum of production, but their work began to focus increasingly on development, financing, marketing, and merchandising. At the same time, each studio more aggressively developed its subsidiary distribution networks (such as Fox Searchlight) to address the diversification of audiences and interests in so-called art house and independent films. These specialty divisions often simply acquired distribution rights to pictures with which the studio had no involvement in production, and the largest part of film production was shipped to other branches of the studios, such as Disney's Pixar (acquired in 2006) and Warner Bros.' New Line Cinema (bought in 2008).

Meanwhile, the independent production and distribution companies that emerged and flourished in the 1990s prospered and grew as the main sources for quality film production and distribution in the United States. These new independent companies—Lionsgate, Summit Entertainment, The Weinstein Company, Overture Films, and others—are often referred to as "mini-majors," and through the course of the decade they successfully competed with the traditional studios in film production and distribution, creating what Thomas Schatz refers to in this volume as "mid-range" companies whose films straddle the gap between art films and big-budget movies. Originally based in Vancouver, British Columbia, for instance, Lionsgate Entertainment moved in 2006 to Santa Monica, California. Founded as an independent production and overseas sales company in 1996, Summit Entertainment became a studio ten years later, with its first major success, *Twilight*, appearing in 2008 and its first Oscar-winning production, *The Hurt Locker*, released a year later. After their departure from Disney's Miramax, Harvey and Bob Weinstein resurfaced in The Weinstein Company in late 2005, and continued their long relationship with Quentin Tarantino with *Inglourious Basterds* in August 2009. Overture Films arrived in the fall of 2006, becoming by 2009 one of the most successful studios in the United States. In 1994 Steven Spielberg, Jeffrey Katzenberg, and David Geffen created DreamWorks SKG, and by the early 2000s it was one of the most renowned success stories of the decade, sometimes described as the seventh major studio.

Across these industrial gyrations, the movie industry vacillated financially throughout the decade, possibly as a result of the weak quality of the films being produced but certainly as a result of expanding competition from other media and the Internet. Attendance at movie theaters grew anemically, with what may have seemed a promising 8.1 percent jump from 2000 to 2004 (attendance was actually down in three of those five years; the figure may simply reflect the sharp increase in attendance in 2002 with the release of *Spider-Man* and *Star Wars: Attack of the Clones*) but slowing considerably in the second half of the decade. By the middle years, the number of moviegoers dropped steadily, falling 4 percent in 2003, 2 percent in 2004, and 8 percent in 2005. Yet by 2008, Hollywood's six majors recorded significant profits, grossing $9.8 billion domestically and $28.1 billion globally, buoyed in part by higher ticket prices and DVD sales.

Fueling the changing economics of the movie industry, the widespread impact of digital technology became a central issue in the decade, transforming not only how movies were made but, more important, how films were delivered to audiences. There is no doubt that digital cameras and editing systems dramatically altered, both financially and stylistically, the ease and costs of making films, but the most revolutionary new directions appeared in how movies began to be viewed and shared as computer downloads, on smaller screens, and according to the demands and choices of individuals. Thus, the convergence of many technological and industrial innovations reshaped movie viewing through the decade—from iPods to video-on-demand—and dramatized the centrifugal spin of the movies as they circulated through different venues and platforms and more active consumer choices (commonly called "agency") about how, where, and when movies are watched.

The traditional theatrical distribution of movies became primarily a way to generate buzz in the promotion of DVD or on-demand sales. Through the course of the decade, Americans spent approximately eighty hours each year watching DVDs as sales and rentals of DVDs soared, exceeding approximately $20 billion a year, far surpassing the declining market for VHS cassettes and making DVD distribution the largest source of revenue for the studios. This foreshadowed a later battle of formats between high-definition DVD and Blu-ray, each claiming to offer higher resolution that could compete with the large theatrical screen. Designed by Sony and first released on 20 June 2006, Blu-ray exceeded the standard DVD in quality with a high-definition image and sound. Toshiba subsequently developed HD-DVD (three months ahead of schedule) but in February 2008 bowed out of the battle with Blu-ray after most of the major content providers chose Blu-ray. (During these battles and transitions, however, the economics and technologies of standard DVD would remain a prominent force through the end of the decade.)

One side effect of the economic shift to DVD occurred in 2007 when the Writers Guild of America demanded financial residuals from DVD sales, as well as compensation for animation programs, reality shows, and new media. More than 12,000 writers participated in a strike that lasted from 5 November 2007 to 12 February 2008, and its complaints and goals brought into high relief the changes taking place across the American movie industry. In the Writers Guild's demand for fair compensation for work distributed through new media, the transition from theatrical to DVD distribution was only a part of larger shifts whereby the distribution of movies would expand into Internet downloads, streaming, smart phone programming, cable and satellite video-on-demand, and other new methods.

Three of the most visible representatives of these technological and commercial changes were Netflix, YouTube, and video-on-demand (VOD). Established in 1997, Netflix created an enormously profitable paradigm for the distribution of DVDs through postal (and later digital) delivery, immediately making over 100,000 film titles available and quickly enlisting approximately ten million subscribers. By February 2007, Netflix had delivered over one billion films through mail subscriptions, and two years later it had doubled that number. In some ways a more radical redirection of movie culture and the potential for digital distribution was the arrival of YouTube in 2005 (purchased by Google in 2006 for $1.65 billion), a video-sharing website through which users can upload and share videos as an MPEG-4 format. While most of the content on YouTube originally featured individual personal videos, media conglomerates begin to take more and more advantage of this rapidly growing distribution site through the 2000s, making both clips of their films and often entire films easily available. A significant part of this expansion was realized through the iPod and iTunes, with Apple making deals with film and television networks and production houses such as Pixar to distribute both short and full-length films. Through an updated version of QuickTime Pro, users were soon able to create their own videos for the iPod and rent selected movie titles in HD from their computers. By the end of the decade, this confluence of forces had drawn more and more attention to video-on-demand as a new force in the remaking of movie distribution. With VOD, the window between theatrical release and availability on cable television or Internet collapsed even further.

At least in part as a consequence of the dramatic shift to DVD, home-delivery platforms, and Internet access, a major debate in the film industry focused on the timing of a movie's release on DVD. One of the most publicized experiments of the DVD revolution was "day-and-date release." With producers Mark Cuban and Tedd Wagner of HDNet Films and 2929 Entertainment, Steven Soderbergh distributed his 2006 film *Bubble*, about a slacker working in a doll factory, across three different venues: theatrical release followed four days later by its appearance on HDNet cable and in stores on DVD.

The Movies: Genres and Trends

The cycles, expansions, and reversals in American culture were quite visible in movie genres, where they absorbed and reworked the new violence, social realities, and image technologies that informed the larger cultural and social movements of the new millennium. Just as Kubrick's *2001* turned the conventional science-fiction film inside-out to explore where new historical pressures and technologies of conquest stretch the rituals of genre, film genres of the 2000s pushed their formulas to question what it means to be human and where the answer to that question can be discovered in lost histories and narratives of women and men. From *The Lord of the Rings* films (2001, 2002, 2003) through *Pirates of the Caribbean* movies (2003, 2006, 2007), the blockbuster, that most contemporary of film practices and arguably a genre in itself, extended itself through international serials threatened by super-villains and monsters. The musical returned in films like *Chicago* (2002) and *Dreamgirls* (2006); westerns took new unexpected twists along the generic borderlines of *There Will Be Blood* (2007) and *No Country for Old Men* (2007); old mysteries puzzled out new stories and new behaviors in the complex interactive narratives of *Donnie Darko* (2001) and *Eternal Sunshine of the Spotless Mind* (2004); and, in films from *Hulk* (2003) to *Avatar* (2009), the human itself was fantastically transformed in animated features, comic book adaptations, and 3D technologies.

Eternal Sunshine of the Spotless Mind (Michel Gondry, Focus Features, 2004) is one of the most successful and engaging examples of a potentially new film genre, "smart" or "puzzle" films. Digital frame enlargement.

As in earlier decades, blockbuster productions drove American cinema, now more than ever spread across serials and sequels and through international financing and audiences. Two of the most successful elicited traditional American anglophilia and the contemporary upswing in film adaptations of literature: the *Harry Potter* and *Lord of the Rings* series. Based on the novels by British writer J. K. Rowling, the first five Harry Potter films became the highest grossing film series of all time when not adjusted for inflation, with $4.48 billion in worldwide receipts (since then overtaken by the James Bond series). The sixth film appeared in 2009; the seventh and final film, *Harry Potter and the Deathly Hallows*, would appear in two parts in 2010–2011. The series depicted the coming of age of Harry Potter (Daniel Radcliffe), who discovers on his eleventh birthday that he is a wizard and is sent to the Hogwarts School of Witchcraft and Wizardry to begin his magical education. At the school Harry becomes part of a community of young wizards, most centrally Ron Weasley (Rupert Grint) and Hermione Granger (Emma Watson).

Based on the three-volume series by J.R.R. Tolkien, *The Lord of the Rings* film trilogy of *The Fellowship of the Ring* (2001), *The Two Towers* (2002), and *The Return of the King* (2003) created astonishing semi-human figures wandering a layered world in a battle between good and evil. Set in the imaginary world of Middle-earth and directed by Peter Jackson, the three films follow the young hobbit Frodo Baggins (Elijah Wood) as he and his comrades embark on a quest to destroy the One Ring and its maker, the Dark Lord Sauron (Sala Baker). Meanwhile, the wizard Gandalf (Ian McKellen) and Aragorn (Viggo Mortensen), heir in exile to the throne of Gondor, unite and rally the Free Peoples of Middle-earth, who are ultimately victorious in the War of the Ring. Distributed by New Line Cinema, the three films became the eighth, fourth, and second highest-grossing films of all time, respectively.

Two other blockbuster series stood out in the decade, both suggesting cinema's near obsession with fantasies of overcoming evil and the power of these fantasies to extend themselves into other cultural spheres. The *Pirates of the Caribbean* franchise, based on a Disneyland theme park ride of the same name, follows the adventures of Captain Jack Sparrow (Johnny Depp) through *The Curse of the Black Pearl* (2003), *Dead Man's Chest* (2006), and *At World's End* (2007). Altogether the three films grossed over $2.79 billion worldwide. *The Matrix* was a trio of cyberspace adventure films written and directed by the Wachowski brothers, with two sequels appearing in this decade, *The Matrix Reloaded* (2003) and *The Matrix Revolutions* (2003). More so than most contemporary blockbusters, *The Matrix* films became an example of significant shifts and expansions in media culture of the new millennium and an instance of what Henry Jenkins has described as "convergence culture," whereby the characters and settings become part of an expanding fictional universe that is re-created in literary stories, comics, video games, websites, and blogs. Finally, in an appropriate example of the progressive regressions of the decade, the James Bond film series, one of the most popular action series that began in 1962 with *Dr. No*, was renewed with *Casino Royale* (2006), becoming the highest-grossing Bond film with a total of $594 million in receipts. With this series and film, movie history again demonstrates that the present and future are often a backward movement to earlier stories and genres, especially in this decade.

Films continued to explore certain traditional genres, but the historical revisions that have always followed genres now tend to re-create those genres in more concentrated ways or to discover the repressed or marginalized figures of those genres. One of the most controversial films of the decade was Mel Gibson's Passion play *The Passion of the Christ* (2004). Based on the New Testament accounts of the arrest, trial, torture, crucifixion, and resurrection of Jesus, the film featured dialogue in Aramaic, Latin, and Hebrew (along with subtitles). The film quickly drew charges of antisemitism while also becoming the highest grossing non–English-language film ever and the most widely seen R-rated film in the United States. A very different sort of genre-bending film, Ang Lee's award-winning *Brokeback Mountain* (2005), described the complex romantic and sexual relationship between two seemingly heterosexual men in the American West between 1963 and 1981. Starring Heath Ledger and Jake Gyllenhaal, the film merged the domestic melodrama and the western to create a powerful drama of gay men struggling to express their love for each other within traditional social and cultural boundaries.

The decade also marked the continuing triumph of Martin Scorsese in exploring and twisting genres: the epic tale of New York in the nineteenth century, *Gangs of New York* (2002), the Howard Hughes biopic *The Aviator* (2004), the crime film about corruption in the Boston police force, *The Departed* (2006), and the rockumentary of a Rolling Stones' concert, *Shine a Light* (2008). For these efforts Scorsese won his second Golden Globe for Best Director, a Critic's Choice Award, his first Director's Guild of America Award, and the Academy Award for Best Director. The last was thought to be long overdue, to the extent that some entertainment critics subsequently referred to it as Scorsese's "Lifetime Achievement" Oscar.

A genre that began in the 1990s and expanded in the 2000s, the smart or puzzle film, or what Thomas Elsaesser has described as "mind-game" films, included movies such as Christopher Nolan's *Memento* (2000), Richard Kelly's *Donnie Darko* (2001), David Lynch's *Mulholland Dr.* (2001), Robert Altman's *Gosford Park* (2001), Spike Jonze's *Adaptation* (2002), and Michel Gondry's *Eternal Sunshine of the Spotless Mind* (2004), the latter two written by Charlie Kaufman. They all share narratives and visual styles that involve the audience in various cognitive and imagistic "games" about what happens and why or, in some cases, about the challenge of distinguishing interior subjective realities from exterior objective realities.

Continuing a resurgence begun at the end of the twentieth century, documentaries were more visible and central in this decade than perhaps in any other era in American film history. The reasons for this turn are many, but chief among them was their somewhat surprising financial profitability: twenty-two of the top twenty-five highest-grossing documentaries in film history appeared after 2000. In addition to revenues, other factors contribute to this resurgence: the popularity of reality television, copyright pressures, and the ease and affordability of digital cameras. Not surprisingly, given the bellicose atmosphere of the decade, many of the documentaries focused on various war efforts and related effects: *The Fog of War: Eleven Lessons from the Life of Robert S. McNamara* (2003), *Fahrenheit 9/11* (2004), *Why We Fight* (2005), *The War Tapes* (2006), *No End in Sight* (2007), and *Taxi to the Dark Side* (2007). Others followed significant shifts in documentary practices to concentrate on the margins or undercurrents of American culture and families as ways to investigate the interaction of a personal point of view and social realities, and to simultaneously stretch the borders of both subjective and objective realities. Some of these documentaries worked within conventional forms and formulas, such as *Dogtown and Z Boys* (2001), *Spellbound* (2002), *The Weather Underground* (2002), *Tupac: Resurrection* (2003), *Super Size Me* (2004), *Murderball* (2005), *Enron: The Smartest Guys in the Room* (2005), *Man on Wire* (2008), and *Food, Inc.* (2009). Others experimented with representational instabilities within the documentary forms themselves to raise questions not only about actual individuals and events but also about the difficulty of adequately representing those figures and events. This type of reflexive documentary included *Bowling for Columbine* (2002), *American Splendor* (2003), *Capturing the Friedmans* (2003), *Born into Brothels* (2004), *Grizzly Man* (2005), *An Inconvenient Truth* (2006), *The King of Kong: A Fistful of Quarters* (2007), *How to Fix the World* (2006), and *How Little We Know of Our Neighbours* (2005).

Perhaps the most distinct trend inthe decade's movieswas the prominence of films fueled by new digital technologies. Two very different examples at the beginning of the decade, *Timecode* (2000) and *Waking Life* (2001), employed digital imagery to, respectively, coordinate the simultaneous actions around a film production office in four quadrants on the screen and create a rambling meditation on art and life through rotoscoped animation. Appropriately, an Academy Awards for the Best Animated Feature was presented for the first time in 2001, won by *Shrek,* a tale that mixes adult humor and a pop soundtrack, including music by Smash Mouth, Eels, Joan Jett, The Proclaimers, Jason Wade, and the Baha Men. Computer-animated films won that award in six of the following eight years, with Pixar leading the way with wins for *Finding Nemo* (2003), *The Incredibles* (2004), *Ratatouille* (2007), and *WALL-E* (2008). At the end of the decade, the marriage of computers and animation produced the enormous success of *Avatar* (2009), whose story of corporate exploitation of an alien planet raised questions about what it means to be human in the new territories of the universe and whose 3D technology offered viewers glimpses of a new way of seeing themselves through movies.

The fascination with animation moved in another direction as cinematic adaptations turned toward superheroes and super-villains from comic books and graphic novels. Traditional adaptations of novels and plays remained a strong current with films such as *Doubt* (2008), the cinematic version of a dark drama about a Catholic priest in the 1960s, or *The Chronicles of Narnia* series (2005–2010), based on the books by C. S. Lewis. Yet the marquee adaptations were less part of a literary tradition than part of a popular culture of video games and comic books. Early in the decade, *Lara Croft: Tomb Raider* (2001) became the first of numerous film re-creations of popular video games, while *X-Men* (2000), based on the fictional Marvel Comics characters of the same name, began a spate of comic book adaptations. *Spider-Man* (2002) was the first installment of a series that would include two sequels (2004 and 2007); the first was the third highest-grossing film of 2002 with $822 million worldwide, while the latter surpassed the first with a gross of $891 million. Ang Lee's *Hulk* (also known as *The Hulk*) was a 2003 superhero film based on the fictional Marvel Comics character of the same name, and *Catwoman* (2004) represented a super-villain and love interest of Batman. Meanwhile, Christopher Nolan helmed two Batman films, *Batman Begins* (2005), a return to the series that told the origin of the character, as well as the commercially and critically successful sequel *The Dark Knight* (2008). Directed by Guillermo del Toro, *Hellboy* (2004) and *Hellboy II: The Golden Army* (2008) were based on the Dark Horse Comics work *Hellboy: Seed of Destruction* by Mike Mignola. Also appearing in 2008, *Iron Man*'s

Perhaps the most resonant film of the decade, *The Dark Knight* (Christopher Nolan, Warner Bros., 2008) struggles with the morality of good and evil, the technologies that support both in a drama, and politics that negotiate human society in a futuristic present. Digital frame enlargement.

superhero was based on the Marvel Comics character of the same name, and Zack Snyder's *Watchmen* (2009), a sci-fi neo-noir film, followed a group of vigilantes amid heightened tension between the United States and the Soviet Union.

Each of the essays in this collection draws on many of the different industrial, social, and technological pressures of the decade, as well as other historical tendencies and generic trends. Nora Alter highlights several 2000 films that teetered on the brink of social satire, fully engaged with the political and cultural violence that would pervade the decade, from *American Psycho* and *Gladiator* to *Traffic* and *Bamboozled*, while Linda Ruth Williams points out that, in 2001, displaced war films, like *Pearl Harbor* and *Black Hawk Down*, appeared prominently alongside so-called "chick flicks" with alternative comedic fantasies, like *Legally Blonde*, *The Princess Diaries*, and *Bridget Jones's Diary*. The following year, as Sharon Willis argues about 2002, these genres and trends were persistently and more generally inflected with troubled and fragile identities, often played out in dramas focused on the gender and family crises of failed fathers and "melancholic mothers" in movies such as *The Bourne Identity* and *Catch Me If You Can*, *The Hours* and *Far from Heaven*. As part of his discussion of 2003, Bob Rehak looks at the "shock and awe" atmosphere that motivated some of the mega-blockbusters of that year, often sharing a vision of "flirting with the powers of God." Anna Everett surveys 2004 through highly successful and inventive sequels such as *The Bourne Supremacy* and *Bridget Jones: The Edge of Reason*, while the year also featured a significant proliferation of political and popular documentaries such as *Fahrenheit 9/11*, *Control Room*, and *WMD*. For Karen Beckman, 2005 continued the decade's investigation of troubled family melodramas in *Junebug* and *The Squid and the Whale*, while Miranda July's *You and Me and Everyone We Know* and Ang Lee's *Brokeback Mountain* all constituted a generic remake of contemporary social problem films of the 1930s. As Nigel Morris notes in his essay, the war drama, not surprisingly, assumed a particularly contemporary bent as the decade proceeded in its recovery of the more recent trauma of 9/11 in *United 93* and *World Trade Center*, counterpointed by meditative and retrospective revisions of the genre in *Flags of Our Fathers* and *Letters from Iwo Jima*. In 2007, Dina Smith discusses how comedies surged in the teen farces of Judd Apatow, such as *Knocked Up*, and in a specific comedic subgenre about bumbling boys and physical humor, as in *Superbad*. In 2008 Thomas Schatz sees the movie industry reflecting the larger economic crisis of the times in which mega-blockbusters like *The Dark Knight* represented a generic investment in movies "too big to fail" and films like *Slumdog Millionaire* blurred the lines between independent production and financial success. For Dana Polan, 2009 described a generic trend that rethinks and remakes questions about identity politics: reconfiguring masculinities as masculine redemptions in movies from *The International* and *The Hangover* to *The Taking of Pelham 1 2 3*; remaking historical personalities to reflect the present in *Public Enemies* and *Taking Woodstock*; and transforming identity politics into identity products in films such as *Hannah Montana*.

Kubrick's *2001* could not have anticipated the complexities of the new American millennium and the all-too-earthly imbroglios of its politics, wars, technologies, and disasters. American movie culture of this decade, however, did seem to recall some of the thematic trajectories of that 1968 film: the cinema moves forward through plots of discovery, through technologies of conquest, through images of expanding worlds, through images of new gender and sexual identities, and through questions about what being human ultimately means.

NOTE

1. Only one major studio changed corporate hands during the decade, but that occurred twice: Vivendi acquired Universal in 2000, and in 2004 General Electric took charge of the studio.

2000

Movies, Anti-Climaxes, and Disenchantments

NORA ALTER

When North Americans awoke on 1 January after a night of partying and celebration to usher in the new millennium, there was an almost audible sigh of relief as they drank their coffee, cleared their foggy (and in some cases pounding) heads, and turned on their computers. Home pages reflecting the accurate date and time opened, records and documents were accessible, the Internet operated smoothly—in short, everything was the same as the day before. The anxiety-producing, long-anticipated super-virus, Y2K, which had threatened to shut down all digital and electronic systems and fling the population back to the Ice Age, had not brought the digital world to a halt. Nor did Millennium apocalyptic predictions that forecast the battle of Armageddon and the end of the world materialize. Instead, the new century appeared to be much like the old one, and the anxieties of dramatic change much overblown.

Americans continued to enjoy unprecedented levels of prosperity, with the Dow Jones Industrial Average closing at 11,722.98 on 14 January, and the NASDAQ peaking at 5132.52 later in the year. Unemployment was at the all-time low of 4 percent. The United States posted a $237 billion surplus at the end of the fiscal year in September, and "experts" forecast that in the next decade the surplus would reach nearly $5 trillion! There were several significant mega-corporate mergers, including Phillip Morris (Kraft) with Nabisco and the Tribune Company with Times Mirror.

Evidence of the expanding purview of the Internet was the purchase of TimeWarner by America Online on 10 January. The launch of the MP3 file format and the popularity of computer games such as Pokemon Stadium, Nintendo, and PlayStation continued to grow as the nature of activities entertainment, and the very concept of leisure, fundamentally changed. However, the hyper-growth in this market placed a palpable stress on cinema that emerges in several films. The events of 1989 that had brought about the collapse of the Soviet Union and the end of the Cold War were

undoubtedly significant. Even more important for the triumphant capitalism of the United States was the dot.com revolution. It seemed that good
old-fashioned American ingenuity had once again led the way. Emerging
out the slump of the 1980s, the full implementation and integration of a
digital way of life helped to reestablish the United States as a world leader
in the realm of electronic communication. Technological global dominance
combined with the massive wealth produced by the deregulation of the
banking and finance industries (that began in the 1980s) promised to
ensure a long period of U.S. wealth and prosperity. Yet those not wearing
rose-tinted glasses could detect cracks in the system, and a number of
movies forecast, in radically different ways, a future when the bubble
would burst.

This was also the year of several noteworthy lawsuits. While the Internet provided the public with an unprecedented accessibility to information
and vast possibilities for downloading amounts of data, including music and
films, the legal profession tried to keep up. A whole array of new legislation
was drafted to protect the commercial interests of corporations. Metallica,
the heavy metal band, filed suit against Napster, virtually shutting it down.
Microsoft lost its first of numerous antitrust lawsuits. There was also a series
of tobacco lawsuits in Florida, resulting in the tobacco industry's being
ordered to pay $144.8 billion (the largest fine to date) in punitive damages.
Early in the year, female employees of the U.S. Information Agency won a
$508 million class-action suit against the agency for discrimination.

Vermont became the first state in the nation to legalize civil unions for
same-sex couples. Women and people of color moved into prominent positions: Hillary Rodham Clinton was elected senator from New York, and
Ruth J. Simmons was hired by Brown University to serve as the first African
American president of an Ivy League university. Incidents such as the outbreak of mad cow disease in England, the discovery of black sludge in the
Mississippi River, and studies indicating the melting of the North Pole ice-
cap brought into focus the need for closer scrutiny of agriculture and the
environment. Many films affirmed that even in a sea of corruption a
grander spirit of idealism would triumph.

Yet, for Americans, the single most important political event of the year
was the controversial presidential election. It would set the course for the
new millennium. Whatever naïveté remained about the fairness of democracy in America was washed away, like a face in the sand at the edge of the
ocean, by the Supreme Court when it decided the outcome of this fateful
event. For many, a hard, cold cynicism set in, with which mainstream
America is still dealing.

The first indication that something was awry was when, on election night, the news media first called Florida (a hotly contested swing state commanding twenty-five Electoral College votes) for Vice President Al Gore, and then backtracked and withdrew that projection. The following day, on 8 November, the election still had no clear winner. Gore and Texas governor George W. Bush were neck-and-neck with results in several states deemed too close to call. In addition, overseas ballots had yet to be tallied, and many in Florida were demanding a manual recount. Irregularities were discovered in Miami-Dade County, where misleading ballots confused voters. In addition, punch machines and computerized readers may have missed countless votes due to hanging chads—incompletely punched circles that did not fall away from paper ballots. Thus began a bitter and acrimonious partisan fight over the presidency that was to last thirty-six days, until 13 December, when Gore conceded the day after the U.S. Supreme Court overturned the Florida Supreme Court to halt the manual recount, leaving in place a margin of 537 votes in favor of Bush. Nationwide, Gore had handily won the popular vote, but Bush had won the Electoral College. The entire process left many disillusioned with the U.S. "democratic" system.

The frenzy leading up to the election and its chaotic aftermath occupied the American public's attention while another consequential incident took place. On 12 October, the USS *Cole* was attacked in the Port of Aden in Yemen by al-Qaeda suicide bombers. Seventeen U.S. citizens were killed in addition to the two perpetrators. This was but the most brazen of attacks on the United States that year. In January, the U.S. Navy reported the attempted destruction of the USS *The Sullivans* (the boat with explosives sank before it reached its target due to the weight of the freight it was carrying), and this event was followed by reports of plans to bomb Los Angeles International Airport and a tourist site in Jordan popular with U.S. visitors. Thus, while most Americans were focused on the pitfalls of domestic politics, new forms of systematic warfare were being plotted and executed against the United States.

Movies engaged and escaped these tensions in a variety of ways. One of the more successful of films of the year about social and political issues, *Erin Brockovich*, tells the tale of a woman in a small working-class community who takes on and defeats a large corporation. Along with weather-disaster films such as *Maelstrom* and *Hurricane*, *The Perfect Storm* sketches the apocalyptic undercurrents of the new millennium in a drama about a fishing boat caught in a mammoth storm. Countering these anxieties are an almost unprecedented number of mass-culture entertainments, nostalgic remakes, and escapist fare, including *Shaft, Mission Impossible II, Scream 3, X-Men, The Patriot, Cast Away, Charlie's Angels, Adventures of Rocky and Bullwinkle, Pokemon the Movie, Digimon*, and, yes, *The Flintstones in Viva Rock Vegas*. Even inventive narrative experiments, such as Christopher Nolan's *Memento*, seem inflected by cultural anxieties: in Nolan's film he immerses the viewer in a confused amnesiac world in which time is reversed and history difficult to locate. At the same time, numerous American films continue to resist easy classification and stretch the borders of Hollywood and its genres: the mockumentary *Best in Show* wittily parodies dog-show culture; *High Fidelity* explores the world of alternative music through the mid-life crisis of a thirty-year-old slacker; Jim Carrey's vehicle *Me, Myself & Irene* follows the madcap adventures of a Rhode Island state trooper with multiple personalities; and in *Miss Congeniality* Sandra Bullock transforms a romantic comedy into the slapstick performance of an undercover FBI agent awkwardly infiltrating a beauty pageant.

Suspicions and Prophecies: *American Psycho* and *The Perfect Storm*

The post–Cold War economic success of Wall Street is satirized in Mary Harron's *American Psycho*, based on the eponymous 1991 novel by Bret Easton Ellis. Supporters of the 2009 bailout of corporations and the continuation of obscene bonuses to bankers and financiers would dislike *American Psycho*. The film is set in the detached capitalist world of young Wall Street executives. With the Twin Towers looming over Lower Manhattan, the plot centers on twenty-seven-year-old Patrick Bateman (Christian Bale), who serves as one of many vice presidents at Pierce & Pierce, his father's corporation. It is not quite clear what Bateman does at his job, as both his office and desk are devoid of any traces of labor. His voiceover, which narrates the film, begins by detailing his age, muscle-crunching capabilities, and personal hygiene regime: "In the shower I use a water-activated gel cleanser, then a honey almond body scrub, and on the face an exfoliating gel scrub. Then I apply an herb-mint facial mask which I leave on for ten minutes while I prepare the rest of my routine." Bateman meticulously attends to every other aspect of his appearance as well. He is dressed and groomed in the height of 1980s fashion. His apartment follows a similar aesthetic, decorated with the work of postmodernist artists Allan McCollum, Robert Longo, Cindy Sherman, and other leading figures of the 1980s. The furniture is high modernist design. Initially Bateman's personality seems affable enough, and when we first encounter him

A pristine and affluent America on the verge of losing control: *American Psycho* (Mary Harron, Lionsgate). Digital frame enlargement.

in conversation with his cohorts he reprimands them for their antisemitic comments.

The film follows a group of young executives as they negotiate the social world of high finance at the height of Reaganomics in late 1980s New York. It is a world of banking deregulations and expanding bubbles, the erosion of social programs and promotion of trickle-down economics— a decade of restructuring that many today hold responsible for enabling the 2008 economic collapse. At one point, Bateman watches the actor-turned-president deliver a speech. The young Bateman's physique, poses, and obsessive body-building evoke Arnold Schwarzenegger, another B-movie actor turned politician in the state of California, where the illusions and dreams spun by Hollywood studios have a tendency to become the nightmare realities of American life. During this sequence we are at once thrust backward into the celluloid past and proleptically forward to a future in which Schwarzenegger becomes governor of California. New York City in the eighties was emerging from bankruptcy; energy (emanating from the financial district) was once again coursing through the city, with the gentrification of SoHo, the proliferation of high-end galleries and boutiques, the popularity of exclusive discos and nightclubs, and plenty of cocaine and martinis. These are the sites frequented by the characters in *American Psycho*. Indeed, several scenes in the film include trendy restaurants with hyperbolic menus featuring items such as "swordfish meatloaf with onion marmalade, rare roasted partridge breast in raspberry coulis with a sorrel timbale, . . . and grilled free-range rabbit with herbed french fries." It is a world before cell phones and personal computers, dominated by empty signifiers that connote value but lack any real substance. This is embodied in a particularly hilarious scene involving business card envy. With deadpan delivery, a group of young executives compare their business cards, sporting background colors with names like "eggshell" or "bone" (in the case of Bateman's), to fonts such as "Silian Rail" or "Romalian Type." They are awestruck as they examine Paul Allen's card (he another vice president at Pierce & Pierce) and are particularly impressed by its watermark. It is a society of spectacle and simulation where the operating law is that of appearance. Thus, the "simulationist" artworks by McCollum hanging on the wall only *appear* to be paintings—in reality they are plaster casts.

The same is true for the characters who lack any depth or development. Bateman adopts the persona of an out-of-control serial killer. Even the detailed musical interpretations he articulates prior to committing his murders ring hollow. His analysis of the music of Phil Collins while engaging in a ménage-à-trois with two prostitutes parodies intellectual criticism: "I think 'Invisible Touch' is the group's undisputed masterpiece. It's an epic meditation on intangibility. At the same time, it deepens and enriches . . . the meaning of the preceding three albums. Christie, take off the robe. Listen to the brilliant ensemble playing . . . of Banks, Collins and Rutherford. You can practically hear every nuance of every instrument. Sabrina, remove your dress."

He executes his murders in a dispassionate and particularly gruesome manner. Even these acts of violence appear to be simulations—derivative of late-night slasher films. Thus in one of the final murders, Bateman chases his victim down a winding stairwell with a battery-operated chainsaw simultaneously evoking the cult-classic *The Texas Chain Saw Massacre* and Fritz Lang's *M*. Like the serial murderer in *M*, Beckert, Bateman pleads insanity. And like Beckert's victims in *M*, Bateman's are initially those from the lower classes. Indeed, Bateman preys on the homeless, prostitutes, and secretaries before advancing to the next register of the social ladder when he kills one of his peers.[1]

The interesting twist in *American Psycho* comes near the end of the film when Bateman tries to confess his crimes to his lawyer. The possibility emerges for the first time in the film that the entire series of murders is his fantasy. Reality is increasingly difficult to discern in Bateman's nightmarish world. Although he may not have literally committed his crimes, there is certainly a lot of symbolic blood on his hands. For in order to stay the course of ruthless finance capitalism, with the disparities between the rich and the poor reaching unprecedented levels, there have to be many victims. The catastrophic annihilation of social spending together with a perverse array of tax and corporate breaks ensured the return of a mandarin class to the United States. The casualties will be the homeless and the working poor who will only continue to grow in numbers into the new millennium. Just as we follow Bateman's character on his killing spree, amazed at how long it goes on, so too economists marveled at the financial bubble, watching it continue to expand until finally it began to burst in 2007. The surprise was not that the economy crashed, but that it took so long.

And crash it did. A spectacular crash—a crash forecast and magnificently constructed cinematographically in Wolfgang Petersen's *The Perfect Storm*. The 130-minute saga chronicles the plight of a group of fishermen at sea who are caught in an enormous storm. It is based on the true story of the *Andrea Gail*, whose Captain Billy Tyne (George Clooney), despite severe weather warnings, set forth in late October 1991 with a crew of five in search of fish off the Massachusetts coast. The audience is told at the outset that the boat will sink with no survivors, but, as in a Greek tragedy, we watch as the drama unfolds, following its narrative detours. The question is not *if* disaster will strike, but how and when.

The similarities between *The Perfect Storm* and Petersen's breakthrough film, the German *Das Boot* (1981), are striking. The theme is once again a group of men alone at sea confronting a ruthless enemy. The only difference is that in the later film nature is the enemy, whereas in the earlier film (set in a U-boat during World War II) it is the British. In both instances, our sympathies are with the crew and the countless perils they face while struggling for their lives. The boats are spaces without women, and initial animosities between crewmembers are overcome by acts of male bonding against a common foe. The resemblance between the two productions reveals Petersen's talent for formulaic filmmaking.[2]

The motivating factors that induce the two crews to place themselves in dangerous circumstances have a common root. In the case of *Das Boot* it is conventional warfare, while for the captain and crew of the *Andrea Gail* it is economic warfare. *The Perfect Storm* opens with Tyne returning from a failed fishing expedition. He is rebuked for not delivering a greater yield of swordfish. In contrast, Christina Cotter, the captain of another vessel, is quite successful, adding a gender dynamic to Tyne's humiliation. Tyne, a white working-class man from the U.S. South, loses his earning power, while a woman whose accent reveals her origins from somewhere in New England forges ahead. (Note that in *An American Psycho*, set in the mid-eighties, women do not pose an economic threat for an executive class that protects men with a glass ceiling.) Facing the prospect of a long winter (it is late October) without financial security, Tyne decides to go out to sea once again; this time farther than usual, where the swordfish are reported to be

In *The Perfect Storm* (Wolfgang Petersen, Warner Bros.), the disasters of a group of fisher-men on the high seas also suggest an apocalyptic burst of the bubble that has been sus-taining the United States for years. Digital frame enlargement.

more plentiful. This is a particularly risky venture given the storms that move through the area in the late fall. But the prospect of poverty is a powerful motivator and, despite warnings, the crew of the *Andrea Gail* sets forth. In a parallel side narrative, a man and two women in a leisure yacht are caught in one of the storms off the Florida coast but are successfully rescued by the Coast Guard. However, the Coast Guard is not as lucky, and one of its crew members perishes. In this instance the leisure class trumps the working class. The *Andrea Gail*'s fate is sealed when three separate severe weather systems come together to produce a "perfect storm," complete with waves over one hundred fifty feet high.

Although the audience knows the outcome, Petersen teases it out. Each adverse encounter and wave is more dangerous than the next. One spectacular feat follows quickly upon another, with an array of sea rescues, including Tyne climbing out onto the fishing spar to solder off the anchor in the midst of high seas and lashing winds. This is not a low-budget film. Petersen filmed many of the scenes during an actual hurricane. The effect of realism is perfectly reproduced in the film right through to the final, ominous wave. The viewer anticipates the wave, much in the same way that the meteorologist in the film who tracks the various storm systems back in the safe haven of a television studio sees the wave coming. But many viewers drew pleasure gauging the ways new digital technologies enhanced and revitalized the disaster film genre, and Petersen demonstrates what the forces of film technology, when expertly executed, can produce: the perfect sensation. As Proximus reminds Maximus in Ridley Scott's *Gladiator*: "You can't just kill, you have to give the audiences a show." And a spectacular show it is. Facing the enormous, towering, cresting wave, the rather pathetic 72-foot fishing boat meets it head-on. There is no question of survival. The wave, which was constructed in a huge studio tank, takes on the role of a character in and of itself. It will resurface six years later with similar destructive force as a 150-foot rogue wave in Petersen's *Poseidon* (2006). The parallel is clear: the economic bubble is a wave that must crash. The question is not if, but when.

▪▪▪▪▪ David and Goliath: *Gladiator* and *Traffic*

If both *An American Psycho* and *The Perfect Storm* leave viewers with a sense of inevitable doom in a world of misplaced values, *Gladiator* seeks to restore a universal faith in noble virtues, and the belief that good will ultimately triumph over evil. The film is replete with profound and weighty lines, such as "What we do in life echoes in eternity," or "You wrote to me once, listing the four chief virtues: Wisdom, Justice, Fortitude, and Temperance." In Scott's Roman Empire, both racial and class barriers can be overturned if the heart is true and a strict code of ethics is followed. *Gladiator* is a historical epic that rewrites the history of Maximus Decimux Aurelius (Russell Crowe, in his first major role), a Spanish farmer who, because of his bravery and skilled leadership qualities, became a general in the army of the Roman emperor Marcus Aurelius. He represents a simple, earnest character, whose eyes and brow are furrowed and brooding, wearing the pain of injurious deeds committed against the Roman people by nefarious elements in ancient Rome.

Gladiator is set around the year 300 (or is it the 1990s in the United States?) and opens during the Danubian Wars against the Germans. Maximus commands the army and secures success for the emperor, who, in turn, decides that Maximus should be his successor. Unfortunately, this means bypassing his own flesh and blood, Commodus (Joaquin Phoenix). The latter, unable to accept Marcus's wish, slays his father before he has the opportunity to publicly announce his decision, and does what he can to murder Maximus. The heroic general manages to escape, and, near death, is sold into serfdom in North Africa. As a slave he becomes a gladiator and uses his military training to organize an extraordinary group of fighters to skillfully vanquish their combatants. In the meantime, Rome under Commodus's decadent rule has sunk into a state of debauchery and unscrupulous behavior. The megalomaniacal Commodus attempts to be rid of the Senate and restore absolute rights to the emperor. He pits himself against the political assembly and plots to assassinate the consul elect and proclaim himself ruler. The historical figure of Commodus was so abusive, both personally and politically, that a wrestler eventually assassinated him during his bath. In Scott's film, Commodus's death is far nobler and occurs during a final duel between Maximus and the emperor in the public view of the spectators of the Coliseum in Rome. Although mortally wounded beforehand by Commodus, Maximus manages to kill him before expiring. Order is then restored with Marcus's young grandson proclaimed emperor, under the strict guidance and counsel of the wise senators. Unlike the historical Emperor Diocletian, a peasant who rose to a general's rank and ultimately became emperor, Scott returns us to a ruling structure predetermined by bloodlines and inheritance.

Gladiator is the Horatio Alger myth of ancient time, staged in the birthplace of democracy. Not once but twice must Maximus rise from nothing to establish himself. In the first instance he has to overcome his farmer origins to become a general, whereas in the second round he advances from slave to the triumphant restorer of order to the state. Maximus succeeds, the film implies, because he is true and uncorrupt. He follows a higher ideal, which is to serve humanity. Although he is obviously not Christian, there are several scenes that depict Maximus praying and demonstrating deep reverence to spiritual forces. In the world in which Maximus inhabits there are no prejudices, all slaves are equal, and indeed his closest friend is African. Geographically, the film emphasizes the far reach of the Roman Empire—southward, from Spain to North Africa and the Nubian Desert, and northward up to present-day Germany. It is also an empire riddled with corruption. Although the Senate, embodied by the character of the noble Senator Gracchus, seeks democratic rule, it is weakened and under constant threat by both internal and external elements. Maximus's higher charge is to empower the noble Senate and render it a legitimate governing branch once again.

Gladiator stresses the point that the Senate is entrusted by the people to represent their rights; it is their voice. The social context of impending catastrophe and crisis depicted in *Gladiator* parallels that of contemporary politics. Government has become mean-spirited in Washington, with rhetorical recklessness and rampant corruption. This condition has been in the making for some time. The Clinton years merely continued the expansion of the number of lobbyists in Washington and the power of special-interest groups set in motion by the Reagan administration in the 1980s. At base there is something deeply perverse, or deranged, as depicted in *American Psycho* or in Darren Aronofsky's tragic *Requiem for a Dream*, in which the promise of a better future barely survives a summer. In the latter film, the hedonism of the American way of life has become fully decadent, and stoned, with pharmaceuticals for the elderly and heroin for the youth. Scott's *Gladiator* calls for a return to less selfish ideals and a more just society. Just as ancient Rome is saved from the brink of disaster by the honorable Maximus, the film suggests that something similar could alter the course of destiny in the United States. Sadly, George W. Bush was no such hero, and the next decade made many yearn nostalgically for the nineties. The popularity of gladiator games and the public's seemingly unquenchable thirst for violence and ever more elaborate bloodbaths serves as a bitter commentary on the power of distraction, the lust for spectacle, and the perversity of real-life politics.

Steve Soderbergh's *Traffic* is another film in which a network of corruption is dismantled and law and order restored by extraordinary individuals who are beyond blemish. The film takes place in four contemporary locations: San Diego, Cincinnati, Washington, D.C., and Tijuana, Mexico. It consists of three interrelated narratives that are connected through illicit drug trade. Each narrative section is separated from the others through the use of different color film stocks and cameras: for Washington and Cincinnati no filter is used, producing a bluish cast; in San Diego the colors are lusher, and warmer; and in Mexico they bear a brownish hue (a tobacco filter). Each vignette concerns the high-stakes money, violence, and corruption connected to the illegal drug trade. In Tijuana, a police officer by the name of Rodriguez (Benicio Del Toro) is determined to squelch the drug cartel and restore peace and hope to youth in a city that has been overrun by drug-related crimes. In San Diego, two undercover drug investigators seek to prosecute one of the leading importers and distributors of drugs north of the border. The story in Cincinnati and Washington, D.C., centers on the new head of the DEA, Judge Wakefield (Michael Douglas), whose private-school, honor-roll daughter is addicted to crack cocaine. Rodriguez is successful in his mission. Yet the viewer is left with the feeling that only one head of the hydra has been cut off, with a new one ready to grow in its place. The film underscores that demand drives the drug industry. In San Diego the trafficker is released and rejoins his wife to rebuild their empire. Back on the U.S homefront, Wakefield rescues his daughter from the clutches of an African American pimp who prostitutes her out to older white men. Coincidentally, the trope of the black pimp preying on white, drug-addicted teenage girls recurs in *Requiem for a Dream*. Whatever such racial stereotyping may mean in these contexts, the two films depart in their conclusions: *Requiem* ends dismally, while in *Traffic* the wealth of the girl's parents allows her to be saved and rehabilitated.

What connects these separate worlds are the drugs that circulate from desperately poor Mexicans to poverty-stricken parts of North American cities to the suburban bathrooms of upper-class American youth. And what makes *Traffic* most interesting is the manner in which the narrative is told. It is structured as three separate stories, each of which is loosely connected through threads of correspondence related to drugs. Each narrative maintains its own separateness, existing as a monad, and, unlike in a conventional narrative, the characters and stories are never brought together at the end. The narrative is thus less like Charles Dickens's *Tale of Two Cities* (1859) than Don DeLillo's *Underworld* (1997). The viewer, like the reader, is placed in an omniscient perspective of looking at all the stories, making the connections, and seeing the totality of the network. In *Traffic* the network is exposed: drug culture is viral. It spreads rhizomatically, immune to borders and boundaries. The spectator is left to connect the dots.

Narrative Experiments: *Timecode* and *Cecil B. Demented*

Along the same lines as *Traffic*, Mike Figgis's *Timecode* experiments with parallel narrative worlds, albeit with an even more pronounced formal technique—the division of the screen into four discrete boxes. Figgis updates a formal innovation first introduced by Andy Warhol in *Chelsea Girls* (1966) and later used by Jean-Luc Godard and Anne-Marie Miéville in *Numero Deux* (1975). It was this millennial year, however, that marked a near completion of the digital revolution in film production, with the first film entirely produced on high-definition digital video—*Videocoq*—completed only months afterward. But until then the procedure was still in the experimental phase. The saturation of media culture by digital production led to the preponderance of split screens, multiple frames, and fragmented viewing experiences that perceptually alter the consumption and processing of information. Digital editing software technically facilitates the use of split screens and the production of simultaneous narrative sequences. *Timecode* anticipates a new mode of spectatorship, one in which the fundamental montage structure will be organized spatially rather than sequentially—"soft montage," as Harun Farocki and Kaja Silverman call it in reference to *Numero Deux* (see Farocki and Silverman). A novel form of cinematic vision emerges in the new millennium, one that is no longer monocular, or even binocular, but rather panoptical (see Crary).

Attention is split in *Timecode*, as four interconnected narratives unfold simultaneously in real time. Tremors from an earthquake that shake the set and interrupt all the characters onscreen remind us of the simultaneity of the four scenes. Each of the narratives is shot in videotape in a single ninety-minute take. The tape was later transferred to film for theatrical release, but the original is meant to be screened in its video format. If *Numero Deux* celebrated the flexibility and degree of experimentation that the relatively new technology of videotape permitted, *Timecode*, a quarter of a century later, stands as a farewell to that medium as we move beyond the analogue and into the digital age. As in *Chelsea Girls*, our attention is directed by subtle adjustments in the amplification of the soundtrack. The viewer follows that which s/he hears the clearest: vision follows sound. The directions that accompanied Warhol's film granted the projectionist the authority to determine the order in which the reels would be screened, thereby making each viewing a unique experience. In the DVD release of *Timecode* the spectator is provided with a similar power to decide which of the sound tracks of each quadrant to follow. This mode of participation parallels interactive games and hypertexts.

Timecode's underlying narrative is rather banal. Priority has been given to technical innovation, to how the narrative is far more interesting than what it tells. But perhaps that is Figgis's point—to demonstrate that content no longer matters in the new regime of cinema. Unlike Kurosawa's *Rashomon* (1950), in which the same story told from multiple perspectives captivates the viewer, in *Timecode* it is the fact of multiple perspectives, and not the story, that is captivating. It is a self-reflexive narrative about a production company, Red Mullet, which happens also to be *Timecode's* production company. The film exposes the behind-the-scenes aspects of making a film, from developing storylines to securing funding, casting actors, and the like. A few romantic affairs and interpersonal tensions are thrown in to heighten the action.

Set in Hollywood, the film is about filmmaking and the entertainment industry, a theme that will resurface in several other films of the year. Unlike late-nineteenth-century culture, which greatly anticipated the year 1900 (Sigmund Freud delayed the publication of *The Interpretation of Dreams* so that it would bear the imprint "1900"), in film culture the year does not appear to have been as significant. This is likely due to the fact that the centenary of cinema was commemorated a mere five years prior in 1995. Yet several significant productions do address the state of the art at the new millennium. In some instances homage is paid to classics, such as E. Elias Merhige's *Shadow of the Vampire*, with its imaginary narrative of the making of F. W. Murnau's *Nosferatu* (1922). Early on, the character of the leading female star, Greta, complains to director Murnau: "Theater gives me life;

Film takes it away!" The comment is telling, for it articulates the anxiety of cinema in the 1920s to find its place among the other more established arts such as theater. Film is vampiric, feeding off other forms; and at the dawn of the new millennium the same anxiety prevails—cinema's role within the entertainment industry and its various competing offshoots.

Ever-so-outrageous director John Waters made sure to start new millennium with a bang with his cinematic missile, *Cecil B. Demented*. The film explicitly lambastes feel-good, righteous, or stoic characters such as Erin Brockovich, *Gladiator*'s Maximus, or other affirmative fare produced by Hollywood. The plot involves a group of rogue film students in Baltimore who, led by director Cecil B. Demented, plot to kidnap a popular Hollywood actress, Honey Whitlock (Melanie Griffith). The terrorist group's mantra is anti-Hollywood, by which they mean the studio system, high production values, formulaic plots, lack of experimentation, and the incessant generation of affirmative entertainment for passive audiences. Each member of Cecil's band, from the lighting technician to the makeup artist, the costume designer to the character actors, has tattooed onto his or her body the name of a filmmaker-artist who defied the system to maintain artistic integrity. These great figures include Rainer Werner Fassbinder, Kenneth Anger, Pedro Almodóvar, and Sam Peckinpah. Cecil proudly bears Otto Preminger on his forearm and nightly leads a group prayer to Andy Warhol. Throughout the film, the characters throw out lines championing Underground Cinema, Guerilla Cinema, and Third Cinema. They decry egregious industry practices such as the reshooting of foreign films into English (necessitated because American's "don't read subtitles"), and maintain that "family" is just another word for censorship.

One particular target is the adaptation of television shows, comics, and interactive games into film. The motley crew of characters blames the fact that they have sold only one ticket to their film on the competition at the local multiplex, *The Flintstones 2*, which is drawing large audiences. It confirms their belief that audiences seek comfort in the tried and true: that which is most predictable and requires little or no work on the part of the spectator. The same formulaic Taylorist production model that avant-garde auteur Hans Richter summoned when speaking about the film industry of the twenties (he wrote that it churned out patterned productions the way that garment factories mass-produced clothes of various sizes and colors) is still in place nearly a century later (see Richter). *Cecil B. Demented*'s band of cinematic outsiders stages increasingly violent events in their attempt to disrupt Baltimore's burgeoning film industry. In the 2000s, Baltimore, like so many formerly industrial cities, including Philadelphia, Pittsburgh, and

Providence, sought to reinvent itself as a cultural center, hoping for revitalization through culture industry investments. Film was just one of the media touted by the myth of the creative economy. Waters spoofs on these initiatives, including a scene with the mayor of Baltimore welcoming filmmakers to the Eastern Shore and celebrating the making of "Gump Again," a sequel to *Forrest Gump*. In one shot, Forrest eats a crab cake (blue crab is a symbol of Baltimore), which he likens to society. In the background we see not the skyline of Baltimore but the Twin Towers of Lower Manhattan, indicating that with green screens any backdrop can be added to a scene. It is precisely this degree of artificiality and manipulation that horrifies the renegade group. Their film, they proclaim, will be based on reality—a reality show. It will be produced outside the scope of a studio and without professional actors (excluding Honey). Reminding the viewer of this "reality" is Patty Hearst, former hostage turned SLA terrorist, who appears in the film as another character's mother. By the film's end, Honey will (like Hearst) be converted by those who hold her captive. Akin to those directors worthy of a tattoo, John Waters is a longtime independent filmmaker who has not sold out and has assumed cult status. *Cecil B. Demented* is his acerbic commentary on the film industry at the turn of the century.

Satire: *Bamboozled* and *O Brother, Where Art Thou?*

One of the team of advisors in *Timecode* criticizes the portrayal of a stereotyped black character with the pronouncement that "Black can be multidimensional." But in order to see that realized in film, we have to turn to Spike Lee's acerbic *Bamboozled*. The film has one of the most striking opening lines: against the music and lyrics of Stevie Wonder's "Misrepresented People," the protagonist, Pierre Delacroix, enunciates the word "Satire" and proceeds to deliver a series of definitions: "1a. A literary work in which human vice or folly is ridiculed or attacked scornfully." The definition continues, ending with various synonyms. *Bamboozled*, then, scathingly critiques American society and its deeply entrenched racist roots. Notably, Lee's tattoo-worthy status was honored in *Cecil B. Demented*, where his name was evoked reverentially.

The narrative of *Bamboozled* follows the character of Delacroix, a writer of screenplays for television, a "creative person" who lives in a room in a clock tower in New York City. The huge arms of the clock face can be seen outside his window. He literally lives inside time. The clock is ticking as Delacroix acknowledges the arrival of the twenty-first century, which he knows will bring about the termination of television—and thus his lifeline. The impact of developments and inventions in mass entertainment, such as interactive games, on the television network has been too great.[3] With the ratings for CSN, the station that employs Delacroix, perilously low, the management concludes that a new program is needed, one that will garner mass appeal and become an overnight success. Delacroix, the one black man on the network team, is charged by his boss to produce a black comedy show. It is made clear that the show should not be about socially integrated and upwardly mobile blacks. The color line has to be clearly demarcated, and innuendos that might confuse an audience and make them think have to be avoided. In order to carry out his new job, Delacroix researches old films and television shows, and Lee splices in archival footage of African Americans entertainers—or, as Henry Louis Gates has it, "signifying monkeys" (see Gates). We see and hear the laughter that follows upon the humiliation of characters in situation comedies such as "The Jeffersons" and "Sanford and Son." Included, too, are recordings from old minstrel shows and classical films. The repertoire is inserted at opportune moments. For instance, when Delacroix presents to the board his concept for "The New Millennium Minstrel Show," the most enthusiastic endorsement comes from a white writer from Iowa who reveals that "The Jeffersons" was his only contact with black America during his youth. The stereotypes of a television program whose sole purpose is entertainment become the reality for a vast majority of Americans whose relative isolation forecloses the possibility of a reality check.

In order for his show to be a success, Delacroix insists that the main players must be unknown. He picks up off the street two marginal characters—Mantan and Sleep'n Eat—who regularly sing and dance in a public space outside CSN headquarters. Delacroix has them perform their comedy routine, not in the projects or other sites of urban blight but, true to the roots of the genre, in a watermelon patch. The first pilot is treated warily by spectators. However, the prompts that command "Applause" or "Howl" gradually provoke a reaction, and, despite just about everyone's expectations, the racist show becomes an overnight success. Even more frightening is that the show appeals not only to white viewers with their deeply ingrained prejudices, but also to African American audiences who, having inculcated white values, laugh at and are entertained by their own degradation. It is the latter public that Spike Lee brilliantly characterizes. This is supported by a parallel scene in a predominantly black nightclub where Delacroix's father, "Junebug," performs a one-man comedy show to the appreciative laughter of patrons. Junebug's final words of wisdom to his son

Outrageous and pointed, *Bamboozled* (Spike Lee, New Line Cinema) satirizes media and race relations that may be far less progressive than the new millennium promises. Digital frame enlargement.

before he passes out from too much drink that evening are "Always make them laugh"—words that Delacroix echoes at the end of *Bamboozled* as he lies dying in a pool of his own blood.

The two entertainers around which the program focuses are not quite dark enough to be true minstrels, so in the fashion of yesteryear blackface is applied. The recipe has been carefully researched and dug out of entertainment industry archives to reveal the tar-like concoction that must be carefully prepared every evening. A thick layer of cocoa butter must be applied to the hands and face in order to avoid chemical burns and skin irritation. Lee includes the ritual of heating up the black paste under a low-level flame (like crack cocaine) and its painstaking application. Cherry red lipstick completes the mask, expanding and enhancing the lips. The result is a purely racist caricature. As the show gains in popularity, Delacroix's collection of the type of early-twentieth-century black sculptures and figurines that would adorn white people's homes grows. A mechanical "Nigger bank" that Delacroix's assistant gives him after the first night is featured. By the film's end such ornaments overpopulate his formerly pristine office. Their bulging eyes and mouths stare and smile at him in his final moments.

Mantan and Sleep'n Eat's comedy routine includes singing and dancing as well as the telling of lewd jokes. They perform their roles as entertainers perfectly. Their humor draws on stereotypes related to African Americans, spanning the gamut from insatiable sexuality to rampant criminal deviance and stunning ignorance. A mass audience of TV viewers, both black and white, expresses their appreciation as they roar in laughter. Their consumption of racism is too much fun. They chant: "Niggers is a beautiful thing!" But not all are amused. Outraged audiences picket the CSN building, accusing the program and therefore the corporation of throwing blacks backward in time to the turn of the twentieth century. Delacroix's own mother tells him that he should be ashamed of himself. Al Sharpton's voice condemning the abuse is crosscut against the smug smirks of white executives. Lee's insertion of Sharpton, a real-life activist and politician, throws the film's fictional narrative into question. Viewers might watch Spike Lee's *Bamboozled* for entertainment, but the director doesn't let them forget that the reality of racism continues today in films, TV, music, and everyday life. This point is driven home by the mock ads shown before the program begins. One of the ads is for a high-octane alcoholic beverage, Da Bomb, which is guaranteed to work on the black man the way Viagra works for whites. Lee includes dancing and gyrating bodies of scantily clad African American women who writhe against the bodies of black men. The ad is reminiscent of the type of rapper aesthetics favored by MTV. Another commercial depicts Tommy Hill Nigger (a pun on the America fashion designer Tommy Hilfiger) as a white racist making enormous profits from the African Americans who buy his clothes. Once again these references to the "real" point to the way in which racism continues today, and how the repetition of degrading images produces a highly problematic view of black people. Where are those ads that feature the many successful blacks in today's America?

But there is one other group that is very critical of the show. The brother of Sloan Hopkins, Delacroix's main assistant, belongs to a militant group, Mau-Maus, which recalls the Black Panthers. Interestingly enough, Mau-Maus does have one white member. Their organization is centered on music and their defiant and angry lyrics decry the plight of African Americans in society. If Sloan has taken the path of education and polish as a way out of these conditions, they have chosen the opposite route. Disgusted and fed up with the success of Mantan, they decide to kidnap him and stage the ultimate show for which white audiences have been waiting: a public lynching.

Unbeknownst to Mau-Maus, however, Mantan has just rebelled while on the air, refusing the blackface and the role Delacroix has assigned him. He comes out on stage to the deafening silence of a disappointed live audience that, in support of his character, wears blackface. Mantan launches the following appeal: "Cousins, I want you all to go to your windows and scream out with all the life you can muster up inside your bruised, assaulted, and battered bodies, 'I am sick and tired of being a Nigger, and I am not going to take it anymore.'" The reference is to the 1976 film *Network*, with its scathing critique of the banality of U.S. television and a protagonist who is similarly fed up: "I am a human being, God damn it, and my life has value. . . . I want all of you to get up out of your chairs, go to the window, open it and yell, 'I'm as mad as hell and I'm not going to take it anymore!'" Of course, in 1976 this message was delivered by and for a white audience. Television programming was the target. The sign that Delacroix places on top of his television set in his home—"Feed the idiot box!"—has a 1960s and 1970s sense to it, but it seems to have lost currency today. "The idiot box" that demands constant nourishment so that it will be able to churn out greater degrees of idiocy is driven by the networks' pursuit of higher ratings—all of which translate into more advertisements and greater profits. Lee evokes a film from a quarter of a century ago to make the point that television as a communications medium has not advanced. Rather, it seems to have moved backward, culling from early-twentieth-century forms of entertainment and thereby perpetuating a loop that forecloses the idea of progress.

Mantan is now fired and thrown out of the studio, where Mau-Maus immediately kidnap him. Upon learning that his television career is over, however, the Mau-Maus rapper group plans a final show. They contact all the major networks to announce Mantan's public execution, which they plan to broadcast during primetime. No amount of ransom money will stay their resolve. In the final moments, and before millions of TV spectators, they force Mantan to do the "dance of death" as he avoids their bullets. This "ultimate show" is actually the penultimate act before they finally hit their target and kill the actor like an animal. Video recordings of his dead face in close-up, eyes wide open, are projected around the nation. The public execution, witnessed by a thrill-seeking audience with an insatiable desire for ever-more spectacular images (not so different from the gladiator spectators during ancient Roman), moves us back in time to the weekly entertainment of public lynchings in the American South (postcards of such events were often made and circulated), and forward in time to the taped executions carried out by al-Qaeda and circulated in the media. Mantan dies before a nation of complicit spectators. His tormenters are caught and killed by the police. Delacroix is shot by his assistant Sloan. In the end we are left with a dozen dead black men, while white society begins its search for the next amusement.

Interestingly, *O Brother, Where Art Thou?* picks up on the minstrel theme, albeit from a radically different point of departure. George Clooney stars as

Everett in Joel and Ethan Coen's contemporary rendition of the *Odyssey*. A recent escapee from a chain gang, Everett and two fellow convicts wander the rural South during the 1930s. The film tracks their many escapades as they evade the law. At one point they pose as a singing group that goes by the name of the Soggy Bottom Boys. They record a song in a ramshackle studio at the crossroads of nowhere—the type of place where so many African American musicians recorded and sold the rights to their music for virtually nothing. This practice continued well into the late sixties, when numerous white musicians appropriated the blues. When Everett and his cohorts find themselves the targets of the Ku Klux Klan, the film makes clear what has thus far been implicit—that although played by white actors, the characters are supposed to be black. The Coens thus seem to acknowledge the impossibility of adequately representing African Americans, especially in film comedy. The directors cleverly get around this obstacle by deftly avoiding it altogether.

For his part, Lee features a brilliant montage of images from the long twentieth century of film and television history before *Bamboozled*'s closing credits. From early clips of African Americans dancing to sections of *The Birth of a Nation*, from Al Jolson in *The Jazz Singer* to Shirley Temple tapping away with two blackface dance partners, and with scenes from "The Jeffersons" and "Sanford and Son" and popular cartoon characters (in blackface) such as Mickey Mouse or in *Song of the South*, a cascade of images depicting blacks as less than intelligent yet highly entertaining rushes across the screen. We see whites putting on blackface and blacks making themselves blacker. We see fears of miscegenation. But above all the shots are intended to be *funny*—to "keep us laughing." This is a humor with roots embedded in racism.

What this montage sequence also makes perfectly apparent is that most of the images are now available on and through the television screen. Old films are replayed and many new series are made for television. Film and television become inextricably entwined and complicit in their crimes against humanity. As the characters in *Cecil B. Demented* complain, no longer is it a one-way street from theatrical release of films to television broadcast; today, television programs, comic book characters, and Saturday morning cartoons are frequently adapted into films. The Ouroborus circle is complete: one medium feeds off of and cannibalizes the content and style of the other. If television was once seen as the enemy of film, today, as Delacroix puts it, with "the onslaught of the Internet, video, and interactive games, 900 channels to choose from, our valued audience has dramatically eroded . . . like rats fleeing a sinking ship."

Of course, the partnership between television and film makes it clear that the fear is also that of the loss of theater tickets. In the era of the "home entertainment system," the public for movies can no longer be taken for granted. (The latest craze for 3D is only the most recent in a string of attempts to remedy this fact in the new millennium.) The feeling one gets from viewing the amazing montage sequence at the end of Lee's film is less one of nostalgia for the golden age of television and film than of disgust for the bad new days. The material chains of slavery have been replaced by the immaterial fetters of entertainment industry ideology. The word "millennium" is repeated more than any other throughout the film. Lee doesn't allow the significance of the new millennium to get away. Racism in the twentieth century was largely propagated by media images. Lee throws down the gauntlet and challenges us to say no in the twenty-first century, to reject the same old stereotypes and images rather than accept themas if they were inevitable. Moreover, Lee targets not only film audiences but producers as well. The film industry, he suggests, can do more than "always make them laugh"; it can do more than evening television or the 24/7 Internet. It can, in short, be more than just entertainment.

NOTES

1. The double nature of an asocial psychotic with a polished veneer of sociality is also developed by the makers of the comedy *Me, Myself & Irene*. Like Bateman, this film's protagonist, Charlie/Hank, epitomizes the schizophrenic nature of the United States at the end of the twentieth century. The nation has a serious personality disorder that is inclined to violent eruptions with deep misogynist, homophobic, and racist roots. What is striking is that at the conclusion of both films no cure is in sight for the personality disorder. The characters are left to adapt to their diseases, to live with their symptoms.

2. Petersen was a member of the same class of Deutsche Film und Fernsehakademie Berlin as avant-garde filmmaker Harun Farocki, Red Army Faction member Holger Meins, and feminist Helke Sanders, though he was schooled in a very different cinematic tradition.

3. In 2011, the gaming industry for the first time surpassed the film industry in total revenue.

2001

Movies, Smart Films, and Dumb Stories

LINDA RUTH WILLIAMS

Though no one knew it as January dawned, this was the year that will forever be divided into Before and After by the events of 9/11. Yet 9/11 was only a brief moment in the stories of the year. George W. Bush was sworn in as president in January, succeeding Bill Clinton; Wikipedia was launched. In April the first space tourist went into orbit. Many terrorist attacks took place across the world—in Israel, Sri Lanka, and Afghanistan; in September anthrax was mailed to U.S. news organizations and two Democratic senators, killing five people. Oklahoma City bomber Timothy McVeigh was executed in June; the "shoe-bomber" Richard Reid attempted to blow up a plane in December. Yet 9/11 eclipsed all else, and Osama bin Laden, along with al-Qaeda, instantly became household names. In October the United States, in alliance with the United Kingdom, invaded Afghanistan with the aim of defeating al-Qaeda, which was based there. Far more people died in earthquakes and storms in India, Peru, El Salvador, Algeria, and Cuba, but 9/11 remained the central trauma for the U.S. collective consciousness.

It was also only a brief moment in the year's cinematic story. The *Variety Top 10* for the opening week in January was frankly unremarkable, largely a mixed bag of holiday season releases carried over from 2000, and by the year's end the widespread critical conclusion had deemed the year one of the worst ever for U.S. film, colored by a summer of lucrative sequels: *Rush Hour 2, The Mummy Returns, Jurassic Park 3, Dr. Dolittle 2, American Pie 2, Scary Movie 2*, all released between April and August, three of which were to secure a place in the year's boxoffice top ten. "If films like *Pearl Harbor* and *Tomb Raider* continue to be useful indicators of the American psyche," wrote Nick James, "few now think of them as aesthetic triumphs on any level. For what it's worth . . . world cinema has been a much richer source this year than the U.S." ("Own Goals All Round").

Four titles in the year's boxoffice top ten were end-of-year holiday season releases, representing a new strategy for Hollywood. Most significant were three lucrative new franchises that opened and cleaned up in November and December. Only one of these giants, *Ocean's Eleven*, was thoroughbred U.S. fare (albeit a remake). The other two were U.S./UK or U.S./New Zealand co-productions. *Harry Potter and the Sorcerer's Stone*, though helmed by a U.S. director, featured a largely British cast and developed from a British literary origin (despite its bespoke U.S. title for audiences alienated by the word "philosopher"). The mighty *Lord of the Rings* series headed up with *The Fellowship of the Ring*. Even within this small group there is little coherence: the slick off-the-peg remake *Ocean's Eleven* is not so much a movie as a starry cast list, while the latter two fantasy adaptations perhaps starred special effects more than personnel. Generically they have little in common, but they do hold a unique place in recent Hollywood history in refocusing the cinematic calendar away from the summer and toward the holiday season.[1]

The few case-history titles I discuss in more detail here do not constitute the year's canon of greats, but they provide interesting examples of a few distinct industry trends. Looked at generically and in terms of target audiences, this was a significant year for variations on the war film, including a range of titles focused on U.S. military and espionage involvement in other nations' politics; the romantic comedies and the neo-woman's film; mainstream "smart" cinema; popular auteur works; and adaptations. Other trends would be well worth further exploration, though I lack the space to follow these through here. In particular, a number of gross-out comedy films developed from Farrelly brothers precedents: *Osmosis Jones* and *Shallow Hal* were both produced and directed by the brothers; *Say It Isn't So* was a Farrelly production directed by J. B. Rogers (who also did *American Pie 2*), while Jerry Zucker's ensemble comedy *Rat Race* showed traces of Farrelly-esque influence. However, the Tom Green vehicle *Freddy Got Fingered* was singled out as falling even below the bottom-scraping of these titles.

A slightly politer route was taken by *A Knight's Tale*, a daft retro-pop sing-along set in medieval Europe, which, in using Queen to accompany a jousting match and vintage David Bowie as the music for a banquet, may have set in motion the vogue for refitting existing pop songs to augment anachronistic stories. Baz Luhrmann's *Moulin Rouge!* did the same in more spectacular fashion later in the year, with the likes of Nicole Kidman, Ewan McGregor, and Jim Broadbent singing Elton John and Madonna songs to each other. The trend continued further into the decade with Marie Antoinette rocking to Adam and the Ants and Abba's back catalog getting its own movie.

Kids' movies also moved into this "borrowed soundtrack" terrain. The venerable Disney-led tradition of original songs punctuating musical-structured films was abandoned with *Shrek* (released in April), the first film by DreamWorks Animation. In addition to its Disney-satirizing storyline, parodic fairy-tale smartness, and innovative CG-animation, *Shrek* appropriated pop classics for its musical soundtrack (a Monkees song performed by rock band Smash Mouth and Eddie Murphy, and a classic Leonard Cohen song performed by John Cale). This "celluloid jukebox" approach to pop history as source material was to see the franchise through to its conclusion in 2010, and became a feature of DreamWorks Animation products such as *Shark Tale*, *Madagascar*, and *Bee Movie* later in the decade. Disney's big release of the year was the smart-scripted *Monsters Inc.*, released for the end-of-year box office and featuring just one iconic song commissioned from Randy Newman. If *Shrek* satirizes DreamWorks's rival Disney (Andrew Sarris called it "the antithesis of everything Disney stands for, from *Snow White and the Seven Dwarfs* to *Pearl Harbor*"), *Monsters Inc.* arguably answers back by satirizing corporate America itself: the monsters of the title generate electricity from the screams of human children, but then see the error of their ways.[2] At the other end of the scale—and certainly not a children's movie—the important Steven Spielberg film *Artificial Intelligence: AI* also read children as commodities, toys for adult consumption.

The films I explore below speak to disparate genres and trends, but each tells a story about the questions being posed by cinema about what women, men, and children want to consume with their popcorn. If 9/11 was a curiously unifying moment in U.S. culture, film releases and audiences continued to be as differentiated as ever, with diverse markets—indies, blockbusters, genres—sustained and developed regardless of the global story that unfolded in Manhattan and elsewhere in September. The attack on the World Trade Center and the Pentagon has lured critics ever since into reading apocalypse—impending or retrospective—into many titles produced in blissful ignorance of what was to come. I return to this issue as I conclude the essay. I want to begin, however, with those films most prone to "9/11 hindsight," focused on war, espionage and foreign policy, and the military.

The Pentagon in Hollywood: *Pearl Harbor* and *Black Hawk Down*

There is a long history of military involvement in Hollywood production, and of Hollywood servicing the military's propaganda arm, but the year threw out some especially interesting cases of this unholy marriage. Such instances have become grist to the mill of conspiracy theorists, inflected by the B.C./A.D. effect of 9/11. Two Jerry Bruckheimer productions, released on either side of the attacks, show the multiple strands of cinema's involvement with the Pentagon and the business of imagining war. The flag-waving, Disney-distributed epic *Pearl Harbor* was directed by blockbuster hack Michael Bay, while *Black Hawk Down* seemed to be a different type of movie—tougher, more ambivalent about war, helmed by the sometimes more cerebral mainstream auteur Ridley Scott (though it looked like something his brother Tony might have directed). Significantly, it is the latter film on which the Department of Defense was most proud to have collaborated.

Pearl Harbor was firmly established as an event movie by the manifold press coverage about its excesses, which emerged over the months of production. The film's escalating costs and historical fudging were the top movie story as the year opened—stars and producers back-ending salaries, U.S. warships masquerading as Japanese ones to the horror of veterans, Bay's alleged desire to redesign naval uniforms because the originals weren't photogenic enough. It had the (then) biggest authorized budget in Hollywood history—figures range from $130 to $140 million, with critics doing what Scott called "reviewing the money rather than the movie," calculating the running-time maths of dollars per minute of screen time ("*Pearl*"). Stories about the shoot, involving a huge attack sequence filmed on the Mexican set that had hosted the *Titanic* production (1997), were largely eclipsed by the spectacle of money leaking like water through the production's fingers. Similar tales also accompanied the *Titanic* shoot, and clearly the filmmakers were hoping for a repeat boxoffice performance. However, with its wooden acting, cut-and-paste script, and a running time of 183 minutes, *Pearl Harbor* became synonymous with Hollywood excess and the Disneyfication of history. Bay was reported as saying—astonishingly—that *Pearl Harbor* could not end on a "downer" (it concludes with a victorious counterattack on Tokyo): "America needed to win this one. . . . People needed to walk out happy" ("*Pearl*"). Decorum only prevailed in promotion where, as *Variety* put it, "the Mouse House decided that it would be tasteless to link Happy Meals to an event in which thousands of people died" (Lyons, "Disney Preps" 87). This bloated profile was consolidated in the style of its premiere. U.S. taxpayers, via the naval budget, funded the six-day trip of the nuclear-powered aircraft carrier USS *John C. Stennis* from San Diego to Hawaii (at a cost of at least $500,000 per day), bleachers were set up on the flight deck, and the ship became what the *New York Times* called "the world's largest and most expensive outdoor theater" (Dao). More complaints were aired about the premiere location itself, which many consider to be a graveyard rather than a red-carpet location. Then there was the editing of the movie so that it wouldn't offend Japanese audiences by producers mindful that 20 percent of *Titanic*'s profits had come from Japan.[3]

Quite simply, *Pearl Harbor* promised to tell the epic tale of the last time America was attacked by foreign nationals on its own territory, while (unbeknownst to everyone) the next time was just around the corner. As might be expected from a Michael Bay film, it plays out rather like a 183-minute trailer for itself: elliptical, constantly on the move, a parade of rapid editing, ponderous slow motion, and tracking shots. Marcia Landy argues that the real Pearl Harbor is often seen as "a yardstick for understanding the 'American Character' in crisis" (96); Bay's *Pearl Harbor* also often stands as a yardstick of contemporary Hollywood. A series of semi-prescient grandstanding speeches mouthed by the protagonists provides anchors in the midst of this stylistic busyness. As Nurse Lt. Evelyn Johnson, Kate Beckinsale concludes with a speech positing a before-and-after function to the Japanese attack on Pearl Harbor and the Doolittle Raid that followed, but here the screenplay rewrites the events as a positive turning point: "This much is certain. Before the Doolittle raid, America knew nothing but defeat. After it, there was hope of victory. . . . America suffered, but America grew stronger. . . . The times tried our souls, and through the trial, we overcame." Earlier, on the brink of taking part in the Doolittle Raid, Josh Hartnett as Captain Danny Walker opines, "We might die doing this and we want to know what it's for," to which Alec Baldwin (playing Lt. Colonel Doolittle himself) responds in a manner worthy of post-Iraq, post-Afghanistan justification: "Victory belongs to those who believe in it the most and believe in it the longest. We're gonna believe. We're gonna make America believe too." Yet the privilege of hindsight enabled subsequent writers to see the excesses of the movie in light of the national disaster that was to strike in September. "While the nation and the administration snoozed in the late spring of 2001, unaware that the next Pearl Harbor was less than four months away," wrote Frank Rich in the *New York Times* in 2003, "the gala premiere party for Bruckheimer's summer extravaganza . . . took place." The explosion-heavy film is then seen as a symptom of a comatose nation so secured by its own jingoism it cannot see it is teetering on the brink. Excessive spectacle becomes a symptom of meretricious waste: "As Ben Affleck and a giddy corps of press junketeers watched, F-15 fighters flew overhead and Navy Seals parachuted onto the deck from a Black Hawk helicopter" (Rich). Even Bruckheimer admitted it was extra-ordinary: "The next premiere will be on the moon," he told *Variety* (Ryan). For the Navy, the costs were offset by the plentiful pro-military publicity the premiere afforded them, with Hollywood fiction doing service as a recruitment aid. Indeed, Disney's poster campaign even featured stars Ben Affleck, Kate Beckinsale, and Cuba Gooding Jr. in mock-ups of 1940s recruitment notices.

For reviewers, the easiest critical strategy was to point to the gap between swollen budget and weak result, often via the rhetorical device of pairing a spectacular adjective with a diminishing term—epic failure, excessively poor, "extravagantly average" (Scott "Pearl Harbor"). Nevertheless, partly because of extremely patriotic subject and perspective during a period of crisis, *Pearl Harbor* was considered critic-proof, opening at over 3,000 cinemas in the United States and in 90 percent of overseas markets in a near day-and-date international release. It was the linchpin in the industry's then highest grossing four-day period ever, contributing $75.1 million to total takings of $176.5 million over the long Memorial Day weekend. This was a short-term effect, however; as the summer progressed, *Pearl Harbor* did not garner the repeat business of a *Titanic*. Negative word-of-mouth ensured that theatrical interest in the film dwindled quickly.

But as the year drew to a close a rather more interesting and perhaps less straightforward title was released from the Bruckheimer stable, accompanied by post-9/11 ballyhoo and a U.S. Defense Department endorsement as one of the releases it was proudest to have helped. *Black Hawk Down*, a grim and violent Ridley Scott–directed feature, was shot before 9/11 and released after, and its story of a military debacle lent it particular resonance in that heated moment. As we have seen, Bruckheimer is no stranger to the Pentagon, and when he visited he told Army Vice Chief of Staff General John M. Keane, "General, I'm going to make a movie that you and your Army will be proud of." In a Defense Department press release, Keane noted, "He did that, so we thank him for it." David Robb calls Bruckheimer "king of the modern, big-budget military movie" who changed the scripts of *Top Gun* (1986) and *Armageddon* (1998) as well as *Pearl Harbor* and *Black Hawk Down* "to satisfy the Pentagon's demands" (94). "'Pro-military' projects are Bruckheimer's speciality," writes Robb (95).

However, I want to read *Black Hawk Down* as a rather more nihilistic film than this would suggest. Based on a notorious intervention in Somalia in 1993 in which U.S. soldiers attempted to remove two senior Somali political figures, *Black Hawk Down* charts the dismal failure of an operation that involved a core military group moving into the most dangerous area of the nation's capital, Mogadishu, for an abduction that was estimated would last one hour. The mission failed, with hundreds dying over many hours of street-level struggle and two Black Hawk helicopters spectacularly shot down by the Somalis. The mistakes, the deaths, the waiting, the rescues—both thwarted and (for some) eventually successful—are charted with the confidence of a director skilled in the marriage of action spectacle and thriller tension. Yet *Black Hawk Down* is, I would say, less sure of the morality of its subject than other war epics, swinging wildly from anxiety about foreign policy interference to spectacular celebration of U.S. might and machismo, overlaid with a bombardment of images of destruction and distress. Much of the film is a rage of spent ammo rounds, spurting arterial blood, and shooting so loud that one character goes deaf (even the actor in question, Ewen Bremner, went partially deaf temporarily as a result of noise on the shoot).

"Visceral" doesn't begin to describe the experience of *Black Hawk Down*. Unlike *Pearl Harbor*, it is a film confident in its power to affect. The spaghetti-western inflected score and cinematography might suggest moral undecidability, but many critics read it as surprisingly even-handed. For Roger Ebert, "The movie's implied message is that America on that day lost its resolve to risk American lives in distant and obscure struggles, and that mindset weakened our stance against terrorism" ("Black Hawk Down"). The focus of the film is on the street-level combat experience of the soldiers, with a final message of fellowship in the ranks (perhaps the only moral it ultimately stands by): "It's about the man next to you. That's all it is." This is powerfully contextualized by two moments, first when a sage Somali businessman advising the Americans tells Garrison (Sam Shepard), a U.S. military leader, "I think you shouldn't have come here. This is civil war, it's our war." The second is perhaps the film's harshest blow, when a closing title tells us that during the depicted operation 1,000 Somalis and 19 Americans died, and one of the corrupt leaders managed to stay alive three more years. An antiwar message emerges through the experience of sitting through this grim soldier's-eye view of combat, especially once we are told it was a waste of life and effort.

More cinematically startling is Scott's treatment of his stars. *Black Hawk Down*—an ensemble film if ever there was one—is replete with them, but beyond the initial establishing sequence where characters are introduced and the mission justified, they are systematically depersonalized. Here star actors are not just deglamorized by dust and costume and confusing cinematography; they are rendered almost entirely unrecognizable in the undifferentiated morass. Hierarchies are erased in the soup of uniform, smoke, and blood. Though the unfolding failed "extraction" of the Somalis and the botched rescue of the U.S. soldiers is carried out by two different military strata (the select Delta Force and the less esteemed Task Force Rangers, respectively), in the midst of the action on the ground even these differences, which hold such sway in the elitism of military rankings, become meaningless. The racist cliché often used to articulate bigoted white people's failure to recognize black individuals ("they all look the same") is here thrown back not just onto white men but onto white Hollywood stars who, via Scott's obfuscating mise-en-scène, do indeed all look the same. Scott even conceded to the historical inaccuracy of having the troops' names painted on their helmets, acknowledging that once in uniform audiences can't tell the difference and might therefore need some help. *Variety* conjectured that it "may well have been Scott's aim to keep the men basically anonymous and interchangeable—to further the point that this is what war is, that it has always been thus and always will be" (McCarthy, "This 'Hawk'" 35). If this is the case, it is a profoundly anti-star strategy. Was it Ewan McGregor or Josh Hartnett or Jason Isaacs who just got shot—and does it matter? This, of course, does not stop the undifferentiated black hordes who threaten the heroes from serving the uneasy politics of the film as it aligns the audience with U.S. invaders rather than Somali nationals.

However, as an unashamed hardware fetish film, *Black Hawk Down*'s overriding interest is not finally in its human stars but in its metal ones: Humvees, mortars, machine guns, Black Hawk and Little Bird helicopters. It is the bodies of machines rather than the bodies of people, hero or enemy, which matter here. Nothing new about that; two years after *Star Wars: Episode 1—The Phantom Menace* (1999), a year before *Attack of the Clones* (2002), and in a decade that saw *Transformers* (2007) return to the screen, the machine as star is a familiar staple of the Hollywood blockbuster. However, Ridley Scott's machines are different—degraded, destroyed artifacts of technology as well as emblems of jingoism. Though I suggested earlier that there are traces of Tony Scott's high-octane action style running through this film, it is its ethical and psychological uncertainty, and refusal to resolve its politics, that makes this a recognizable Ridley Scott film. In *Top Gun* Tony celebrates dog-fighting F-14's high on glorious victory; here Ridley aestheticizes Black Hawks *down*, crashed and disintegrating, like his alien spaceship of 1979 or his dying replicants of 1982, each all the more interesting because they are caught in the moment of defeat.

Women are largely absent from *Black Hawk Down*; when they do appear they are usually either picturesque wallpaper or symbolic devices. But *Pearl Harbor*, which orchestrates the central attack sequence around male victimage and female action, differs in this regard. Once the Japanese attack unfolds, an extended sequence of explosions, high-octane aerial chases, and sinking ships, punctuated by gratuitous jingoistic flashes (forlorn U.S.

Pearl Harbor (Michael Bay, Touchstone Pictures): war movie meets woman's film. Digital frame enlargement.

flags drift across the water strewn with bodies; the heroes donate blood using the only vessels available in the chaos—all-American Coke bottles). Yet *Pearl Harbor*, extraordinarily, also juxtaposes male victimage with female practicality: male bodies are blown up, dismembered, and bleed copiously, while plucky nurses run hither and thither taking action. In a movie in which men do such a lot of shouting, it is refreshing to see women being effective. Yet this was not enough to secure female audiences, and *Pearl Harbor* needed to secure everyone. The blockbuster template set by *Titanic*, which wedded "romance and disaster, fiction and history, chick flick and action pic" (Garrett 149), was in place with *Pearl Harbor* through its glossy romance subplot organized around a doomed love triangle intended both to better Kate and Leo in *Titanic* and to replicate that film's winning recipe of character-led romance and epic action: women's picture married to man's movie.[4] One iconic moment is emblematic of these genre hybrid aspirations: as they prepare to consummate their relationship under a billowing canopy of parachute silk, a prone Kate Beckinsale pulls Josh Hartnett down onto her by tugging at the military ID tag dangling from his neck.

The Feminization of the New Century: *The Princess Diaries* and *Legally Blonde*

Pearl Harbor was not *Titanic*, of course, and female audiences went elsewhere. Gender separation at the box office was reinforced with the release of a cluster of female-targeted titles that explored the sometimes evolving, sometimes reactionary views of women's roles and relationships as the new century got under way. *The Wedding Planner, The Mexican, Say It Isn't So, Sweet November, Town & Country*, and *Kate & Leopold* spoke to a range of issues, audiences, and themes and were diverse enough to show that any of the terms commonly used to describe them (chick-flick, women's film, rom-com) are unhelpful, though audience remains a common definer.[5] As varied formations on the star vehicle, the date movie, the teen movie, and the 'oldies' rom-com, this handful of titles shows how misleading it is to think of movies loosely targeted at 50 percent of the population in one critical or marketing bracket. Each performed moderately at the box office and, though none received plaudits in the awards game, interesting issues emerge in the reviews, reception, and subsequent academic analysis of new kinds of women's cinema.

Three films rise above this list as the most successful female-focused movies of the year by far, each of which would come to generate sequels, and it is these that have also garnered the most academic attention. *Legally Blonde, The Princess Diaries*, and *Bridget Jones's Diary* were all based on books by women (Amanda Brown, Meg Cabot, and Helen Fielding, respectively); *Bridget Jones* was also directed by a woman (Sharon Maguire),[6] while *The Princess Diaries* was co-produced by Whitney Houston. Much of the writing around these films refers to them as chick-flicks, though "postmodern women's cinema" is becoming a popular term. The almost universal PG-13 rating has identified them as much with tweenie and teen/girl audiences as with women viewers, so there is also a case to be made for reading them in the frame of the family film. *The Princess Diaries* is perhaps the "youngest" of this cluster of films in that it features a teen heroine and is based on a best-selling novel targeted at the lucrative YA market (young adult fiction, for readers between early teens and early twenties). Its protagonist (played by upcoming star Anne Hathaway as Californian misfit Mia) lives out a classic girl's fantasy when it is revealed that she is really a princess, heir to the throne of the fictional European country Genovia. Of course *The Princess Diaries* contains the customary romantic subplot involving potential boyfriends both feckless and faithful, but its primary focus is on women's relationships with each other. With an absent (dead) father, Mia's universe comprises women who influence her in a variety of ways—her bohemian artist mother, her left-wing ecologically minded best friend Lilly, and the new woman in her life, the aristocratic grandmother who grooms her for leadership (Julie Andrews revisiting Mary Poppins and prefiguring her role as the queen in the *Shrek* sequels). Indeed, it is remarkable that a film could be so successful in the mainstream given its central focus on the relationship between a teenager and her grandmother. The fantasy package of designer clothes, good grooming, and sudden popularity is turned to liberal political ends when Mia is persuaded by the politicized Lilly that she can now be a force for good.

These contradictions of liberal and conservatism run through the genre and the year and have stretched critical discussion. Chick-flicks are associated with various women's movements caught under the umbrella of post-feminism or third wave feminism—girl power, girlie-culture, the "New Girl Order," and reframing equality struggles through consumerism and sexual and individual pleasure. Suzanne Ferris and Mallory Young describe the chick-flick as both "reinscribing traditional attitudes and reactionary roles for women" and as providing "pleasurable and potentially liberating entertainments, assisting women in negotiating the challenges of contemporary life" (1), while Roberta Garrett argues that the "new romantic comedy" is both "appealing and successful" because of how it offsets a "'feminine' romance fantasy" with "a cooler framework of postmodernist irony" (105).

While in some films women choose conventional pleasures over independence, others refigure prefeminist happy endings through distancing strategies and humor. The singular example of this is that feast of pink girliness and astonishingly overt cosmetics product placement *Legally Blonde*, a film which Ferris and Young argue bears out the third wave premise that "femininity and feminism aren't mutually exclusive" (7). Other critics have found it a bit of a stretch to read Elle (Reese Witherspoon) as a feminist. Ditsy Elle gets into Harvard Law School after hiring "a Coppola to direct my admissions video," and she rises to the top of her class on the basis of facts about haircare that "any *Cosmo* girl would have known." Elle is a parodic image of extreme postmodern femininity, and, perhaps, in her undecidability (is Elle critique or celebration? ironic or guileless?) she exemplifies attitudes to postfeminism itself. On one level it's perfectly possible to read the movie as a film about sisterhood: Elle's Harvard is at first a place where upper-class women betray and humiliate each other, and men can only see the intellectual potential of the heroine once they've finished admiring her physique. However, Elle's best friend is a trailer trash nail beautician who becomes self-confident and confronts an abusive partner thanks to her new friend's support. Elle succeeds in turning attitudes around in the classroom, too, befriending a former rival and overturning preconceptions about herself and her sex. She emerges as both classy and classless, in a film that galvanizes a range of political responses and requirements, from soft feminist to traditional chick-flick viewer. Yet *Legally Blonde* starts and ends with the promise of marriage proposals: despite her hot legal career, Elle still considers the perfect end to a perfect graduation day would be a marriage pro-

Legally Blonde (Robert Luketic, MGM): postfeminist irony or prefeminist wish fulfilment? Digital frame enlargement.

posal. Irony or conservatism? That both readings are possible shows the canny way in which this film—like its British sister *Bridget Jones's Diary*—played the widest possible marketplace.

Smart and Smarter: Auteurs and Adaptations

The successes of these chick-flick adaptations underline a key focus for cinema at this time—these were only part of a much wider, lucrative trend. The literary/fictional best seller was enthusiastically mined for boxoffice gold this year. The first installments of both Peter Jackson's *Lord of the Rings* trilogy and the series of *Harry Potter* adaptations held the challenge of appeasing fans of the literary texts (which Jackson took particularly seriously; Chris Columbus, director of the first Potter, less so). To make a full cinematic transition from a bestseller usually requires either a dedicated (and large) readership curious to see how it's been done (the J. K. Rowling/J.R.R. Tolkien readers/audiences) or marquee-hogging A-listers. Riding an adjacent "prestige" crest were biopics such as *Iris* (based on John Bayley's memoir of his wife, novelist Iris Murdoch) and arm's-length adaptations such as *O*, which reconfigured Shakespeare's *Othello* in a North Carolina high school with the eponymous tragic hero as basketball player.

The years' most lucrative adaptations more typically fall into two camps. On the one hand were those aimed at the family market, while on the other were adaptations which laid claim to that much disputed term, "quality"—often allied to heritage filmmaking and focused on an older demographic. In its end-of-year round-up *Variety* linked the literary adaptation to the family film, which "ruled the box office like playground bullies in 2001, generating close to 10% of the year's overall $8 billion take and kicking off lucrative pic franchises," at the same time awakening "a voracious appetite for a literary genre that studios have long overlooked: children's classics . . . the perfect fuel for the synergy machine." One ICM agent called Rowling's series the "'Star Wars' of children's fiction" (Bing and Dunkley 38) for its merchandise potential, but it was not alone. In a separate article arguing that the year's kids' films had usurped the more lucrative teen market, Charles Lyons quotes Disney producer Robert Simonds as saying, "Kids are not going to buy 'Pearl Harbor' toy planes. . . . But if they go to 'Monsters [Inc.]' there's a certain nag factor that will prompt parents to go out and buy a Babbin' Boo" ("Family" 69).Clever as the *Monsters Inc.* and *Shrek* screenplays were (arguably far smarter than this first cinematic *Potter*), literary underpinning helps to sell a notion of quality and educational added value in the hyper-popular market. Producer Jane Startz has said, "As a parent, if I were going to buy some spin-off product from a movie, I think it would be great to have something based on a book" (Bing and Dunkley 69).

But this phenomenon was not just for kids. Though based on an original screenplay rather than a literary source, *Gosford Park* looked like a classic adaptation and provided an adult version of this claim to "quality." A tale built around the social codes, snobbery, and sexual shenanigans of a group of British aristocrats and their servants at a 1930s house party does not seem like the typical project for the director of *M*A*S*H* and *Nashville*, or more recently *The Player* and *Short Cuts*. However, the film's intricately woven storylines and judiciously weighted ensemble performances are vintage Robert Altman, as is the ironic attention to hypocrisy and self-deceit. This U.S./U.K. co-production set in the period just prior to the outbreak of World War II was then distinguished by many hallmarks of the "Altmanesque." U.S. cinematic years really end with the following year's Oscars ceremony, and along with *Monster's Ball*, *A Beautiful Mind*, and *In the Bedroom*, *Gosford Park* featured strongly in the 2002 Oscar nominations and found an audience that was both discerning and multiplex-familiar. It also rivaled *Harry Potter* and *Lord of the Rings* for its showcasing of a huge cast of "quality" actors with résumés that read like a Who's Who of stage and screen achievement. In the *Potter* case, these were higher on the marquee because its three child stars (Daniel Radcliffe, Emma Watson, and Rupert Grint) were then complete unknowns. Commenting on the sheer quantity of "quality" actors employed by Altman, Nick James wrote, "It's as if a whole genre of film, and the generation of great actors who made it, had been teetering on the edge of extinction until Altman came along" ("To Be" 15). The same might be said for Chris Columbus and Potter, though there the film's actorly

Britishness may have had more to do with J. K. Rowling's casting influence than Warners' preference—only Maggie Smith did double service, appearing in both *Potter* and *Gosford*.

The "quality" quality was also seen in other costume dramas. Such films have long spoken to class and gender issues and are interpreted as having a classy if middlebrow appeal that straddles the multiplex and art house markets. They have also been associated with the spectacular women-focused pleasures—a fetishism of textile, color, and design—which writers such as Pam Cook, Sarah Street, and Stella Bruzzi have addressed. Katja Hofmann called Gillian Armstrong's *Charlotte Gray* "a woman's movie that seems to exist for its costumes . . . through [it] we can see how the romanticism that feeds the fashion industry leaks into movies" (10). This year also saw the successful release of three other period-setting stablemates, each of which nostalgically reflected on distinct moments in mid-twentieth-century history, with costume and nostalgia at the fore. *Enigma* and *Captain Corelli's Mandolin* were also literary adaptations; Alejandro Amenábar's *The Others* not strictly so, though it was received as a latter-day revisiting of *The Turn of the Screw*. All (including *Charlotte Gray*) are thrillers set during World War II, though not the World War II of *Pearl Harbor* (the latter is a supernatural-thriller, while the first three are historical drama/romances). All four were U.S./European co-productions[7] and, with the exception of *Corelli*, are centrally focused on strong female protagonists (played by Cate Blanchett, Kate Winslet, and Nicole Kidman), with storylines squarely aimed at a grown-up, discerning audience demographic. War here is a place where formations of identity are questionable—nationality and loyalty, sexual identity, what it is to be a child or a mother, what it is to be alive or dead. As the uncanny sequence in *The Others* in which Grace's husband emerges from out of the pervasive mist evidences, war is a space in which certainties are undermined rather than reinforced. Some certainties are eventually fixed, however, as these films come to exonerate the players suspected for much of their running time as irrational or untrustworthy—spooky children inflected by the gothic in the case of *The Others*; a femme fatale inflected by *noir* in the case of *Enigma*. In each, women, children, and to some extent insane men are established first as a problem and are then reclaimed as heroic, honest, secure.

Perhaps because *Gosford Park* is set before World War II broke out, perhaps because it is a Robert Altman film, its take on history, and humanity, is rather bleaker and less heroic. Looking darkly at the 1930s with its backdrop of fermenting fascism, it provides a series of interweaving metaphors for class struggle, sexual hypocrisy, and moral relativity. Reviewing the film in *Cineaste*, George Rafael called its upper-class protagonists "genetically inbred legatees of grafted privilege . . . planning their spring holidays in Berlin to catch glimpses of the New World Order." The film, he adds, "serves as a microcosm of English society between the wars in the low, dishonest decade of the 1930s, and as a harbinger of things to come." A number of writers cite it as the "smarter" version of the heritage film; Rafael, for instance, explicitly distinguishes it from "the usual period trifles such as Alan Brooks's *The Shooting Party*, the frilly Laura Ashley productions of Merchant/Ivory . . . , Agatha Christie adaptations and, of course, *Upstairs Downstairs*." Yet Altman acknowledges that if it weren't for the heritage precedent of Merchant-Ivory, "*Gosford Park* wouldn't have been made, as there wouldn't have been a reference" (196–97).

It might then be more interesting to read *Gosford Park* as a formation of the "smart film," a term first coined by Jeffrey Sconce in his 2002 article for the journal *Screen*, which he revisited and updated in 2006. As a form, smart cinema is associated with key writers or directors and has an "indie" aesthetic. As Sconce puts it, "Smart cinema describes a mode of cinematic practice that emerged among a new generation of post-baby boomer film-makers during the 1990s. Relying heavily on irony, black humour, fatalism, relativism, and occasional nihilism, this cinema became a particularly active battleground in a larger moral debate over the place of cynicism, irony, postmodernism, secular humanism, and cultural relativism in contemporary popular culture" (429).

Rafael's review unwittingly confirms *Gosford Park*'s "smartness"—its individualistic director, its ironic detachment, its ensemble-cast synchronous narrative: "As an outsider (bona-fide American maverick, last of a dying breed), Altman has no interests to protect, no weight of history on his back, no tribal myths to defer to nor archaic traditions to cherish . . . ; he comes to Perfidious Albion afresh." "Smart" in Sconce's formulation is then explicitly contrasted to "dumb"; he writes: "Not quite 'art' films in the sober Bergmanesque art house tradition, nor 'Hollywood' films in the sense of 1200-screen saturation bombing campaigns, nor 'independent' films according to the DIY outsider credo, 'smart' films nevertheless share an aura of 'intelligence' (or at least ironic distance) that distinguishes them (and their audiences) from the perceived 'dross' (and 'rabble') of the mainstream multiplex" (430).

Gosford Park sits squarely in this slippery category, not just for its ironic take on class within the text, but for its marketplace position as "classier," more thoughtful, made for a more discerning audience. Altman himself argues that the cinematographic style of the film, with the camera constantly on the move and in an arbitrary relationship to key elements of the action, makes the viewer work harder: "You make the audience find the drama in the situation, rather than serve it up to them" (Thompson and Anderson 197). Sconce cites exemplary "smart" late-boomer and Gen-X directors as Todd Solondz, Hal Hartley, Richard Linklater, and Richard Kelly, all of whom released films this year (*Storytelling, No Such Thing, Waking Life,* and *Donnie Darko,* respectively), as well as Todd Haynes, Sam Mendes, Quentin Tarantino, and Alexander Payne. But perhaps the clearest cluster of "smart" talent is Paul Thomas Anderson, Spike Jonze, Michel Gondry, and writer Charlie Kaufman. Anderson had already released *Boogie Nights* and *Magnolia,* seminal works deploying ensemble casts performing synchronous, multi-stranded stories in an episodic structure (very "Altmanesque"). As Sconce writes, "The favoured narrative structure is no longer the passive observer of an absurd world who eventually experiences some form of epiphany, but rather a range of characters subjected to increasing despair and/or humiliation captured in a rotating series of interlocking scenes in which some endure while others are crushed" (435). In terms of narrative structure this might also be said to be the form favored by soap opera—or by *Black Hawk Down,* for that matter. Yet with his bleak perspectives and arbitrary focus, it is no accident that Sconce reads Altman as the godfather of smartness, and then that Paul Thomas Anderson, who provides a preface for a book of interviews with Altman, would revere him as a primary influence. What Anderson says about Altman is coterminous with what Sconce says about smart cinema: "There didn't have to be lessons or a moral to the story; things could drift in and out and stories could ramble and be more effective in glimpsing moments of truth rather than going for the touchdown. . . . Beginnings, middles and ends could all flow delicately together in any order, and weren't even needed to be a great film. . . . It's hard to find heroes in Bob's movies" (Thompson and Anderson xvi).

Anderson on Altman might then be as useful a measure as any for understanding other key smart films of the year: both Terry Zwigoff's *Ghost World* and Wes Anderson's *The Royal Tenenbaums* exemplify this synchronous antiheroic form. Both are also infused with the literary in its widest sense. Directed by a documentarian-turned-smart-cinematic darling, *Ghost World* was based on a graphic novel (by Daniel Clowes).

Now a huge cult hit that has been treated to a 2004 director's cut revamp, *Donnie Darko* is a multiple smart film: the hero is an alienated, perhaps psychotic Gen X-er (the film is set in 1988, making the seventeen-year-old Donnie just a little older than director Kelly) who takes on organized religion, unearned authority, small-town Americana, and the

Donnie Darko (Richard Kelly, Pandora Cinema) as smart film: psycho-drama, science fiction, or magic realism? Digital frame enlargement.

family. Donnie (Jake Gyllenhaal) is haunted by psychotic visions of Frank, a giant menacing rabbit who tells him that the world will end in twenty-eight days and saves his life when a jet engine falls on Donnie's bedroom. The twenty-eight days through which Donnie then lives culminate in the deaths and presumed deaths of various characters. Yet Donnie has been given a mysterious book called *The Philosophy of Time Travel*, and this gives him the tools to jump back to the beginning of the story, twenty-eight days earlier; he chooses to die courtesy of the jet engine in order to save those he loves. Many viewers end the initial experience of this film in what we might call exhilarating confusion, situating the film itself in a kind of exhibition loop—repeat viewing is practically a requirement, if any sense is to be made of it. Yet it is also a deeply pleasurable film, perhaps because of its canny deployment of a zeitgeist song, perhaps because it is ultimately moral; perhaps because of career-making performances (Jake's sister Maggie Gyllenhaal plays Donnie's sister Elizabeth). The synchronous and multiple narratives of many smart films present coterminous events as coincidental, coincidences that are not meaningful, underpinned by purpose, or God. However, the tricky narrative of *Donnie* enables its anomic hero (as conventionally drawn as any antihero since the 1950s) to manipulate time and act ethically within his alienated milieu.

This enigmatic narrative that loops back on itself and leaves many questions unanswered is one reason why *Donnie* has become such a cult hit, inspiring prolific fan responses, art, and dedicated websites, and, crucially, requiring a larger quota of reception smartness than your average Michael Bay film. Sconce has highlighted "dampened affect" as a smart hallmark, but *Donnie* is finally a deeply affecting, even romantic film. In particular, it adopted a specifically American cinematic form of magic realism, or what we might call ironic fantasy, as did the collaborations between writer Charlie Kaufman and directors Spike Jonze and Michel Gondry (Sconce uses the phrase "'matter-of-fact' surrealism" to describe the fantastic play with realism). *Donnie* thus sits happily alongside a range of other cinematic enigmas of the year that traded in uncertain realities, double narratives, time loops, and unreliable narrators: Cameron Crowe's *Vanilla Sky* (one of the top earners of the year), Michel Gondry's *Human Nature*, and most significantly David Lynch's *Mulholland Dr.* Reviewers found this last film brilliant and mystifying in equal measures, but it has since emerged as the stand-out film of not just its year but its decade: in the 2010 round-up of films since 2000, the *Village Voice* placed it on top, as did *Time Out New York*, *Cahiers du cinéma*, *Film Comment*, and the Los Angeles Film Critics Association.[8]

A surreal and erotically charged nightmare, *Mulholland Dr.* charts the mystery of an amnesiac femme fatale, Rita (who takes her name from a poster of the 1946 movie *Gilda*), and a bright-eyed wannabe actress, Betty, who together investigate Rita's true identity, fall in love, and then switch into two entirely different women, successful and failed actresses Camilla and Diane (Rita and Camilla are played by Laura Elena Harring; Betty and Diane are played by Naomi Watts). Other characters, both genuinely connected to the four women's stories or haphazardly connected to each other or to nothing at all, slide into the narrative(s) with little explanation but much resonance. This is vintage Lynch, dazzling and seducing bemused audiences with doubles, archetypes, half-understood connections conveyed through luscious visuals. Starting life as a pilot for a TV series that was rejected, then rescued by Studio Canal and revived as a feature, it again eschews the standard three-act blockbuster narrative template: "It's the continuing story thing that has the stupid pull," says Lynch of *Mulholland Dr.*'s episodic, televisual beginnings; "In a continuing story, not knowing where this is all taking you is thrilling. Seeing and discovering the way is a thrill. That's why I like the idea of TV, to go on a continuing who-knows-where story" (281). In an interview, LAFCA president Brent Simon described *Mulholland* as a "beautiful, woozy mystery for the id—portions of its meaning are readily apparent, while others dance along its edges, deliciously up for substantive argument and debate" (qtd. in *Screen Daily*, 12 January 2010). It is also the quintessential exploration of the underbelly of Hollywood and Los Angeles as a noir-landscape: if *Pearl Harbor* is one indicator of Hollywood's psyche, this is another.

I started by observing that after 9/11 it became increasingly hard to read films without this intentional inflection. Even the enigmatic *Mulholland Dr.*

ostensibly addressed the disaster: "Can there be another movie that speaks as resonantly—if unwittingly—to the awful moment that marked our decade? Viewers grappled over the meaning of the movie's 'blue box,' finding little purchase. But in the troubled autumn of this psychodrama's 2001 NYC release, we might have understood it all too well" (Rothkopf). J. Hoberman also saw *Donnie Darko* as strangely appropriate: "The events of September 11 have rendered most movies inconsequential; the heart-breaking *Donnie Darko*, by contrast, feels weirdly consoling. Period piece though it is, Kelly's high-school gothic seems perfectly attuned to the pres-ent moment" ("Meet the Depressed"). Yet despite the media's desperate desire to find historical precedents (see Landy)—CBS anchorman Dan Rather referred to 9/11 as "the Pearl Harbor of terrorism"—no one looked to Michael Bay's film for comfort or understanding. So what impact did the attacks have on cinema and its interpretation? Perhaps it isn't surprising that a film that starts and ends with part of a passenger plane falling into a house would be troublesome for distributors on its release a month after 9/11. Though *Donnie Darko* premiered at Sundance in January 2001, it received only a limited general release in October 2001, and would have to wait for its slow-burn cult following to build over subsequent years. Yet while 9/11 impacted on wider culture and audience perceptions, it had only a local effect on boxoffice and production patterns. The cases of movies pulled from release, or altered due to their serendipitous relationship to real events, were few and far between. The trailer for *Spider-Man* was reedited, its spectacular sequence involving a giant web spun between the Twin Tow-ers excised. Shots of the World Trade Center were similarly edited out of *Zoolander*. The release of Arnold Schwarzenegger's *Collateral Damage*, with terrorism and hijacking themes, was reedited and delayed until 2002. A poster for *The Last Castle* was pulled because it depicted the U.S. flag upside down (a distress signal), while *Men in Black 2*, which was to feature the Twin Towers hosting swarms of aliens, was rewritten.

The video games industry also briefly adopted a more sensitive stance toward representations of violence in their products, pulling titles featuring the Twin Towers and redesigning products with resonant material (Graser). In the longer term Hollywood was cautious about what to greenlight: "Pro-duction slates are virtually blank as studios fret about release schedules and marketing plans in the wake of the Sept. 11 terrorist attacks," wrote Tim Swanson in *Variety*. Shelved projects included *Truck 44* (about imperiled firefighters), *Big Trouble* (a Tim Allen vehicle, in which a bomb is smuggled onto a plane), *Boaz the Great* (in which Adam Sandler was to play a Mossad agent), and *Designated Survivor* (a disaster movie set in Washington). Film festivals also suffered because of withdrawal of corporate sponsorship as well as logistical security issues (McNary "Fests").

For a brief time 9/11 brought audiences together in front of the small screen, and cinema attendance suffered as people watched the events live on television and then in endless replay. Television, wrote *Variety*, "became a metaphor for all of showbiz. As schedules were scrambled, execs wondered: Will people want escapism, or will anything that's entertaining seem trivial?" (Adalian, "Shell-Shocked" 1).[9] We must also not forget that it was television that first planted the thought that the attacks were "just like a movie," as CNN and Fox News anchors put it as the live horror unfolded rather like a real-life disaster movie. Robert Altman said in 2006, "I don't think there is a policeman alive today who didn't learn his behaviour from looking at films. Nor a gangster. . . . And when the World Trade Center was attacked, everybody said, 'What's going on? Are they making a movie?'" (Thompson and Anderson 197). However, within a few days the studios were working again, and TV schedules were nearly back to normal—even if there was then much second-guessing about where cinema was to go next. Martin Grove, boxoffice analyst for the *Hollywood Reporter*, told CNN, "I think in troubled times, we're going to see the same genre that worked during the depression—comedy. . . . People need to escape" (Vercammen). This was endorsed by a *Variety* "insider": "There's been a paradigm shift. . . . The age of irony will be over. You'll see more escapism, more warmth, more heroism, more patriotism" (Adalian, "Shell-Shocked" 36). Perhaps the end-of-year returns, boosted by the wizards of Las Vegas, Hogwarts, and Middle-earth, bear this out—certainly *Ocean's Eleven*, *Harry Potter*, and *Lord of the Rings* provide escapism aplenty, with dashes of warmth and elements of heroism in the mix. In his 2008 book on U.S. politics on screen, Michael Coyne noted that films dealing with 9/11 have "focused on the heroism of Americans in crisis . . . rather than on the negligence that allowed this tragedy to occur" (197). Whether 9/11 spelled the end of Hollywood's "age of irony," however, is left to the rest of this book to tell.

NOTES

1. For totals for films made this year see http://www.boxofficereport.com/ybon/2001 gross.shtml.

2. Various other live-action and computer-generated family-focused fare appeared this year, including *Dr. Dolittle 2*, an Eddie Murphy vehicle that arguably killed off the franchise in theatrical form, and the rather more interesting *Spy Kids*, which spawned two sequels in the next two years.

3. "Disney has reedited *Pearl Harbor* for its Japanese and German releases in order not to offend America's World War II enemies, the British tabloid *The Sun* said today (Tuesday).

. . . They are a huge market and accounted for 20 per cent of profits for *Titanic*," the source said. "The film barely refers to the Germans but we have cut the speech for them, too. It won't make a big difference, most people know who won the war." http://www.studio briefing.net/, 22 May 2001.

4. *Variety* also saw *Black Hawk Down* as a specialist ride in its perceived exclusion of women: "War film buffs and Scott fans will turn out, but general audiences, and women in particular, will approach with extreme caution."

5. One working definition of the term chick-flick is "a sappy movie for women that men don't like" (Ferris and Young 2).

6. Although *Bridget Jones's Diary* is a British production based on a British novel set in Britain and directed by a British woman, it was a huge Miramax-distributed success in the United States and famously starred Texan Renée Zellweger as the thirty-something London office worker.

7. Nick James wrote in June 2001 that *Charlotte Gray*, *Gosford Park*, and *Enigma* "are star-driven U.S./UK co-productions budgeted above £10 million and with the air of the popular literary package about them—much like, say, *Captain Corelli's Mandolin*, a film whose blandness has given birth to a new category: the natopudding. By which we mean films that combine U.S., UK, and European stars in order to manufacture a catch-all appeal."

8. See http://www.villagevoice.com/filmpoll/index/best_of_decade/2009; http://newyork.timeout.com/articles/film/80947/the-tony-top-50-movies-of-the-decade/6.html; and http://www.filmlinc.com/fcm/jf10/best00s.html.

9. "Movies were shuffled or replaced in TV lineups. Viewers tuning into ABC would not see *The Peacemaker*, about nuclear terrorists, but the romance *Hope Floats*. Instead of airings of the conspiracy-laden *X-Files* movie and *Independence Day* this weekend, Fox will broadcast the pregnancy comedy *Nine Months* and Robin Williams's *Mrs. Doubtfire*. . . . 'We're looking at programming that is more family-oriented so people can watch it together,' Fox network spokesman Scott Grogin said" ("Hollywood Lights Dim After Attack," archived at http://www.foxnews.com/story/0,2933,34295,00.htm). See also "Fall Movies Undergo Changes," CNN.com, 26 September 2001, archived at http://edition.cnn.com/2001/US/09/26/rec.fall.movies/index.html.

2002

Movies and Melancholy

SHARON WILLIS

In the wake of the 9/11 attacks on different U.S. sites by al-Qaeda terrorists, it may have seemed to many Americans that, for the first time since Pearl Harbor or the Cuban missile crisis, violent history had come to us. It had been more common in the post–World War II period that our aggressive participation had shaped world events elsewhere. The attack on the Twin Towers that had become iconic both of New York City and of U.S. financial dominance aimed, among other things, to produce staggering and haunting images. Our collective fantasies of the national image were—if not shattered—then radically reframed.

This year witnessed vigorous contests over images and interpretations. An atmosphere still marked by a sense of uncertainty, exposure, and vulnerability generated contending versions of national identity, refashioned out of collective mourning and fear. Alongside official and popular preoccupations with terrorism, new discourses of patriotism arose. Battles of interpretation erupted over everything from basic legal questions to the meaning of words like "torture" to the classification of persons and acts, such as "enemy combatant" and justified war. Across the year the government's relentless repetition of baseless charges that Saddam Hussein possessed weapons of mass destruction, and that his country had been centrally connected to the World Trade Center and Pentagon attacks, took hold and made a war for "regime change" in Iraq inevitable.

Terrorism continued to erupt outside the United States. *Wall Street Journal* reporter Daniel Pearl was kidnapped in Karachi, Pakistan, on 23 January; his captors beheaded him on 1 February and released a horrific video of his execution three weeks later. On 12 October, bombings of a Bali hotel and club killed more than two hundred people. Chechen rebels occupied a Moscow theater on 23 October, taking some 850 people hostage. Domestically, the "Beltway Sniper" attacks terrorized motorists in the Washington, D.C., area in October.

It was difficult to gain perspective in this anxious year. Official rhetoric emphasized fear and even paranoia, often under the heading of "security."

By 25 November, we had a cabinet-level Department of Homeland Security. In his first State of the Union address, President George W. Bush's labeled Iran, Iraq, and North Korea the "axis of evil" and declared his commitment to expand the War on Terror to include them. The Guantanamo Bay detention camp opened early in the year. American John Walker Lindh, who had been apprehended with the Taliban in Afghanistan, was indicted on charges of terrorism and conspiracy and convicted on 4 October.

On 2 March, the United States launched Operation Anaconda, a renewed attack on al-Qaeda and Taliban forces remaining in Afghanistan. Hans Blix led a U.N. arms inspection team into Iraq in November for the first such visit in the four years sincea U.N. blockade there had begun. After President Bush addressed the United Nations, calling for regime change in Iraq, Congress passed the "Authorization for Use of Military Force in Iraq Resolution" on 16 October. Even as this vote, for many, seemed to register a failure of political will, it also signaled a collapse of public debate. As the executive branch frequently characterized criticism as delusional and dissent as unpatriotic, the standard arenas of public contention, from Congress to the mainstream press, retreated to an increasingly timid and homogenous discourse about "national security."

Beginning with Kenneth Lay's resignation from Enron, the year saw a parade of corporate scandals and government investigations, including those of Arthur Andersen, Tyco, and Halliburton. WorldCom filed for the largest bankruptcy in U.S. history. Robert Hanssen, a double agent for the FBI and the Soviets, was sentenced to life in prison. But there was another side to this case: a devout Catholic family man, Hanssen obsessively videotaped his marital sex life to share with a male friend. His sensational hypocrisy struck a chord that resonated not only with mistrust of the FBI, but with the significant publicity the Catholic Church was receiving.[1] *Boston Globe* coverage of Father John Goeghan's trial sparked a wave of accusations and revelations of both sexual abuse by priests and the Catholic Church's systematic collaboration in its concealment. As a consequence, Archbishop Bernard Law of Boston resigned on 13 December.

On the international front, numerous events affected the United States: Slobodan Milosevic went on trial for crimes against humanity in the former Yugoslavia on 12 February at the International Criminal Tribunal for Yugoslavia; by 1 July, the International Criminal Court had been established. East Timor became a nation. In April, a coup d'état deposed Venezuelan president Hugo Chavez, replacing him with pro-U.S. Pedro Carmona; when Chavez was reinstated within forty-eight hours, the United States hastened to condemn the coup. Brazil, winner of the World Cup for the fifth time, elected

Luis Ignacio Lula da Silva president. Jimmy Carter won the Nobel Peace Prize for his efforts at international peacemaking and his work as a human rights advocate. In the literary world, the Pulitzer Prize went to Richard Russo's *Empire Falls*; Alice Sebold's *The Lovely Bones* remained on the *New York Times* bestseller list for a year; Ian McEwan's *Atonement* won the National Book Critics Circle award; Canadian Yann Martel won the Booker Prize for his *Life of Pi*; and the Nobel Prize for literature went to Hungarian Imre Kertész.

Television entered rapid, finance-driven transition, as game and reality shows took off. "Survivor," which began in 2000, had already become the top-rated series by this season. "The Bachelor" premiered on ABC, and Fox debuted "American Idol." MTV's "The Osbournes" became the highest-rated program on cable this year. "CSI" (2000–) had recently rocketed to the top of the ratings, and this year saw the launch of the first of its franchise spin-offs, "CSI: Miami." As networks reduced their investment in dramatic series, quality writing migrated to cable. HBO's writerly series garnered enthusiastic popular and critical attention: Alan Ball's "Six Feet Under" (2001–2005), "The Sopranos," created by David Chase (1999–2007), and "Sex and the City," created by Darren Starr (1998–2004), based on Candace Bushnell's book, dominated television in 2002.

Two popular shows in particular presented worlds paralleling contemporary reality. Aaron Sorkin's "The West Wing" (NBC, 1999–2006) sustained the fantasy of a traditional liberal president in Martin Sheen's Jed Bartlett. Fox's "24," debuting in 2001, propelled its hero, Jack Bauer (Kiefer Sutherland), head of a government counterterrorism unit, into ever more radical testing of the moral and juridical limits of his tactics.

In the wake of the 9/11 attacks, any film released this year was likely to take on unexpected meanings, its reading inevitably framed in some relation to that event. Of course, some filmmakers made adjustments in order to avoid evoking that trauma frivolously. Others worried their work might produce unintended effects in the current context. Everyone in the industry wondered how responsibly—and profitably—to entertain in the post-9/11 landscape. History, both distant and proximate, preoccupied a number of films, and its exploration frequently took on a nostalgic, melancholy tone, turning on a central loss. A number of films explored the relationship of image to identity. Many movies, from the very popular to those garnering more narrow critical respect, from *The Bourne Identity* to *The Quiet American*, seemed inflected by struggles over the meaning of American identity at home and America's image abroad.

Meanwhile, a number of prominent screenwriters and writer-directors translated literature into film. Adaptation emerged as a prominent theme as well as a practice. Spike Jonze's film of that name stages Charlie Kaufman's attempt to adapt Susan Orlean's book *The Orchid Thief*, with the result that he makes the author a character in his psychodrama. In another mode entirely, *Spider-Man*, Sam Raimi's adaptation of Stan Lee's Marvel comic book series, explores an ordinary teenager's adaptation to his body's adjustment to its acquisition of spider's capacities.

Fathers loom large this year: disappeared, damaged, failing, or failed. Many films organize their stories around paternal memory, around tenacious compulsions to redeem the father. The plot of M. Night Shyamalan's top-grossing supernatural thriller, *Signs*, is ultimately about restoring a traumatized widower to his proper paternal place. *Road to Perdition*, also an adaptation (based on the graphic novel by Max Allen Collins), traces a son's melancholy memories of going on the lam with his hit-man father, Michael Sullivan (Tom Hanks). In the deeply melancholy *About Schmidt*, the title character (Jack Nicholson) takes stock of his failure as a husband and father after his wife's death while pursuing a bleak and lonely road trip to his daughter's wedding, where he fails to achieve any reconciliation. Even *Spider-Man*'s nerdy, regular-guy adolescent superhero, Peter Parker (Tobey Maguire), has father issues: an orphan, he learns that his primary antagonist, the Green Goblin (Willem Dafoe), is really none other than his best friend's father, a man he had idolized.

It was an unusual year for women, presenting an array of work by women directors and a range of roles for actors, especially older ones. Both Meryl Streep and Julianne Moore played two major roles. Mira Nair's *Monsoon Wedding* offered a complex portrait of a Punjabi extended family. *My Big Fat Greek Wedding* was written by Nia Vardalos, who also played its protagonist. Julie Taymor directed *Frida* (with Selma Hayek as Frida Kahlo opposite Alfred Molina as Diego Rivera). *Chicago* provided substantial roles for Renée Zellweger, Catherine Zeta-Jones, and Queen Latifah.

Identity and Violence

Michael Moore's *Bowling for Columbine* is one of the only films to make explicit reference to 9/11. In this well-received documentary, Moore sets out to explore the American passion for guns and the culture of fear it seems to perpetuate. This film terrifies on several counts, most notably for the number of interlocutors who assert that their insistence on bearing arms is fundamental to American identity. If these speakers generally alarm through the tautological circularity of their thinking, equally troubling is the bafflement of non-gun owners and gun control advocates, who seem unable to produce solid analyses of the American penchant for violence. Moore's own persona in this film unsettles as well; at times, as when he interviews Timothy McVeigh's brother, or members of a gun club that looks strikingly like a militia, he seems cautious to the point of timidity. Particularly when he deals with his home state of Michigan, as in these cases, Moore presents himself as entirely alienated, stunned by his distance from his fellow citizens.

Moore seeks to demonstrate that racism and xenophobia remain powerful features of the paranoid, gun-dependent American identities that white militia sympathizers claim. His film goes on to sketch a consistent connection between our violent domestic culture and America's tendency to resort to armed force—or its threat—when dealing with the rest of the world. At the end of a historical montage on this subject, he introduces footage of the World Trade Center bombings. A later segment adumbrates the messages and images through which, Moore contends, "the media, the corporations, and the politicians have done such a good job of scaring the public they don't need to give a reason at all." Here he introduces the George W. Bush press conference in which the president "explains" the reasons for unexplained "terror alerts," which are necessary, given the "attitudes of the evildoers."

Moore's film concludes with melancholy irresolution, as if the filmmaker himself had run out of ways to pose his questions about the violence that so many see as characteristic of—if not foundational to—American identity. He retreats from NRA chair Charlton Heston's Los Angeles mansion, where the actor has briefly dithered with him before abruptly cutting off the interview. Returning to Littleton, Colorado, site of the Columbine events in which two high school seniors killed twelve students and one teacher on 20 April 1999, Moore concludes with a report on a bowling alley shooting that left three dead in the same town. He's returning, he tells us, "to an America living and breathing in fear." "Yes," he muses bitterly, "it was a glorious time to be American." Interrogating American identity, Moore seems, in this film, to have traded his usual incisive aggression for a melancholy resignation. But the picture he has presented sharply captures the cultural polarization that seemed only to grow starker this year, as the Iraq invasion approached.

In *Gangs of New York*, a film that refers to the missing Twin Towers, Martin Scorsese focuses centrally on the development of American identity among Irish immigrants. Reconstructing the Five Points neighborhood that received the largest concentration of Irish in the period, this film extends Scorsese's longtime fascination with ethnic "tribalism" into an excavation of mid-nineteenth-century New York, layers buried beneath the "mean streets" so many of his earlier films explored. Resonating with its context, *Gangs of New York* posits violent tribalism at the origin of modern American identity.

Protagonist Amsterdam Vallon (Leonardo DiCaprio) remains obsessed with avenging his father, Priest Vallon (Liam Neeson). A stunning early sequence, whose montage and choreography evoke both Kurosawa and Eisenstein, depicts a decisive battle of 1846 that secures the ascendency of the "Nativist" gangs over the Irish gangs. This sequence also establishes the bitter oedipal antagonism between Amsterdam and the Nativist chief, Bill "the Butcher" Cutting (Daniel Day-Lewis), who slaughters his father. Originating in New York City in the 1840s, the fiercely anti-immigrant Nativist movement formed a political party that came to be known as the "Know-Nothing" party, a name that produced stark irony in this year of stifled debate and resolutely repeated misinformation.

This film literalizes its historical excavation in the underground caves and endless little warrens the Irish inhabit. Space becomes allegorical: the Irish and the Nativists struggle beneath the very ground of the city, as if contesting its very foundations. As the narrative develops, the Irish slowly begin to emerge from underground and into the public political sphere. Shifting American identity emerges in the agglomeration of ethnic groups together in the Five Points—Chinese, African, and Irish. But its instability also figures visually in a proliferation of mirrors into which no one ever looks.

We follow the collective story of identity formation through the parallel development of Amsterdam's personal revenge plot. One of its most powerful threads emerges in his oedipal transference onto the Butcher, whose trust he must acquire and retain in order to achieve his aim. In this thoroughly oedipalized story of identity formation, we hear nothing of a mother; Amsterdam triangulates with the dead and the living fathers. Significantly, this film presents the Butcher as a figure preoccupied with the visual. In a grotesque underlining of the oedipal drama, the Butcher wears a prosthetic glass eye, which he occasionally taps with the point of his knife for emphasis. This spectacular dandy asserts that spectacle itself accounts for his ability to maintain power in the anarchic environment of gangs. "Fear," he tells Amsterdam, "the spectacle of fearsome acts, that's what preserves the order of things." He terrorizes the neighborhood through the public display of brutally murdered corpses and the mutilation of his adversaries.

As an identity plot, this narrative drives toward resolution in a second murder of the "father." But tangled around the edges of this replay of oedipal gangster tropes, the film manages a compelling excavation of New

York City history, as the final and belated (now a generation after the first) battle between Nativists and Irish is outstripped and overrun by history. The New York City draft riots (1862) erupt in the middle of this conflict and entirely displace it. Those riots, the largest in U.S. history, pitted draftees against police and military as they violently expressed their rage about the surrogacy program that allowed the wealthy to avoid the draft by paying a substitute. Bringing these riots and their class and racial elements to the fore, emphasizing the number of lynchings perpetrated on New York's black citizens, Scorsese pictures the origins of modern New York City in ongoing ethnic conflict and violence, very much in keeping with the story of the nation itself. In the process, he supplies a more adequate history of the rifts and upheavals that marked the culture of the "Union" side as anything but unified.

In *Gangs of New York*'s elegiac conclusion, Amsterdam and his girlfriend, Jenny (Cameron Diaz), contemplate the devastating aftermath of the riots from a graveyard across the river. Amsterdam reflects on the skyline of the "city born of blood and tribulation." Burying his father's blade between his grave and the Butcher's, between the bodies of his two fathers, he continues: "It was like everything we knew was mightily swept away." "And no matter what they did to build the city up," he speculates, "for the rest of time it would be like no one even knew we was ever here." As digital effects figure the architectural transformations of New York's skyline from the nineteenth century through the addition of the Twin Towers, the gravesite gradually recedes into vegetation. Haunted by this ghostly image, this melancholy moment seems to assert as inevitable a cycle of violence and its erasure, the amnesia at the heart of national identity, and perhaps of the city itself. In its context, this moment surely evokes concerns about the erasure of Ground Zero that so preoccupied contemporary discussion about its proper memorialization.

Image Problems and Problem Images

Steven Spielberg's two releases this year produce a kind of inverse mirroring effect. Both *Minority Report* and *Catch Me If You Can* are grounded in a chase; both narratives are motivated by troubled paternity and dreams of restoration. Though these films couldn't be more different in genre, or in affective and visual feel, they circle around similar preoccupations with identity, images, and technology.

The darkly dystopian *Minority Report*, based on a Phillip K. Dick story, extravagantly displays that author's obsessions with paranoia and surveillance, memory and identity, and optical apparatuses. Here, as in *Blade Runner*, eyes guarantee identity, as all manner of scanners deploy to determine it. When John Anderman (Tom Cruise), the chief of the Washington, D.C., pre-crime unit, becomes a fugitive from his own organization, he must "swap out" his eyes to avoid detection. Eerily, as he moves through public space, he finds himself repeatedly hailed by the name of his eyes' originator, as store displays and digital advertising boards address him personally to pitch their product. The body has become its own barcode, complete with an inventory of previous purchases. Identity has become one among the many commodities circulating in the mall.

Perhaps more shocking, John's own detached eyes, which he carries in a plastic freezer bag, function as a prosthetic identity, through which he gains access to secure locations in the pre-crime facilities. This creepy effect strikes a stunning resonance with a central plot line of seeing through another's eyes. John's pre-crime unit has virtually eliminated the crime of murder in the D.C. area, since it employs a team of three "pre-cogs," specially adapted humans who live suspended in a milky medium that supports their labor. This eerily embryonic image anchors the narrative in anxieties about the relationship of the organic to the technological and evokes stem-cell research controversies. These three pre-cogs, male twins Arthur and Dashiell and the stronger female, Agatha (Samantha Morton), who seems to keep them organized in their visions, themselves function as mediums. They anticipate future homicides—at this point almost all unpremeditated—viewing the future point at which a perpetrator is taken by surprise by his own actions. Pre-crime then "catches up with the future," interrupting the completion of a spontaneous intention, arresting the precriminal and relegating him to "containment," where his life is suspended indefinitely.

Fascinated with the optical, this film fascinates optically, as we watch the pre-cogs and their unit work. Apparently working through identification with both victims and perpetrators, the pre-cogs generate a series of fragmentary images that eventually resolve into a coherent sequence on the enormous glass computer screens that the detectives observe. We watch as the detectives manipulate the digital images into a legible "movie"; their task amounts to editing the crime in progress, editing the future. These sequences are visually riveting because they occur in spaces composed entirely of glass, where the viewing subject is also reflected on the screen. Layers of mediation occupy the visual field, even as characters drive toward transparency and display a rigid confidence in the unambiguous "truth" of the visual "evidence." Further complicating the film's temporal grounding,

John Anderton (Tom Cruise) confronts his virtual future self in *Minority Report* (Steven Spielberg, Twentieth Century–Fox/DreamWorks SKG). Digital frame enlargement.

the pre-cogs are regularly haunted by memories—"echoes"—of future events their visions have caused to be averted.

Significantly, the film regularly reminds us that Anderton's motivation for joining this unit has been his young son's kidnapping. Obsessed by his paternal failure, he engages in a melancholy ritual, repeatedly watching images of his estranged wife and lost child. He seems to have turned his overpowering longing to change the past, to make it "not have happened," into an urgent desire to prevent future events from unfolding. Anderton abruptly becomes the pre-crime unit's target when his own image emerges in a vision that appears on his screen. Visually, this moment literalizes his split identity: he is now both investigator and the future murderer of a man completely unknown to him.

He has entered the "film" the pre-cogs project; he is now seeing himself through another's eyes. Similarly, the pre-cogs produce fragmented identifications, as they see these future scenes first in the third person and then shift to subjective point-of-view. This instability governs the images themselves, of course; as the digital projection of thoughts, they trouble the boundary of subjectivity and they raise the question of "objectivity" itself. As it unfolds, the film foregrounds questions about images' authorship, authenticity, and agency as well as their uses, since Anderton must gain control of an image that remains estranged from him by becoming its author and editing it.

As the thriller develops, Anderton discovers that his mentor and boss, Lamar Burgess (Max von Sydow), has managed to plant the images that "frame" him. Founder and director of the pre-crime unit, and charged with negotiating its future funding with Congress, Burgess will guarantee its perfect success by continuing to conceal evidence of one crime it failed to prevent. This is his own crime, originary to the founding of his unit: he has murdered Agatha's mother who had tried to reclaim her from his custody. Cleverly gaming his own system, Burgess has staged a fake pre-crime, whose images mirror those of his own act. Agatha's apparently "echo" memories of this murder provide Anderton the clue to his "father"'s foundational crime. In this struggle between them, the film figures surveillance turning against its own agents. In surveillance gone wild, proliferating its reach through technologies of image and identity, this film brushes against timely anxieties about governmental and policing agencies and their accountability. This dysfunctional security apparatus begins to devour its own, very much in the mode of *The Bourne Identity*.

But once the mystery is solved, the bad father having committed suicide and his unit discredited and dissolved, the film retreats from its anxious exploration of the status of images and identity and turns instead to the restoration of paternity. It ends with a light-suffused portrait of Anderton and his obviously pregnant wife back together. Restoring the loss his earlier "home movies" had replayed, the future redoes the past and disappears as a problem. *Catch Me If You Can*, by contrast, takes more interest in deception than in its unmasking. This film begins amusingly with a retrofitted episode of "To Tell the Truth,"where contestants try to distinguish the "real" imposter from the two imposters.[2] Flashing back to Abagnale's arrest, the film then moves back further to 1963, as Frank and his parents celebrate Christmas in their luxurious home in a New York suburb. Frank Jr. (Leonardo DiCaprio) watches raptly as his father, Frank (Christopher Walken), dances with his mother, Paula (Natalie Baye). As they dance, the father recounts meeting her in liberated France. This could not more emphatically register as a primal scene: Paula even spills some red wine on the white carpet while dancing.

In the next scene, we learn that the IRS is pursuing Frank Sr. for tax fraud, and he trades in his Cadillac for a cheap used car and sells his house to move to a dingy apartment in Queens. He and his wife soon divorce, in a legal proceeding that requires the son to choose which one will gain custody. This forced choice—posed here as originary trauma—propels him to leave home altogether at age sixteen. Structurally, this film casts the shock of his parents' unmasking at the origin of Frank's career in fraud. Made with the cooperation of the author on whose memoir, *Catch Me If You Can: The True Story of a Real Fake*, is based, the filmgrounds his turn toward deception in paternal failure. His urgent desire to restore or remake the paternal image leads him, in a sense, to join the family business, adopting his con artist father's central aphorism. According to him, "the Yankees always win," not because of Mickey Mantle, but because "the other teams can't stop staring at those pinstripes." Frank will become master of surface and style. Part of this film's pleasure, indeed, is its resolute commitment to the surface, limiting our access to interiority. Covering the period between 1963 and 1974, while focusing centrally on the height of Abagnale's activities between 1964 and 1967, this film minutely scrutinizes details, just as its protagonist does. And, like Frank, it revels in the stylish finesse with which he outwits and eludes authority of all kinds.

Catch Me If You Can invites us to share its own fascination with this protean creature of constantly shifting identities, and it anchors this fascination to the figure of Carl Hanratty (Tom Hanks), the FBI agent whose relentless pursuit finally brings Frank into custody. In this film's ironic oedipal obsessions, fathers and sons remain reciprocally captivated with each other's image and the mysteries it may conceal. Carl becomes obsessed with Frank Jr. Likewise, Frank Jr. remains committed to restoring his father's lost image, promising to buy him all the things he had when he was rich. In turn, his father takes every opportunity to "show off" his visiting son. Their relationship trades in and on images.

This film's limitless fascination with details is absorbing, and it is through details that it constructs Frank. As he works scrupulously to create fake checks, we watch every step of the process. In this pre-digital age, the sureness of his hand crafts the forgery; this is *graphic* mastery, which would be useless today, since images and electronic transfers have largely replaced checks. *Catch Me If You Can* matches Frank's meticulous detail work with its own attention to the design features of the apartments he inhabits, the clothes he wears, the brands he prizes. Luxuriating in the look and sound of the 1960s—dial telephones and their rings, typewriters and keystrokes— this film seems illuminated by nostalgia.

In place of interiority, surface: this fascinating imposter appears to shape himself into the images he sees. He embarks on his career as an "airline pilot" for Pan Am after contemplating a pilot's uniform on display. He never flies the planes; he flies on them, "deadheading" his way to millions of miles' worth of trips and encounters with flight attendants—he is pure image. In the various impersonations of professionals that he stages, his identity itself seems improvised, keyed to the contexts he inhabits, the reflecting surfaces he confronts. Identity is something he occupies, like an apartment.

More than anything, this is a film about flight, emphasizing the trip, not the destination. Countries and sites visited become so many commodities, or conquests, in a life of luxury. But in this emphasis the film nostalgically recalls a period when air travel was itself a pleasurable adventure and when the pilot's profession was glamorous and highly paid. Perhaps the most thrilling of Frank's flights comes when he eludes the FBI, which is closing in on him at the Miami airport. Alighting from a limousine with a bevy of eight Pan Am flight attendants, Frank strides through the airport surrounded by these light-blue-uniformed beauties. Underlining the pre-feminist moment when airlines strictly regulated flight attendants' appearance, the camera aligns itself with the group and focuses on the appreciative reactions of police and FBI agents entirely distracted by this feminine display. This exhilarating sequence is inflected by Frank Sinatra's "Come Fly with Me," which plays through to a shot of a plane taking off over the head of an exasperated Carl Hanratty, once again outwitted by Frank's decoys and distractions.

In the course of his career, Frank runs through an inventory of middle-class dream careers for boys, aimed at wealth, prestige, and authority. At the same time, he consistently maintains the material features of the *Playboy* lifestyle, with its emphasis on specifically masculine commodity culture. The professions here figure as image and lifestyle, making light of their authority, just as Frank and the film itself delight in his consistent ability to outwit Hanratty and to elude capture. In the naïveté it attributes to the 1960s, this film treats its FBI agents almost playfully, emphasizing the slightness and faultiness of their surveillance technologies.

Alongside the glamorous con man he pursues, Hanratty strikes us as rigid, bland, unimaginative. Like his adversary, he seems to lack an interior. But, as the film unfolds, Frank initiates more regular contact with Hanratty than he does with his own father; he consistently places a Christmas Day phone call to the agent. Notably, we don't see him call his father on the holiday. Christmas necessarily invokes the primal scene with which this story begins, so it is not surprising that the chiasmatic exchange of fathers—from Frank Sr. to Hanratty—should pivot on this annual celebration.

In this universe of relatively benign authority, Hanratty and the FBI translate Frank's consummate skills at fraud into expertise in its detection, and he serves out the bulk of his prison term working for that very agency. In its emphasis on reconciliation with authority, as a "good" father rescues Frank from the perpetually shifting identity provoked by the failed father, this film seems oddly out of joint with the period it represents. Stabilizing its protagonist's identity through benign paternal authority, this film seems to read cultural change as a generational style gap. *Catch Me If You Can*'s approach to its period remains strikingly detached; even as it scrupulously details the style and texture of a certain affluent singles lifestyle, its principals are isolated from their social context: it is as if there were no war in Vietnam, no antiwar protests, no civil rights movement, and no incipient feminism.

Paul Schrader's *Auto Focus* strikes an echo with *Catch Me If You Can*, concerning itself with roughly the same timeframe. It, too, seems oddly detached from key events and issues that mark its historical moment, fascinated as it is with the preoccupations of actor Bob Crane (Greg Kinnear), who became a household name through his starring role in "Hogan's Heroes" (CBS, 1965–1971). That hit comedy series ran through the height of the Vietnam War, appealing to a kind of ironic, cool, anti-authoritarian sensibility, organizing its gags around the suave, unflappable, wise-cracking Colonel Hogan.

Auto Focus revels in exploring the underside of Crane's Hogan persona, exploring his "image problem," as the actor trades on his star image to pursue his addiction to sexual promiscuity. While he represented himself as a devout Catholic family man, Crane became obsessed with documenting and exhibiting his sexual exploits, with disastrous effects on his career. Tracking that decline, this film elaborates its central preoccupations with the image, both literal and figurative—Crane's "private" videotapes and his celebrity—and with the technologies that generate and maintain it. Of course this image of the autoaffective environment that Crane builds figures in the film's title. But "autofocus" also suggests the film's, and its director's, own self-referentiality.

Focused on Crane's lack of interiority, inscribed in the obsessive exteriorizing of his self-display and his apparent dependency on ever-renewed images of himself, this film remains resolutely confined to surfaces, its voiceovers and flashbacks only enhancing our sense of distance and superficiality. At the same time, because *Auto Focus* confines itself to tracking Crane's increasing obsession with producing and consuming his own image, it comes across as strangely interior. Rarely do we glimpse an outside to this world. It is as if this film had "recorded over" the period it covers, leaving us with only "Hogan's Heroes" and Crane's "swinging" lifestyle.

Melancholy Mothers

As if in counterpoint to the 1960s period films, two films released late in the year revisited the genre of maternal melodrama, exploring and adapting its conventions in stories centered on the plight of a 1950s wife and mother. Both *Far from Heaven* and *The Hours* starred Julianne Moore in this role. The latter, directed by Stephen Daldry with script by

David Hare, adapts Michael Cunningham's 1999 novel of the same name, while director Todd Haynes's original script of *Far from Heaven* explicitly reworks elements of Douglas Sirk's most famous 1950s melodramas, *Imitation of Life* (1959), *All That Heaven Allows* (1955), and *Written on the Wind* (1956), with a bit of Rainer Werner Fassbinder's *Ali: Fear Eats the Soul* (1974). Clearly sympathetic to feminism, each film apparently seeks to mine both the resources of melodrama and of the 1950s itself as they highlight erotic and social conflicts its popular culture could only hint at, if not repress altogether. We could characterize both as undertaking the project of "articulating affect and analysis," to cite Mary Ann Doane's claim for Haynes's work (18). In this articulation, both films seek to restore to the image of the 1950s housewife the complexity of her context.

To this end, they deploy soundtracks that, far from immersing the spectator, or amplifying a scene's affective force, work instead to provide a certain contemplative distance. Phillip Glass's score for *The Hours* weaves together its three embedded storylines through its circling repetitive motifs. Its minimalist restraint supplies affective tonality that does not adhere to the image content but holds us at a distance. In this film's most intense moments, music falls away. The scene seems to empty, bereft of aural support, in moments of stark isolation, as its characters contemplate loss. Elmer Bernstein's score for *Far from Heaven* works similarly: its amplified obtrusiveness distances us and reminds us of its mediating function. Ending on a single, strikingly sour note, this soundtrack provides a final ironic punctuation to the film's development, recalling its sustained meditation on the ironies of Sirk's melodramas.

The Hours links its stories through fragile, glancing intersections: through objects like flowers and books, but also through missed encounters, unrealized meals, parties failed or cancelled. Holding this tissue together is a poet, Richard (Ed Harris), immobilized in his apartment by HIV/AIDS. He functions as the relay between Virginia Woolf (Nicole Kidman) as she begins to write *Mrs. Dalloway* and her protagonist's contemporary counterpart, Clarissa Vaughan (Meryl Streep). Richard has long ago dubbed her "Mrs. Dalloway." Like her namesake she is planning a party, which will honor Richard for having received a poetry award. Embedded more deeply—almost buried—in its enframing narratives, the film's pivotal focus emerges around the conflicts of Laura Brown (Julianne Moore), a 1950s housewife, who seeks refuge from her alienation in reading Woolf's novel.

Late in its progress, the film confirms our suspicions that Laura is Richard's mother. In a stark sequence, Laura leaves her young son with a

Richard Brown (Ed Harris) mourns the mother who abandoned him in *The Hours* (Stephen Daldry, Paramount). Digital frame enlargement.

sitter and then later returns to collect the confused and mournful child. Before her return, she has retreated to a hotel room, only to abandon her plan to commit suicide. This separation triggers the son's violent grief; he struggles and screams, and presses his face to the window wailing, in sharp contrast to her rigidly silent composure. On the ride home, the camera registers the distance between them through rack focus, as they mutely ponder each other. An abrupt cut to Laura's wedding picture midway through this sequence weaves it into the present, as Richard raises his gaze from the image to stare out the window. We see him from outside, through the glass, as the film cuts to his younger self, as if in flashback, seen through a picture window as he screams for his mother.

Richard's contemporary moment of grief, as he weeps over this photograph and its memories, almost immediately precedes his suicide. In Clarissa's presence, he will shortly let himself fall from the window to his death. She has come to pick him up, characteristically early, only to be too late to prevent his suicide, for which she arrives accidentally on time. At the film's end, in an aching parallel, Laura Brown arrives at Clarissa's apartment. She returns too late for Richard, too late for the party they have all already missed on account of his death. An uneasy scene with Clarissa restores Laura's voice. Throughout the film, her utter incapacity to inhabit her role as 1950s suburban wife and mother has registered in her rigid affectlessness, her strained and disjointed monosyllabic speech. This moment renders her tormented conflict discursive as she recounts her decision, in her own words, one that "no one will forgive," to abandon her family. The "bad" mother, who failed to accommodate herself to the demands of middle-class suburban family life, returns as the repressed mother of 1950s popular culture, finally to tell her story in the contemporary moment. Melancholy gives way to mourning.[3]

Far from Heaven's much more assertive heroine, Cathy Whitaker (Moore again), appears at first as the ideal image of the 1950s mother, having internalized the repression that she imposes on the family. Because Cathy so richly embodies the contradictions of that maternal image, continually disappointing in her role even as she relentlessly performs it, she might appear to be the ideal figure for feminist sympathy or identification. As she fails to sustain the boundaries of white middle-class domesticity, she becomes the vehicle by which the film explores terrain that 1950s family sitcoms, and melodrama, including Sirk's, largely deflected or outright foreclosed.

In a key early scene Cathy is giving an interview to the local "society" paper. A poster above the TV set shows her posing with her husband as "Mr. and Mrs. Magnatech" to promote the brand of television for which he works as an advertising executive. Cathy's domestic world, then, both depends on and reproduces the consumer culture nexus of TV and advertising, and the film casts her literally as a poster girl for 1950s consumer culture. This scene's irony redoubles as she demurs that she's "like any other wife and mother," since in the film's previous sequence her husband, Frank (Dennis Quaid), has been arrested for "loitering," that 1950s euphemism for cruising that escapes Cathy's, but not the spectator's, understanding. Before the interview can proceed, it is disrupted by the characters' alarm at the unexpected presence of a black man in the garden. When Cathy confronts him, she learns that he has replaced his father as her gardener. Having watched this encounter with Raymond Deagan (Dennis Haysbert), the interviewer incorporates it into her copy, deeming Cathy "a devoted wife and mother" who is also "kind to Negroes." This slogan sticks to her throughout the film, as friends and neighbors mockingly reference it.

Bookended as it is by the revelation of Frank's sexual "problem," and by the arrival of Raymond, with whom Cathy will develop an intimate friendship, this scene stages a picture of domestic stability while highlighting the fragility of its boundaries. From this point, the film follows Cathy as she pushes beyond the secure center of home and family toward the margins, what lies off the map of white middle-class heteronormativity.

Far from Heaven carefully constructs a sort of symmetry within its own architecture, bringing together the violent repressions of both racial mobility and sexual choice. Its drama works through a play of visibility and invisibility. Raymond emerges from his invisibility as a service worker in this white suburb into scandalous hypervisibility when he appears in public with Cathy. Frank's "deviance," on the other hand, stays invisible as long as he remains with her and erupts as scandal and vulnerability when he ventures into illicit homosexual spaces. Cathy thus becomes the film's switch point, the central pivot that links its parallel and repressed worlds: homosexual subculture and the black community.

Presenting a drama of marital impasse between Cathy, in her wishful heterosexual blindness, and her husband, who struggles with the escalating unmanageability of his homosexual urges, *Far from Heaven* filters this disappointment and failure through Cathy's scandalous relationship with Raymond. That is, it reframes its drama in a broader social frame, as Cathy consistently exceeds the purview of white suburbia, venturing out with Raymond and finally visiting his context. On the one hand, Cathy breaches domestic and racial boundaries, while on the other hand she relentlessly pursues therapeutic strategies to re-secure her husband's heterosexuality.

Building its parallels around Cathy's fascination with the mystery and inaccessibility of her two "bad" object choices, the film establishes a tenuous analogy between their positions. It also follows Cathy's awkward blundering, as her ignorance gives way to a more analytical curiosity and to a sense that there is much that escapes her. Her uncertainty and her questioning steadily dislodge her from the homogeneous community that surrounds her. Frank's agonized internal struggles in the face of brutal homophobic repression, along with the violent public reaction to her and Raymond as a couple, render Cathy's private proclivities inevitably social; her personal world becomes politicized. Her conflicts begin to become legible as proto-feminist.

Far from Heaven's story ends in loss; its final musical note registers the melancholy of lost possibilities. Cathy is forced to break with Raymond, and he is forced to leave town, his business ruined by the scandal of their public appearances. Her husband leaves her for a pretty boy, and we leave her retracing the route home from the train station where she has said goodbye to Raymond, returning to her irrevocably changed home. But if Cathy's story ends in disappointment, the film's own project finds other possibilities in this reworked 1950s maternal melodrama.

This film imagines what would happen if the 1950s "mother" deviated from her popularly assigned tasks. What if she failed to manage her man and her own transgressive desires? What if she refused to collaborate in the management and repression of what lay just beneath the surface of her home and her culture? What if she sought not just to support equal rights in the abstract, but to establish an actual connection across racial lines? And what if all these things were linked, and her personal "politics," prefiguring feminism, eroded the boundaries of suburban middle-class convention? Such a project of reelaboration aims to expose underlying textual and cultural architecture to retrieve the fullness of the films'—and their period's—meanings.

Partial Views

Roman Polanski's sparse, starkly haunting *The Pianist* also inscribes mourning in music. This film follows the grinding contraction of the world of Warsaw's Jews, carefully exploring daily life details and rhythms as they shift radically during the Nazis' accelerating pursuit of the Final Solution. It tracks the increasing deterioration of life in the ghetto through the perspective of Wladyslaw Szpilman (Adrien Brody), a composer and concert pianist who worked at Polish Radio before and after the war (he served as its music director from 1945 to 1963).[4] While it stays within the ghetto until the deportation of Szpilman's entire family, for its later two-thirds *The Pianist* follows his solitary, claustrophobic life in hiding. Its tension and suspense hinge largely on small movements, muffled sounds barely discerned, subtle shifts in the actor's expressions. Devastating in its bleak melancholy, this film explores some of the terrain that preoccupied Polanski in *The Tenant* (1976) and *Repulsion* (1975), both films that depict protagonists confined to apartments and slowly going mad. It is as if those films had internalized the madness that threatens Szpilman's clandestine world. But this film also echoes Polanski's own experience as a child who escaped the Krakow ghetto and survived the war in hiding.

Musical performance frames the film: in its opening sequence, Szpilman's live broadcast is interrupted as explosions shatter his building; at its end, he has returned to play the same piece. For much of its course, however, the film remains pointedly bereft of diegetic music, which comes to mark the melancholy memory of normal life. At first, Szpilman continues to play piano in restaurants. As his family's life becomes restricted to the ghetto and the ghetto itself constricts, filling with ever more people, his musical interludes in its remaining restaurants provide momentary relief to both spectator and characters. Shortly, however, the contraction of Szpilman's world is expressed in the sale of his piano and the absence of music.

Instead, in the ghetto's streets, raucous, chaotic clamor prevails, as people scramble to feed themselves under ever more dire conditions. Frequently, we hear, as do the characters, menacing sounds whose source we can't see. Likewise, later, in Szpilman's isolated apartments, oppressive, anxious silence reigns. Obliged to maintain this silence to avoid detection, Szpilman is reduced to hyper-alert listening. Sounds of daily life, like a couple arguing, a chair scraping, or the occasional amateurish piano playing indicate that things go on somewhat as usual in the building. But they also pointedly emphasize Szpilman's utter separation from that everyday life. Meanwhile, ominous, terrifying sounds regularly punctuate this imposed silence: military vehicles, gunshots, German voices yelling, boots scraping on stairs. We remain anxiously aware, like Szpilman, of the stark limitations on our view, as we watch him strain to gauge the nearness of danger by sound.

These apartments limit his range of motion. Before a frequently static camera, which confines itself to frontal angles, Szpilman moves little, only performing the most rudimentary tasks. When he sits before the piano in one room, we briefly hear the piece he plays in his mind as his fingers hover above its keys. In this melancholy moment, musical memory haunts the image. In contrast to the empty stillness of Szpilman's hiding places, the ghetto remains constantly in motion. Following Szpilman through it, the camera registers the press of the crowd, a flow that imposes its pace on him, propelling him forward or abruptly blocking his passage. Fits and starts of movement mark this chaotic, brutal space, as its diverse populations struggle for space and resources. Congestion impedes our passage, jostling the camera along with characters. Like them, the camera confronts protracted waits, its movement frozen into cramped stillness for uncertain periods.

This frequently shaky camera inscribes uncertainty and anxiety; sometimes moving urgently as if to see better. A number of low angles both suggest the fearsome brutality of police and German soldiers, or the frightening press of moving crowds, forced along by their own momentum. But these angles also suggest a child's point of view, perhaps inscribing Polanski's own memory images. In this sea of bodies churning in desperate activity, we register a world expunged of color. Across its muddy browns and leaden grays, buildings and sky, bereft of color or light, match the clothing of its inhabitants. In this space it becomes difficult to differentiate people and places. Similarly, in the sparse, bleak interiors Szpilman occupies, little visual detail interrupts the expanse of grayish white walls. He lives in spaces with few markers of specificity or meaning. A stopped clock is nothing but a marker, since it no longer keeps time. But, then, Szpilman cannot really keep time either.

In this radically reduced world, Szpilman, like the camera, focuses intently on small details, everyday objects: a knife, a teacup, the rotten potato that is all that remains of his larder. Later, several scenes are anchored to a large can of pickles that Szpilman finds in the house to which he retreats after the Germans' destruction of Warsaw has blasted his previous hiding places to rubble. We watch him struggle desperately to open it with a fireplace poker until he drops the can. As it rolls away, the camera follows, holding it in medium shot until it leads us to the boots of a German officer. When he learns Szpilman's profession, he asks him to play the piano. It is the only piece of furniture in this room, and as Szpilman shuffles to it, he places the can on top. Two isolated, abandoned objects, then, anchor this space. In a haunting scene, the pianist plays an entire piece, his breath condensing in the cold, dark room, for the appreciative officer who will help him by securing his hiding place. When the officer delivers Szpilman food the next day, the camera notes pointedly that he has included that missing necessity, a can opener, in the package.

Such banal daily objects code the stark reduction of life to bare necessity in Szpilman's world. But they also mark the traumatic points where the banalities of ordinary life coexist, coincide, or collide with the cataclysmic history of this moment.[5] In one of its more wrenching sequences, the film follows Szpilman after a Jewish policeman has roughly separated him from the line of deportees heading to the trains. After a horrifically slow rendering of the vicious violence with which soldiers force people into freight cars, the film cuts to a long tracking shot. In long shot, Szpilman walks toward the camera, wailing, in the one moment he shows extreme affect. This sequence starkly registers collective absence through objects, details: the piles of furniture, housewares, and personal objects that strew his path as he makes his way through the empty streets. Returning to the Umschlagplatz, the staging ground for the deportation, the film captures in long shot the empty square littered with suitcases, clothing, and toys. We remember that the film's first images have been black-and-white archival footage of Warsaw in 1939. Carefully matching his own locations to resemble what we see there, Polanski creates a ghostly effect, as if to reconstruct what no longer exists, as this archival film marks the absence of so many from the city.

Another of ·The Pianist's compelling effects involves its windows. Repeatedly it returns us to a view of Szpilman from outside his window. We watch this confined spectator attempting to assess the situation on the ground through his sharply limited vantage. Framed in his window, he struggles to see what goes on beyond its frame, to match sight to the sounds he is hearing in the streets. From an apartment near the ghetto, he watches, helpless and anguished, as the Ghetto Uprising continues until its bloody defeat. We spectators share Szpilman's compulsion to watch this scene

In *The Pianist* (Roman Polanski, R. P. Productions/Focus Features), Wladyslaw Szpilman (Adrien Brody) waits, watching the street in Warsaw. Digital frame enlargement.

unfolding. Later, he anxiously observes what little he can see of the Warsaw Uprising, pacing anxiously, and finally escaping through a blasted wall. In his new refuge in an abandoned hospital, his partial view is reduced to a tiny, jagged triangular chink that has been blown out of one of its frosted glass windows. This extreme limitation excruciatingly intensifies our sense of partial view, of near blindness, as he anxiously watches the fighting outside and tracks the progress of explosions and fire bombings with which the Germans are leveling Warsaw.

Emphasizing the partial—and particular—view, this film comes to closure by restoring Szpilman to his place at Polish Radio, where he plays the same piece with which the film began. As he begins to play, he begins to weep. Music as memory here opens the possibility for mourning. This moment seems to stress the beginning of a mourning suspended throughout this film. In a sequence that functions as coda, running through the final credits, Szpilman again plays Chopin, this time with a full orchestra. Trauma is perhaps not liquidated so much as it is attenuated in a mourning that remembers. For its own difficult moment, this was a film that rewarded renewed willingness to reflect on history.

NOTES

1. His story was substantial enough to warrant a book, Adrian Havill's *The Spy Who Stayed Out in the Cold: The Secret Life of FBI Double Agent Robert Hanssen*, which later served as the basis for a film, *Breach* (2007).

2. This game show ran on CBS from 1956 to 1968, on which celebrities attempted to determine which of three contestants claiming the same identity and unusual story was authentic.

3. On this point, see Michael Leblanc's reading of this film, "Melancholic Arrangements: Music, Queer Melodrama, and the Seeds of Transformation in *The Hours*." He writes: "Mourning is not the complete elimination of a melancholic conflict, but a mode of renarrating that conflict that offers a degree of distance and control over it" (138).

4. Szpilman wrote the first version of *The Pianist* in 1945; it was not published in translation until 1999 in England and 2000 in the United States.

5. In *Traumatic Realism: The Demands of Holocaust Realism*, Michael Rothenberg considers that status of such objects as indexical, writing that "the index in traumatic circumstances functions differently than in the traditional version. . . . Instead of indicating an object or phenomenon that caused it, and in that sense making the referent present, the traumatic index points to a necessary absence" (105).

2003

Movies, "Shock and Awe," and the Troubled Blockbuster

BOB REHAK

On 20 March, the nighttime skies over Baghdad lit up as cruise missiles and bunker-buster bombs blasted locations where Saddam Hussein was rumored to be hiding. The U.S.-led invasion of Iraq had begun, with a spectacular display of might designed to quickly and decisively undermine the enemy's will to fight back. It was the world's first taste of a doctrine known as "shock and awe": a mission as much about emotions as explosions, about fireworks as firepower, about control of information and perception along with airbases and oil fields. Based on a 1996 defense report advocating "rapid dominance" to gain the upper hand in military conflicts (Ullman and Wade), the calculated show of force launched a long-running war even as it concluded a long build-up choreographed by the administration of President George W. Bush, promoted by a largely uncritical mainstream media, and sanctioned by a Congress all too conscious of the public hunger for vengeance.

Certainly it is in poor taste to call the invasion and subsequent war a "sequel" to the Gulf War of 1991 prosecuted by a previous George Bush (though the narrative of vengeful sons grappling with paternal legacies has structured many a blockbuster franchise, from the *Godfather* films to the *Star Wars* series). But it is less far-fetched to compare the effects of shock and awe abroad and at home—both its immediate, sugar-rush successes and its simmering, long-term failures—to the dynamics that shaped the year's cinematic landscape, which saw media conglomerates behaving in new ways and blockbuster movies adopting new strategies in an attempt to achieve their own "rapid dominance" in the marketplace. At times, the assault on the box office seemed as intensive and unrelenting as those on Baghdad and Basrah, with one wave of TV advertising and tie-in promotional products ebbing just in time for a fresh onslaught. Like the build-up to the invasion, Hollywood's marketing and publicity efforts centered on selling their products in advance, pumping up excitement in order to generate monumental profits on opening weekend. Yet beneath their highly technologized surfaces—the bombast of visual effects, cranked-up audio, and high-concept franchise building—the year's major films shared a strange ambivalence toward the very powers that had made them possible: unease about assuming the abilities of God, distrust of the morality and correctness of our guiding authorities, and yearning for a more traditional past in which the anchoring truths of a pre-9/11 era had not yet been destabilized.

The year's news was full of dour visions that were sometimes difficult to distinguish from filmed fiction. Befitting an emerging style of promotion in which publicity spread laterally through word-of-mouth and the nascent social-networking movement (Friendster launched in 2002, MySpace in 2003; Facebook was just around the corner), it often seemed as though the dramatic *Sturm und Drang* of big-budget action had leaked into the real world—as though the twenty-four-hour news cycle had been conscripted into the infectious spread of viral marketing. The space shuttle *Columbia* disintegrated over Texas on 1 February, splintering into glowing streamers upon reentry. (The image of a shuttle crash-landing would recur, played for thrills, in *The Core*, one of the year's less commercially successful science-fiction films.) This tragedy was bookended by an apparent victory when, on 13 December, Saddam Hussein was found hiding in a "spider-hole" in Tikrit. (The military operation that located him was code-named "Red Dawn"—the title of a 1984 film about a Soviet invasion of the United States—suggesting the thoroughness with which the political and the cinematic had become intertwined in the years since Ronald Reagan.) Other significant events mirrored plotlines of the prior decade's thrillers. A global alert on Severe Acute Respiratory Syndrome (SARS) was issued on 12 March, echoing movies like *Outbreak* and *Twelve Monkeys* (both 1995); on the same day, fourteen-year-old Elizabeth Smart was recovered nine months after being abducted from her home in an eerie parallel to kidnapping storylines like those in *Ransom* and *Fargo* (both 1996). Early May saw a rash of nearly 400 tornadoes across nineteen states, like something out of *Twister* (1996); Eric Rudolph, suspected Olympic Park bomber, was captured in North Carolina on 31 May, reminiscent of the urban terrorists in *Arlington Road* (1999). On 14 July, Robert Novak "outed" CIA operative Valerie Plame in his *Washington Post* column—allegedly in retaliation for her husband's role in discrediting WMD claims—in a convoluted saga straight out of *Conspiracy Theory* (1997) or *Enemy of the State* (1999).

On the cultural front, Britney Spears created controversy by engaging in a three-way kiss with Madonna and Christina Aguilera at the "MTV Music Video Awards" on 28 August. Lifestyle guru and publishing giant Martha

Stewart was indicted in June for her role in the ImClone stock-trading case and sentenced in July to five months in a federal correctional facility. His hand forced by a story in the *National Enquirer*, right-wing firebrand Rush Limbaugh confessed in October that he was addicted to prescription pain-killers. In July, Los Angeles Lakers superstar Kobe Bryant found himself at the center of a sexual-assault case in which he was accused of raping a hotel employee named Katelyn Faber. (Following a public apology and an out-of-court settlement, the case was dismissed.) As though to counterweight these scandals, Arnold Schwarzenegger—perhaps the biggest action-movie icon of the 1980s and early 1990s—was elected governor of California on 7 October. Schwarzenegger's political profile was from the start inseparable from his stardom: he announced he was running on "The Tonight Show with Jay Leno" in August, labeling the recall election in which he would go on to defeat incumbent Gray Davis "Total Recall," after the science-fiction film of the same name in which he starred in 1990. Following suit, the media tagged Schwarzenegger as "The Governator"—referencing his iconic role in *The Terminator* (1984)—and murmured that his electoral victory was due in part to the publicity he received from starring in the July release of *Terminator 3: Rise of the Machines.*

In the world of science, Dolly the sheep—the first mammal to be cloned—died on 14 February at the age of six after developing lung disease and severe arthritis. And on 14 April, scientists announced that the Human Genome Project had completed its goal of successfully mapping nearly 100 percent of human DNA. Yet even as new frontiers were being broken, the frailty of human life and its dependence on technology were made clear in a series of devastating disasters, both natural and man-made, across the globe: huge earthquakes struck Algeria on 21 May and Iran on 25 December, killing more than thirty thousand people, while a major power outage struck the eastern United States and Canada on 14 August, affecting an estimated fifty million people from Ontario to Michigan, Ohio, New York, and Pennsylvania. Meanwhile, Europe experienced one of its hottest summers on record, with an August heat wave killing more than forty thousand and creating a crop shortfall that impaired the European Union's total production that year by ten million tons.

In cinema, smaller movies and independent releases broke new ground for filmmakers. There were an unprecedented number of films directed by women and whose focus on women's lives and concerns departed from the traditional Hollywood focus: Catherine Hardwicke's *Thirteen* explored the complex relationship between mother and adolescent daughter, while *Monster*, directed and written by Patty Jenkins, painted a wrenching portrait of serial killer Aileen Wuornos through the determinedly unglamorous performance of Charlize Theron. Sofia Coppola's *Lost in Translation* detailed, with quiet, ironic precision, the ambiguous bond between a washed-up actor (Bill Murray) and a young woman (Scarlett Johansson) against a Tokyo backdrop that was both distantly alien and dreamily romantic. *In the Cut*, directed by New Zealander Jane Campion, adapted a 1995 novel by Susanna Moore about a woman's relationship with a detective whom she suspects of being a serial killer. British director Christine Jeff's *Sylvia* was a biopic about poet Sylvia Plath, who committed suicide in 1963. Contrasting with these offbeat—and downbeat—movies, the romantic comedy *Something's Gotta Give*, written, produced, and directed by Nancy Myers, was a mainstream success.

Another trend in the year's films suggested that reality was making ever more aggressive incursions into the darkened theater, with an unusually large number of documentaries receiving public attention. Some, like *Touching the Void*, focused on the dangers of nature; others, like *The Corporation*, on the dangers of culture, in this case the excesses of omnivorous, uncaring capitalism. Errol Morris's *The Fog of War* looked back at Vietnam through interviews with former secretary of defense Robert S. McNamara, marking a revisionist intervention in the nation's memories of what had been, until Iraq, its most uncertain and traumatic war effort. Trauma on a more personal scale structured *Capturing the Friedmans*, an exploration of a family torn apart by allegations of child sexual abuse, and *Tupac: Resurrection*, about the rapper Tupac Shakur who was shot to death in 1996. But the most interesting eruptions of the documentary spirit took the form of hybrids and crossovers—"mockumentaries" like the Christopher Guest comedy *A Mighty Wind*; *American Splendor*, an adaptation of Harvey Pekar's autobiographical comic books that featured, in an act of self-conscious reflexivity, the real Pekar alongside the actor Paul Giamatti who plays him; and Gus Van Sant's *Elephant*, not-so-loosely based on the 1999 Columbine High School shootings, a film that won the Palme d'Or at Cannes. Another line of documentary-like titles adopted *verité* stylings as branding strategies (*The Real Cancun*, promoted as a "reality film") or as a means of generating suspense and thwarting generic expectations (the shark-attack thriller *Open Water*).

From Sequels to Transmedia: Rethinking the Blockbuster

The year marked a unique time in the country's collective response to the events of 9/11. It was the moment at which the U.S.

government's official reply to the attacks unfolded on the global stage, in a summer of combat that toppled the Iraqi regime while fueling a violent and stubborn insurgency. Some of this was due to the timing of production schedules; it was the first year to be dominated by films that originated after, or whose productions substantially overlapped, the attacks on the World Trade Center and Pentagon. Of the top ten boxoffice successes, four titles belonged to franchises that had been in production since the early 2000s: *The Return of the King* concluded the *Lord of the Rings* trilogy that had started in 2001 and continued in 2002; the two-part *Matrix* sequels completed an arc begun with 1999's *The Matrix*; and *X2: X-Men United* continued the saga of *X-Men* (2000). *Finding Nemo*, following the painstakingly slow development process characteristic of Pixar, had been in preproduction since 1997. All the remaining titles in the top ten began shooting in 2002, as did the majority of the 506 movies released in 2003. Unlike films released in 2001 and 2002, which due to their production schedules inevitably bore the stamp of a pre-9/11 era, the year's films were among the first to speak not just of trauma, but its aftermath: capturing through the lens of popular fantasy a nation seeking explanations for the injuries it had suffered, raining vengeance upon the parties it believed to be guilty, and grappling with both its suddenly exposed vulnerabilities and its newfound appetite for destruction.

Some of the year's successes seemed inevitable. Given the strong performance and committed fan base surrounding *The Fellowship of the Ring* and *The Two Towers*, few doubted that *The Return of the King* would find favor with audiences. Other successes were unexpected, like New Line Cinema's holiday comedy *Elf*, which returned $173 million domestically and an additional $47 million globally on a relatively small budget of $33 million. Still other blockbusters looked like safe commercial bets but failed to find either public or critical acclaim, often in spite of their profitability: *The Matrix Reloaded* and *Revolutions* were widely judged to have fallen short of their potential, as was *Terminator 3*. And some of the year's blockbuster hopefuls ended up among the most derided critical failures in history, such as the comedy *Gigli*, born under the ill-fated sign of Jennifer Lopez and Ben Affleck's brief celebrity romance. But what many of the top-grossing films shared was membership in the latest generation of blockbusters, an evolving mode of production and marketing geared toward high-concept, visual-effects-dependent storytelling; dense tapestries of commercial tie-ins and product placements' giant opening weekends; and a strong afterlife in the ancillary markets of home rentals and purchases as well as TV airings on broadcast, cable, and subscription networks (Bordwell 2–3). Although the basic model of the New Hollywood blockbuster has been with us since the mid-1970s—with *Jaws* (1975) and *Star Wars* (1977) as paradigmatic cases—the year exemplified three trends that, to differing degrees, have come to characterize contemporary blockbuster filmmaking: sequelization, adaptation, and remakes; transmedia storytelling; and multipart productions.

A rush of follow-ups to prior hits dominated the year. Alongside the aforementioned *X2* were *Bad Boys 2, 2 Fast 2 Furious, Legally Blonde 2: Red, White, and Blonde, Final Destination 2, Jeepers Creepers 2, Spy Kids 3D, Scary Movie 3, Tomb Raider: The Cradle of Life, Shanghai Knights*, and *Dumb and Dumberer: When Harry Met Lloyd*. Not all the sequels were to recent films: *Terminator 3: Rise of the Machines* succeeded in resurrecting a franchise many had considered definitively concluded a dozen years before, with 1991's *Terminator 2: Judgment Day*. And the theatrical release of Disney's *The Jungle Book 2*, originally intended to go straight to video, picked up the story begun in 1967's *The Jungle Book*. In addition to movie sequels, other media were mined to extend, exploit, or reinvent existing brands. A number of books made the leap to the big screen: *Dreamcatcher, Runaway Jury, Holes, The Cat in the Hat, Cold Mountain*, and, with multiple Academy Award nominations and wins for Sean Penn and Tim Robbins as Best Actor and Best Supporting Actor, one of the year's most acclaimed films, *Mystic River*. Film adaptations of defunct TV series included *S.W.A.T., Charlie's Angels: Full Throttle*, and *Rugrats Go Wild*. Several films adapted comic books and graphic novels: *Hulk, Daredevil*, and *The League of Extraordinary Gentlemen*. *The Haunted Mansion* and *Pirates of the Caribbean: The Curse of the Black Pearl* were based on theme-park rides from Walt Disney, suggesting not so much adaptation as "narrativization," the linear taming of interactive and immersive sensory experiences into a more-or-less classicallystructured story. Hollywood also continued its long-running practice of remaking earlier films, evident in the release of *The In-Laws* (based on the 1979 original), *Freaky Friday* (from 1976), *The Texas Chainsaw Massacre* (from 1974), *Willard* (from 1971), *The Italian Job* (from 1969), and *Cheaper by the Dozen* (from 1950).

Another dimension to blockbuster engineering could be found in transmedia storytelling. As defined by Henry Jenkins, "A transmedia story unfolds across multiple media platforms, with each new text making a distinctive and valuable contribution to the whole" (96). That is to say, certain kinds of stories and their associated characters and "worlds" extend beyond an individual film or even series of films to encompass print novels, comics, TV, videogames, and other media that would once have been dismissed as mere spinoffs and tie-ins. Different audiences with different tastes can come together around the same media property, experiencing it through the multiple channels of transmedia storytelling, a way of spinning singular tales at enormous scale (and, not incidentally, profitability and brand control). While Jenkins traces the origins of transmedia storytelling to 1999's *The Blair Witch Project* and notes that "few, if any franchises [have achieved] the full aesthetic potential of transmedia storytelling—yet" (97), his exemplar is *The Matrix* and in particular the cluster of interconnected media that reached critical mass with the release of the sequels. Dubbed by a *Newsweek* cover story "The Year of the Matrix," 2003 saw not just two follow-up feature films but a collection of short animated stories (*The Animatrix*) and the launch of a videogame (Shiny Entertainment's *Enter the Matrix*) timed to coincide with the release of the first sequel, *The Matrix Reloaded* on 15 May. To fully comprehend the story and appreciate the artistry at work in the *Matrix* saga, the argument goes, one would have to consume all its transmedia extensions—a seemingly Herculean task, making necessary the collective clue-sifting, debate, and exegesis of a large interpretive community connected via the Internet.

A final trend in the evolution of the blockbuster was the prominence of multipart film production, in which two or more films are shot simultaneously or back-to-back. While this practice dates back many decades—*Superman* and its sequel *Superman 2* were shot simultaneously in the late 1970s, *Back to the Future 2* and *3* in the late 1980s—this year was unusual in that it saw the culmination of two franchises shot in this fashion, along with the launch of a third. The two *Matrix* sequels were filmed together from 2000 to 2002, while the three films in the *Lord of the Rings* cycle were filmed in one large chunk between 1998 and 2000. By contrast, *Pirates of the Caribbean: The Curse of the Black Pearl* was a standalone production whose back-to-back sequels were greenlighted after the first film's unexpected longevity at the box office. Giant productions such as this tend to occur with properties involving elaborate production design and heavy use of visual and special effects—primarily the science-fiction and fantasy material favored by blockbusters. But a related trend, in which a film conceived and shot as a single entity is split into two smaller "chapters," shaped the fortunes of Quentin Tarantino's *Kill Bill*, which producer Harvey Weinstein decreed should be released as *Volume 1* in late 2003 and *Volume 2* in spring 2004.

Taken together, these trends suggest a double logic operating within the year's blockbusters. In one sense, they continued practices such as sequelization and opportunistic adaptation that were commonplace in the industry's search for big box office. Yet beneath this appearance of business as usual, everything seemed to be changing, often in counterintuitive ways.

The tools that had worked in one year were no longer capable of producing the same results. Hollywood, by definition, always wants the same results (it relies on the replication of past victories, the continuation of successful trends, and the avoidance of past mistakes), so on the surface this year might seem little different from those that preceded or followed it. But things were changing. Consider, for example, the death of traditional 2D cel animation—a practice with more than a century of history behind it—signaled by the failure of *Sinbad: Legend of the Seven Seas*, which made approximately $27 million on a $60 million investment, prompting DreamWorks to cease production of films animated in the traditional style. Alongside *Sinbad*'s failure, *Finding Nemo*—a fully computer-generated film largely set at sea—was among the year's most profitable films.

Flirting with the Powers of God in Middle-earth and the Matrix

The term "blockbuster" was first used by British forces in World War II to refer to the aerial bombs dropped on cities in Germany (Bowles). Later, of course, the name became associated with the long lines of theatergoers that stretched around the block, waiting to gain entrance to much-anticipated shows. By contemporary definitions, in which a movie must exceed $100 million in ticket sales, more films attained blockbuster status this year than in any previous year: twenty-five releases in all. Pressure to create the giant opening weekends that guarantee this level of performance drove filmmakers to ever greater heights of invention, expense, and excess, marshalling armies of technicians, artists, publicists, and finally audiences: creation on a godlike scale. Yet, like the warring mutants in Bryan Singer's *X-Men 2*, newfound abilities came with new worries, and the year's blockbusters seemed unusually conscious of the drawbacks to unlimited power, their storylines preoccupied with risk, loss, and destruction on both a societal and personal scale.

Perhaps no movie was more emblematic than *The Return of the King* of the possibilities of blockbuster production as a seemingly unstoppable trend on the one hand, and the singularly inward and troubled nature of large-scale cinematic fantasy on the other. The third installment in Peter Jackson's ambitious adaptation of J.R.R. Tolkien's *Lord of the Rings* marked the culmination of a moviemaking adventure on a scale almost without precedent: a total production cost in excess of $300 million, shot together over a 274-day period of principal photography between 1999 and 2000 with pickup shooting, visual effects, and scoring proceeding continuously for the next several years. The resulting three films ran a total of nine hours and seventeen minutes in their theatrical versions, with extended editions released on DVD containing additional footage and extensive documentary material. The two previous installments, *The Fellowship of the Ring*, released in December 2001, and *The Two Towers*, released in December 2002, had together grossed just under $2 billion internationally. *The Return of the King* itself took in $1.1 billion internationally, placing the trilogy third on the list of all-time successful film franchises, behind the *Star Wars* series and the James Bond films.

While the first two films were widely praised, it was *The Return of the King* that yielded a crop of Academy Awards, winning every category—eleven in all—in which it had been nominated. It was difficult to escape the sense that, in fact, the awards were being given to the complete set of films, director and co-screenwriter Peter Jackson being recognized not simply for the final chapter but for the entire epic journey. As Peter Travers wrote in *Rolling Stone*, "After four years, a $270 million budget and three films that add up to more than the sum of their parts, the Rings trilogy is more than a movie. It's a colossus on the march into screen legend" (76). And this would have reflected Jackson's own perspective, which paralleled Tolkien's in that both saw the work as a single, giant story, broken into smaller units only at the insistence of publishers and film distributors.

The Return of the King completes the story of Frodo Baggins (Elijah Wood), a Hobbit tasked with the unenviable mission of carrying the One Ring—a mystical object that grants invisibility to its wearer but whose true power and influence extend much further—to the fires of Mount Doom, where he attempts to destroy it. The first two films had seen the formation and dissolution of a fellowship to assist Frodo in his mission, a group that includes the wise wizard Gandalf (Ian McKellan), the dwarf Gimli (John Rhys-Davies), and the elf Legolas (Orlando Bloom). Yet in the end, it is only Sam Gamgee (Sean Astin) who remains to assist Frodo, along with the troubled Gollum (Andy Serkis), a wretched being transformed by his lust for the One Ring. The trio face dangers from malevolent Orcs to a giant spider, Shelob, but the quest to destroy the ring is ultimately a battle waged within the soul, as Frodo struggles to stay free of the ring's corrupting influence—its promise of unlimited power. It is, ultimately, a personal and psychological drama, despite the gigantic tides of mythic history sweeping through the events of the narrative, such as the ascendency of the titular king Aragorn (Viggo Mortensen) to the throne of Gondor and the stewardship of mankind amid the epic battle of Pellenor Fields that constitutes *Return*'s most spectacular setpiece. Steve Vineberg of *The Christian Century* characterized Middle-earth

Frodo (Elijah Wood) struggles to resist Middle-earth's "weapon of mass destruction" in *The Lord of the Rings: The Return of the King* (Peter Jackson, New Line Cinema). Digital frame enlargement.

as a place "where the moral battle is fought on the grand scale by Aragorn's army but on a smaller one by every individual" (41).

That Tolkien persistently disavowed any allegorical meaning to *The Lord of the Rings* has not dissuaded interpretations tying it to the fearsome weapons of World War II or the nuclear age, with which the publication of his original novel coincided. *New Yorker* writer Alex Ross reminds us that the roots of the concept run even deeper. "It is surely no accident that the notion of a Ring of Power surfaced in the late nineteenth century, when technologies of mass destruction were appearing on the horizon," he observes. "Nor did the ring have to be understood only in terms of military science. Mass media now allowed for the worldwide destruction of an idea, a reputation, a belief system, a culture" (161). In the various types of nefarious agency it brings together—control of vision, control of thought, control of will—the One Ring encapsulates the hybrid essence of power in the modern era, expressing itself discursively and semiotically as much as militarily. And in Frodo's piquant but ultimately steely resistance to its lure, a choice is made between isolation and community—a testament to a true fellowship, one that embraces difference even among different species, human, elf, hobbit, and dwarf.

The Return of the King functioned as a palimpsest of the year's concerns in other ways. Denethor (John Noble), steward of Gondor, is a leader who makes foolish choices that send his armies to certain destruction. A vain, gluttonous, and short-sighted ruler, Denethor epitomizes the deadliest of the seven deadly sins, pride, ultimately going mad as he attempts to burn his presumed-dead son Faramir (David Wenham) on a funeral pyre. Igniting himself instead, Denethor commits suicide by hurling himself from the wall of Minas Tirith onto the battlefield below. His tragic characterization in the film differs radically from how he is shown in Tolkien's source material and bears more than a faint resemblance to George W. Bush—at least as Bush was caricatured by his critics as a belligerent and unwise leader. At the other pole of military power, Sauron, the dark lord whose quest to control the ring motivates the narrative, is pictured as a flaming eye atop a gigantic tower, acting through his legions of minions or the mind-controlling palantir but himself a mute and distant figure—literally a feature on the horizon. The film's refusal to personify its primary villain echoes the changing antagonists at the center of the United States' response to 9/11 and Iraq: first Osama bin Laden, then Saddam Hussein, working through their shadowy networks of al-Qaeda and insurgents. Sauron's lack of embodiment renders him a protean and omnipresent foe, one whose influence extends beyond corporeal death, reflecting the endlessness of what Vice President Dick Cheney had termed "a new kind of war against a new enemy."

The *Village Voice* praised the film's timing along with its technology: "Even if the movie hadn't had the mystical good fortune to coincide with the wars against the Taliban and Saddam Hussein, its complex mythology would still have the inevitability (and superior CGI) of a perfect storm" (Hoberman). Not everyone agreed with the interpretation, of course. "The invasion of Iraq makes a poor match with the War of the Ring," wrote Steven Hart in *Salon*. "It only works if we can imagine Gandalf as having cut business deals with Sauron back in the Second Age, even providing him with the seed cultures for breeding his legions of orcs. There is no question of imminent threat in *The Lord of the Rings*—the armies of Mordor come looking for trouble. Had Gondor marshaled its troops only to find Mordor bare of weapons, and Barad-dur ready to crumble at a touch, then we might find parallels with George W. Bush's grand venture." But the quieter and more profound idea running through *The Return of the King* is that, presented with the chance for ultimate power, Frodo turns away, preferring to retain his humanity (or its hobbit equivalent), shaky as its moral foundation may be; as one critic wrote, "In Tolkien's world the ring is the instrument of evil; humans are inherently weak and corruptible, susceptible to greed and lust for power, but not inherently bad" (Vineberg 41).

The conundrum between godlike power and human nature appeared in other films, most notably *The Matrix Reloaded* and *Revolutions*, which together conclude the epic odyssey of Neo (Keanu Reeves), a human in rebellion against the cybernetic evil of the virtual-reality prison known as the Matrix. In the paired movies, Neo confronts successive layers of the Matrix, including, toward the conclusion of *Reloaded*, a mystical encounter with the computer entity that built the construct in the first place. Perched before an endless bank of monitors, the bearded old man dressed in a white suit identifies himself as the Architect, telling Neo, "Your life is the sum of a remainder of an unbalanced equation inherent to the programming of the Matrix." The ponderous speech highlights one of the central themes of the sequels: free will versus preprogrammed restriction, Neo's nature as a mere "anomaly" weighed against his potential to escape the rules of his scripted reality and attain transcendence. (Presumably, something like the same conundrum faced the filmmakers, burdened with astronomically high expectations from fans as well as the financiers of the enormous production.) It also suggests an interesting conception of god-as-controlling-white-man, contrasting in race- and gender-laden imagery with the other powerful deity at the heart of the simulation, the Oracle (played by Gloria Foster in *Reloaded* but recast, following Foster's death, by Mary Alice in *Revolutions*).

Neo's main nemesis, however, remains Agent Smith (Hugo Weaving), who has developed the ability to multiply himself, virus-like, into an army of clones. In *Reloaded*, Neo fights a swarm of Smiths to a standstill in a visual-effects setpiece codenamed "the Burly Brawl" by the production crew. And in *Revolutions*, Neo and Smith do aerial battle, hurtling through a lightning-streaked sky to land titanic, shockwave-inducing blows on each other. True to producer Joel Silver's promise that the sequels would raise the bar so high that the bar would cease to exist, the two *Matrix* sequels abounded in spectacular fights and car chases while serving up plentiful helpings of the postmodern metaphysics that had captivated fans of the original film in 1999. But by granting Neo the powers of a god, they undercut their own drama. What many reviewers saw as an excess of visual effects was in fact the logical outcome of a aggressive four-year program of R&D by the Wachowski siblings—what one might metaphorize as a kind of visual-effects arms race. In the end, Neo's strange plight, stranded by his own omnipotence, seemed a metaphorical reflection of their own apparently unlimited power to warp cinematic reality. By the same token, the battle that dominates *Revolutions*, in which swarms of computer-controlled "squiddies" lay siege to the underground human city of Zion, suggests an all-consuming technological peril, familiar as a science-fiction trope (indeed, on ready display in *Terminator 3*) but given fresh urgency in the context of a production underpinned by advanced visual effects.

Good and Evil Fathers in *Hulk* and *Finding Nemo*

Though each were orphans in their way, Neo and Frodo appeared to have many "fathers" in the symbolic sense. Some were good—Gandalf, Morpheus (Laurence Fishburne)—and some were evil—Sauron, Saruman (Christopher Lee), Agent Smith. But all of them represented paternal authority in some form, forces of ethical guidance, cultural law, or physical coercion with which the heroes had to grapple as they forged their paths through worlds grown uncertain and threatening. Reflecting the vexed political and moral principles of the United States in the first full bloom of its aggressive answer to the terrorist attacks, the year's films were replete with divisive father figures who, like Bush and Cheney, promised on the one hand protection and salvation and on the other a vengeful, vindictive punishment. The fantasies of fatherhood offered by the year's blockbusters suggested a distrust of authority as profound and deep-seated as the desire for a firm guiding hand in troubled times.

One of the most unusual releases of the summer, *Hulk*, reflected and amplified this fear through a strangely inward tale of fathers, destructive emotions, and traumas buried in the past. Created by the tried-and-true partnership of writer-producer James Schamus and director Ang Lee, who had previously specialized in commercially successful middlebrow cinema, *Hulk* was an ambitious attempt to interbreed the superhero movie—a genre undergoing rejuvenation thanks to digital visual effects and the popular success of films such as *Spider-Man* (Sam Raimi, 2002)—with the high-minded art film. Translating into cinematic form a Marvel Comics character introduced in 1962, the film tells the story of Bruce Banner (Eric Bana), a geneticist whose own genes contain a monster: when angered, he mutates into a giant green-skinned behemoth, the Hulk, capable of smashing through walls, leaping miles through the air, and flinging armored tanks as though they were Frisbees. The Hulk's mute and animalistic nature is a dialectical counterpart to Banner's gentle, introverted personality, and in the narrative's beauty-and-the-beast subplot, Banner's relationship with Betty Ross (Jennifer Connelly) deepens as the Hulk emerges from its "puny" human shell. Their love seems doomed, however, as the Hulk is hounded by the military in the form of Betty's father, "Thunderbolt" Ross (Sam Elliott), as well as his own troubled past, personified by Bruce's renegade-scientist father David Banner (Nick Nolte). Though on opposite sides of the legal fence, *Hulk*'s two fathers act in unison as conservative, imprisoning forces, intervening in Bruce's and Betty's desires and ultimately threatening Bruce's very existence.

A further layer of complexity stems from the film's Oedipal structuring. As a child living on a New Mexico army base, Bruce is experimented upon by his father, and in a key scene—arriving late in the film as a recovered memory—witnesses his mother's murder by his father. In a Freudian nightmare, David emerges from the bedroom where the two have been arguing and stabs his wife with a knife meant for his child. Bruce watches as his mother stumbles into the desert to die, set against a glowing green explosion on the horizon: a gamma-ray bomb whose radiation will further push Bruce's cells toward their monstrous mutation. Invoking Condoleeza Rice's dire warning about WMDs in Iraq—"We don't want the smoking gun to be a mushroom cloud" (quoted in Ricks 58)—*Hulk*'s primal scene conflates fears of nuclear devastation with the fear of a punishing father, burying these linked terrors in Bruce's subconscious, where they will fester into adulthood until they finally erupt in explosive rage.

Earning $62 million in its strong opening weekend, *Hulk*'s box office dropped a startling 70 percent in its second week. It went on to make $254 million worldwide, but measured against its $137 million budget, the movie's performance was judged a disappointment. Even more damning were the critical responses, which found *Hulk*'s combination of quasi-avant-garde editing techniques (designed to mimic the panel-to-panel dynamics of comic books), noisy action sequences, and psychological exploration an awkward and unpalatable mix. "It's certainly serious—deadly serious," wrote David Edelstein in *Slate*. "Battling against Dad (and Dad's legacy) could be a great theme for a monster picture, but the writers have built in too many Freudian wheels and pulleys to give the film a more conventional structure." Some critical voices centered on the film's reliance on CGI to generate its lead performance, drawing unflattering comparisons with the year's other computer-generated characters, such as *The Return of the King*'s Gollum and the entire cast of *Finding Nemo*: "On the evidence presented by *Hulk*, however, [CG effects are] not ready to furnish a live-action film with a full-fledged antihero who compels pity, awe, or even steadfast interest" (Morgenstern "Incredible"). But it was Andrew Sarris who drew the most explicit connection between *Hulk*'s story and the prevailing political climate. "Curiously, *Hulk* seems to be considerably out of sync with what is perceived in many quarters as the public's triumphant pride in the feats of our armed forces," Sarris wrote, calling one of the film's antagonists "a likely candidate for C.E.O. of Halliburton, à la Dick Cheney and the rest of the military-industrial complex," and pointing out that the Hulk primarily rains destruction on American tanks, planes, and soldiers. "This isn't a foreign enemy or a traitorous domestic foe he's

Fishy friends or foes? Joining a new coalition in *Finding Nemo* (Andrew Stanton and Lee Unkrich, Walt Disney/Pixar). Digital frame enlargement.

sweeping away like tenpins," Sarris observes, "it's our own glorious boys in uniform."

The vicissitudes of fatherhood—its challenges, risks, and rewards— were a central theme in *Finding Nemo*, the fifth in Pixar Animation Studios' extraordinarily successful run of computer-animated features and, with its worldwide box office of more than $800 million, still the studio's most successful film. An undersea parable about parenting and protection, *Nemo* presents a nightmare scenario in the long tradition of Disney tales that mix the tender with the traumatic. Clownfish Marlin (voiced by Albert Brooks), neurotic single parent to his only surviving offspring, Nemo (Alexander Gould), is horrified when one day Nemo ventures beyond the reef where they have made a comfortable, if restrictive, home. The young fish's curiosity draws him to a boat, where he is captured by a scuba diver. From there, the bifurcated narrative follows Marlin and Nemo on their twin odysseys: the son eager to explore uncharted waters and make new friends, the father desperate to return him to safety and protect him from dangerous strangers such as a group of guilt-ridden sharks in recovery from their own carnivorous appetites. Nemo's destination—a crowded fish tank in a dentist's office in Sydney—represents both a dead-end for his growth and a perverse apotheosis of Marlin's fantasy of armored isolation from a natural environment full of predatory threats. (Although completely accidental, *Nemo*'s search-and-rescue storyline paralleled the unfolding drama of Private Jessica Lynch, captured by Iraqi soldiers on 23 March and recovered on 1 April by

U.S. Special Operations forces. The account of Lynch's heroics during her time as a prisoner of war was spun by a Pentagon eager to foreground success stories of U.S. efforts in the Middle East; Lynch would later disavow much of the official story, rejecting the master narrative put forth by the country's leaders.) The film's conclusion, of course, finds a happy equilibrium, reuniting the family back at home while demonstrating Marlin's newfound ability to take the occasional risk.

Nemo shares with *Hulk* a singular anxiety about the smothering, controlling influence of patriarchy and the need to transcend one's fears in confronting a world of difference. At the same time, the ultimately conservative narrative affirms the sanctity of the homeland and the need to choose one's allies wisely; the various friends that Marlin and Nemo make on their parallel hero's journeys, from the memory-challenged Dory (voiced by Ellen DeGeneres) to a group of surfer turtles riding the East Australian Current, echo the coalition assembled by the United States as part of its War on Terror.

Sailing the Seas of Tradition and Honor: Samurai, Soldiers, and Pirates

If movies such as *The Return of the King* and *The Matrix* sequels addressed the problem of overwhelming power and the moral responsibilities that attend it, and *Hulk* and *Finding Nemo* concern leadership and security through the metaphor of fatherhood, a final group of films evidenced a desire to turn away from the turbulent present and seek comfort in years gone by—even if that edenic time was a purely cinematic construction. In Tim Burton's *Big Fish*, for example, the past comes alive through a set of tall tales told by a dying salesman (Albert Finney) to his disaffected son (Billy Crudup); in these fantastical flashbacks, elaborately designed settings and baroque visual effects play up rather than hide the unreality of the stories, yet assert, beneath their artifice, a core of genuine if sentimental emotion, as father and son move toward reconciliation. A similarly frank approach to the past as both artificial construct and a repository of basic decency was seen in *Down with Love*, which self-consciously remediates the Rock Hudson/Doris Day romantic comedies of the 1950s and 1960s to infuse that era's sexism and heteronormativity with a more enlightened, postfeminist take on women's career possibilities and independence from men. These films are not precisely conservative—they do not invoke the past uncritically—but instead attempt to bridge past and present, establishing continuities by which we can frame the chaos of the twenty-first century through the lessons (sometimes inadvertent) of the twentieth.

This was particularly evident in a trio of films that spoke in different ways about militarism, warfare, and codes of honor. Edward Zwick's *The Last Samurai* was a prestigious December release that, like other films that year (*Gods and Generals, Cold Mountain*), returned to the era of the Civil War to tell a story of heroism forged not because of, but despite, the brutalities of the battlefield. Captain Nathan Algren (Tom Cruise) begins the film as a broken-down alcoholic, deep in the grip of what will, more than a century later, be diagnosed as Post-Traumatic Stress Disorder (PTSD) for the atrocities he witnessed—and committed—against Native Americans while an active member of the U.S. Army. Drafted as part of a mission to modernize the Japanese military, Algren travels to Tokyo, where the Imperial Government is locked in conflict with a holdout group of rebel samurai living in the mountains. Captured by the samurai and forced to live as one of them over the course of a long winter, Algren grows close to the samurai leader Katsumoto (Ken Watanabe) and undergoes a kind of spiritual purification: he stops drinking, gives up his army uniform for the robes and sandals of the country folk, and learns the ways of meditation. Along the way, he exchanges one form of military prowess for another, training in combat and swordplay as his inner nature—symbolized in the film by Katsumoto's repeated visions of a white tiger—emerges. Algren's evolution from "barbarian" to enlightened warrior corresponds to an encompassing narrative arc of historical shifts, as the Imperial Japanese Army (under the command of a duplicitous politician, Omura) adopts Western technologies of war such as howitzers and Gatling guns. Against the callous mechanization of these weapons, the sword-wielding samurai on their horses represent an older "way of the warrior" based on discipline and honor.

That Algren survives the climactic battle (a prolonged, bloody clash involving thousands of troops and bearing the clear visual influence of the *Lord of the Rings* setpieces) and returns to the mountainside village to live out his days with the beautiful Taka (Koyuki) is somewhat surprising, given the film's theme of redemption through self-sacrifice. Like *Dances with Wolves* (1990) before it, however, and anticipating the science-fiction epic *Avatar* (2009), *The Last Samurai* invokes cross-culturalism as a balm for the white man's troubled soul, suggesting that in any encounter between East and West, both cultures are improved through the intermediary of the protagonist, who acts as a relay between two apparently incompatible ideologies. *Samurai*'s performance at the box office—earning $456 million worldwide—demonstrated the apparent attractiveness of this message on a global scale, perhaps by presenting to the rest of the world a more positive picture of the U.S. military spirit through its handsome protagonist: Tom Cruise, in one of his more serious roles, sells the idea of a photogenic killer who in more reflective moments expresses shame for his actions and disgust toward the "arrogant and foolhardy" Custer, "a murderer who fell in love with his own legend."

A more forthright endorsement of the notion that warfare can be honorable was *Master and Commander: The Far Side of the World*, an elaborately detailed adaptation of Patrick O'Brian's seafaring adventure stories set in 1805, when, as a title card informs us, Napoleon is expanding his power and "oceans are now battlefields." Directed by Peter Weir, this co-production from Twentieth Century–Fox, Miramax, and Universal spared no expense in mounting its tale of Jack Aubrey (Russell Crowe), captain of the HMS *Surprise*, a frigate engaged in a hunt for the French privateer vessel *Acheron*. Ordered to "sink, burn, or take her a prize," Aubrey and his crew of 197 alternately chase and elude the *Acheron* throughout the course of the film, with bursts of cannon-fire combat only an infrequent punctuation to the rituals of nautical life. The film's primary emphasis, in fact, is more sociological than historical, bringing microscopic attention to conflicts among the crew, who believe one of their number to be a cursed "Jonah"; to the camaraderie and apprenticeship shared by the officers; and to the codes of (specifically masculine) bravery and honor with which each sailor meets the challenges placed upon him, whether in the ingenious feints and misdirections by which the *Acheron* is tricked and finally caught, or in the amputation of twelve-year-old Lord Blakeney's arm—a grueling operation following which Aubrey makes the boy a gift of Lord Nelson's military biography. When Blakeney pleads with his captain to describe the sort of person Nelson was, Aubrey replies simply, "Read the book," suggesting that to know the battles is to know the man.

The most meaningful relationship in the film is that between Aubrey and the ship's doctor, Stephen Maturin (Paul Bettany): an incongruous but intimate friendship between the masterful strategist and the quietly pacific man of science. In their encounters, Aubrey and Maturin trade jests, debate disciplinary procedures, and play string duets on cello and violin. Conflict erupts between them when the *Surprise* arrives at the Galapagos Islands, whose varied animal life the doctor—anticipating Charles Darwin's voyage aboard the *Beagle* by thirty years—desperately wishes to explore and catalog. Aubrey's need to resume pursuit of his own quarry, the *Acheron*, puts them fiercely at odds. But ultimately the worlds of science and warfare are recon-

The crew of the H.M.S. *Surprise* confronts an uncertain future in *Master and Commander: The Far Side of the World* (Peter Weir, Twentieth Century–Fox). Digital frame enlargement.

ciled when the mimicry shown by one of Maturin's samples, a stick insect, inspires the captain to disguise his own ship as a helpless whaling vessel, luring the enemy ship close enough to attack and capture. Through this storyline, *Master and Commander* suggests that culture and learning are not necessarily incompatible with government-sponsored aggression, but will always exist in tension nonetheless—a tension embodied by Aubrey and Maturin's complex relationship. "Men must be governed," Aubrey insists at one point, "often not wisely, but governed nonetheless." Maturin counters, "That's the excuse of every tyrant in history, from Nero to Bonaparte."

Completing this set of films was *Pirates of the Caribbean: The Curse of the Black Pearl*. Directed by Gore Verbinski, this adaptation of a Disney theme-park attraction had been in development for more than a decade, its fortunes shadowed by the prevailing Hollywood wisdom—following the notorious failure of *Cutthroat Island* (1995)—that pirate movies were a dead genre. Originally conceived as a direct-to-video feature, *Pirates of the Caribbean* went forward as a Jerry Bruckheimer production, with Johnny Depp controversially cast in the lead role of Captain Jack Sparrow, a dissolute, mascara-wearing scoundrel. Sparrow's grand joke of an entrance, astride the mast of a sinking ship from which he steps onto a dock, reflects the deft, light touch of the entire enterprise, as the film goes on to blend adventure, romance, and ghost stories with postmodern élan. The intricate yet streamlined narrative sets Sparrow, along with romantic lead Will Turner (Orlando Bloom), on a quest to rescue Elizabeth Swann (Keira Knightley), who has been kidnapped by the crew of a mysterious ship, the *Black Pearl*. The crew of the *Pearl*, like their captain, Barbossa (Geoffrey Rush), exists under a curse that has stranded them in a state of half-life, with moonlight revealing their true skeletal selves. Eventually, the fates of Barbossa, Swann, Turner, and Sparrow collide in a series of battles aboard a desert island, in a cave filled with treasure, and between sailing ships, whose exchanges of cannon fire are the only moments where the comical fantasia of *Pirates* resembles the more sober and historically accurate *Master and Commander*.

Both films, however, share a concern with the overlapping and contrasting codes of behavior and morality that structure human conduct. The world presented in *Pirates* is divided into three spheres: the lawful (represented by the stiff-necked Norrington, also in love with Elizabeth); the lawless (represented by pirates in general and Jack Sparrow specifically); and the supernatural (represented by Barbossa and his spectral crew). For all the film's circuslike play with genre tropes and self-conscious shout-outs to classical Hollywood adventures like *Captain Blood* (1935), the movie functions as a commentary on promises and commitments—including those that we would rather escape—as well as on the lust for material gain that drives individuals, and often nations, to violate those trusts. Movie studios, too: at one point, Barbossa describes the curse placed on the stolen treasure in terms that might characterize the Disney producers eager to monetize their amusement-park properties: "If anyone took so much as a single piece, as he was compelled by greed, by greed he would be consumed!" But the company's fortunes, like the film's sunny conclusion, were blessed with good luck. *Pirates'* unlikely but crowd-pleasing spectacle accomplished something unusual at the summer box office, maintaining strong ticket sales throughout the season, inviting repeat viewings, and ranking in the top five most profitable pictures over a course of twelve weeks (Stewart 440). The movie's success, along with those of *Finding Nemo* and the remake *Freaky Friday*, placed Disney in the top earning position among distributors by the end of the year (Diorio).

Meanwhile, against the surrealistic and heightened backdrop provided by the year's troubled blockbusters, the larger drama of the Iraq War continued as invasion gave way to occupation. Suicide bombers targeted public gathering places, while insurgents planted IEDs (improvised explosive devices) as roadside bombs to thwart the ground forces of the U.S.-led coalition. Although George W. Bush would declare on 1 May the end of combat operations in Iraq in his infamous "Mission Accomplished" speech, the facts on the ground suggested that the United States was moving into a much deeper conflict: a truly long-lived franchise of quagmire.

Similarly, this year in film showcased the film industry at the height of its technological powers, with new models of blockbuster cinema emerging to take advantage of the large-scale integration that made mega-productions possible, as well as the cross-pollinations of transmedia storytelling, the recognition of the importance of fan audiences and participatory culture, and the canny adaptive strategies by which franchises mine content from existing properties. Despite all this, however, it was not a terribly success-ful year for the blockbuster, either financially or ideologically. Our collec-tive fantasies seemed to turn inward and grow unstable, symptomatically announcing a new distrust of the authorities that guided us, an anxiety over personal and collective agency, and a quest both for assignable villains and a recovery of national innocence. That this innocence was itself some-thing of a mirage is reflected by the twin movement toward a historical purity and outright fantasy. The year's blockbusters demonstrated a response to traumatic shock and terrified awe at the new world in which we lived. They marshaled our greatest resources of imaging and imagining, yet failed, finally, to convince.

2004

Movies and Spectacle in a Political Year

ANNA EVERETT

The wide spectrum of films produced this year feature pure escapist entertainment, earnest political documentaries, family-friendly cartoons and animated fare, dazzling visual effects often with state-of-the-art computer-generated imagery (CGI), and biopics, among others. By far, according to Box Office Mojo's "2004 Domestic Grosses," the overwhelming majority of the top-grossing films during the year were Hollywood's spectacular sequels and remakes, including *The Bourne Supremacy*, sequel to *The Bourne Identity* (2002); *Bridget Jones: The Edge of Reason*, sequel to *Bridget Jones's Diary* (2001); *Alfie*, remake of the original film *Alfie* (1966); and more. There also were numerous offerings of other blockbuster and well-performing films emanating from original screenplays, well-known literary adaptations, and historical narratives that audiences eagerly patronized, such as *The Aviator* (about aerospace and movie industry pioneer Howard Hughes), *Kinsey* (about the famed sex researcher Alfred Kinsey), *Ray* (about legendary musician Ray Charles), and *Alexander* (about young warrior king Alexander the Great), for example. The most surprisingly successful offering of the year was the controversial political documentary *Fahrenheit 9/11*, most likely attributable to the fact that it was a highly contested presidential election year.

Still, considering their titles alone, and their huge popularity with audiences, most of these spectacular, twenty-first-century technology-driven films suggest a persistence of what Guy Debord famously identified in 1967 as the "Society of the Spectacle." This association comes to mind because in this highly polarized election year, such a preponderance of popular light-hearted and escapist fare comports well with Debord's contention that "the spectacle, grasped in its totality, is both the result and the project of the existing mode of production. It is not a supplement to the real world, an additional decoration. It is the heart of the unrealism of the real society" (6).

In fact, many of the notable occurrences this year that a number of films capture could be considered symptomatic of certain unreal and spectacularized strands existing within American civil society alongside the highly fraught realpolitik operating within the nation. This was especially true of the dramatic and oft-lamented expansion of film and celebrity culture (see Turner; Currid-Halkett; and Holmes and Redmond) and the nation's looming presidential election, replete with increasing doubts about the Bush administration's commencement and subsequent conduct of the unpopular Iraq War (see Hoskins; Chomsky). For on one side was the nation's preoccupation with celebrity scandals and gossip; on the other hand, serious media matters involving politics and other weighty issues of the day riveted the nation as well. With the encroachments of new digital media technologies and practices such as social networks into the political firmament, America's *vox populi* became increasingly amplified and influential as traditional media hegemony fragmented significantly.

Politics and celebrity found expression in several of the year's top-grossing biopics, which *The Aviator*, *Kinsey*, *Ray*, and *Alexander* illustrate rather handily. And while star vehicles and celebrity-driven blockbuster films were boxoffice powerhouses and thus indicators of the public mood to consume escapist and visual effects–driven spectacles, a sizable audience welcomed other, more intellectually engaging specular pleasures. For this was also the year that adult film fare proliferated, especially in the political documentary genre.

Sequel and Remake Nation:
The Bourne Supremacy,
Bridget Jones: The Edge of Reason, and *Alfie*

Not only are sequels and remakes a dominant mode of film-making praxis in Hollywood during any year, and especially this year, but this mode of cultural production also parallels a dominant feature of our political economy. That "humans are creatures of habit" is widely accepted, resonating throughout our concern with sequels and remakes in both films and politics this year. So, taking into account a representative sample of films to which audiences and studios became habituated, now let's consider, for example, *The Bourne Supremacy, Bridget Jones: The Edge of Reason*, and *Alfie* for their meaningful discourses along specific tracks relevant to America's post-postmodern, post–civil rights, postfeminist, and post-9/11 new normal conditions, as it were.

In *Spider-Man 2* (Sam Raimi, Columbia), the superhero (Tobey McGuire) exhibits amazing powers and derring-do atop a rapidly moving train speeding through the cityscape. Digital frame enlargement.

What is striking about *The Bourne Supremacy* is its ability to capture the new, post–Cold War geopolitical terror anxiety gripping the nation and clearly animating our electoral politics. Further, as a fitting Matt Damon star vehicle, the film showcases a new masculine mood and troubled male personality that counterbalance the two-dimensional, simplistic cartoon superhero males of such films as *Spider-Man 2*, *The Incredibles*, *Van Helsing*, and even *Walking Tall*, whose heroes represent essentialized goodness through and through, with no complexity, no moral or identity confusion. In the wake of 9/11, it is understandable that audiences respond well to film narratives with clearly outlined good and evil contests and recognizable good and bad guys to love and hate. At the same time, audiences also could enjoy the kick-ass, take-no-prisoners, super-spy rogue antics of Jason Bourne, a recoded antihero character suitable for the new millennium. Todd McCarthy, in a review entitled "Spy Pic's Bourne to Be Wild," puts the film in perspective, arguably, along new, post-9/11, normal parameters:

> Based on his actions alone, Bourne is a nasty piece of work, hardly a protagonist worthy of one's emotional interest; but once he's seen clearly enough for what he is, a pawn in a deadly game whose resourcefulness in

staying alive is impressive, the story becomes more engaging. . . . Once again, Damon scores in the title role by never courting audience sympathy and playing his all American good looks against the hard-shell brutality of the character. Much of the film's pleasure stems from its many atmospheric locations, some of which—particularly Berlin and Moscow—carry extensive Cold War resonance.   (54, 63)

McCarthy's critical but largely affirmative review of *Supremacy* identifies certain elements of Bourne's character and the film's discourse that are in step with American society post-9/11. And, Manohla Dargis's *Los Angeles Times* review of the film enables us also to assess how Bourne's morally compromised, violence-prone, and amnesiac former CIA agent persona is symptomatic of America's terror-stricken culture of distress in an uncertain contemporary geopolitical reality. As Dargis notes, "Much of what happens plot-wise involves the CIA, which in its fumbling resembles the agency of recent headlines" ("Just Try" E1). For Claudia Puig, writing in *USA Today*, the film's lure is its success as a sequel, and especially one that captures the era's obsession with taking out or killing our political and military enemies abroad (Osama bin Laden and his countless second-in-command cronies). She specifies the spy thriller genre and its "edge-of-the-seat

In *The Bourne Supremacy* (Paul Greengrass, Universal), Matt Damon as super-spy Jason Bourne spectacularizes the contemporary antihero, whose flawed masculinity is constantly tested in this quintessential action thriller. Photofest.

action," the impressive cast, namely Joan Allen as a compassionate CIA official and, of course, Matt Damon, and notable others (Julia Stiles and Brian Cox) as essential components assuring the film's popularity. Of Damon's centrality, Puig contends, "The movie belongs to Damon, whose Bourne is manly, exquisitely tough and oddly endearing, given he's a cold-blooded killer" (1E). That she underscores Bourne's flawed masculinity and his guilt and grief over past crimes he has committed is another strength of Puig's assessment of the various registers on which the film connects with cynical and even jaded audiences, following the highly publicized failings of our government's top intelligence operations at home and abroad.

Sequels and remakes were generally a good bet for the film industry this year. They also provided clues to the nation's collective attitudes about certain topics and cultural shifts. Boxoffice hits and misses, then, while not deterministic, can be revealing. Whereas Matt Damon's imperfect CIA assassin in *The Bourne Supremacy* humanizes and effectively repurposes the James Bond super-spy type for sophisticated filmgoers unimpressed with such dated masculine and politicized icons, *Bridget Jones: The Edge of Reason* misses its mark as a measure of audience affect for the beloved title character and her quirky narrative of anxious and insecure love. Actually, the sequel garnered mixed reviews. Most interesting about the Bridget Jones films, however, is the casting of American actor Renée Zellweger in the lead. A small project that adapted Helen Fielding's novel *Bridget Jones's Diary*, itself loosely based on events and characters from Jane Austen's *Pride and Prejudice*, the first film was a European co-production that became a surprise Hollywood and international blockbuster, generating U.S. returns of more than $71 million and approximately $282 million globally. A user review for IMDb sums up this unlikely 2001 success, contrasting it with some reviews of the sequel not based upon Fielding's novel and discussing what made the original film work:

> Her name is Renee Zellweger, seriously, if the actress was British, this film would've been—been there, done that. Instead, this clever casting has made Bridget Jones a wonderful little picture. Renee Zellweger is an actress who changed to suit the screenplay, now that is ACTING! Her mannerisms, her weight, her enthusiasm and cutesy style are a wonder to behold. Colin Firth does a great job, he plays his role well. . . . Hugh Grant finally gives us something different, he was actually quite funny at times. . . . The Super 35 widescreen frame is used well, bravo! The screenplay is lightweight, but written well, plenty of ad-lib and spontaneity transcend the script. As a male, sit back and have a laugh. Quality!   (Darth Sidious)

After stealing the show in *Jerry Maguire* (1996) with her signature line "You had me at hello," Zellweger's character in that film now suggests a younger Bridget in formation. Rather than the third member of a brilliant triangle ensemble, as in *Jerry Maguire*, in the *Bridget Jones* films Zellweger is the bankable Hollywood ingénue opening the films, supported by Britain's most powerful and charismatic male stars Firth and Grant. The suggestion that males "sit back and have a laugh" is insightful, especially for the sequel, since the film aims to extend its primary focus to include male characters and male audience members.

It is not apparent that male filmgoers did in fact sit back and laugh at the sequel, but *Los Angeles Times* critic Carina Chocano gives us a sense of U.S. female audiences' affection for the British Bridget Jones and their resulting disaffection with the less-empowered agency of their returning heroine: "The movie might be British, but its attitude toward girls is still pure Hollywood. This is a shame" (E1). For unlike the original *Diary*, a small film on a modest budget ($25 million), *Reason* was a co-production, this time with substantial American studio involvement, a budget of $40 million, but domestic boxoffice earnings that barely exceeded production costs. Nevertheless, despite American audiences' cooling to the nascent franchise, international grosses nearly matched those of the first film.

What was clearly amiss for American audiences generally and for women audiences in particular was Bridget's devolution, as Liz Braun puts it: "Everything endearing about the plump little-diarist-who-could has been made pathetic. . . . Bridget . . . stops being endearing and starts being infuriating in a story that is endlessly (and needlessly) complicated" (E2). For a generation of third wave feminists and postfeminists, the presumed target audience, it is understandable that they might resist the "Hollywood" treatment of this once empowered if neurotic heroine now caricatured beyond recognition for the sake of "a rare comedy that lets the girl play the clown" (Chocano E1); but at what price, given women's continual frustrations about full parity with men across all sectors of U.S. society? Without a doubt, for the U.S. audience at least, the irreverent fun of *Bridget Jones's Diary* was not recaptured by the mocking absurdity of *The Edge of Reason*. One popular IMDb reviewer explains this sequel-to-audience disconnect:

> The film relies completely on Zellweger's star power. She's game, but gives quite possibly the worst performance of her career. Bridget's become a daft twit. She's lost any semblance of intelligence. With nothing genuinely funny to fall back on, director Beeban Kidron gets Zellweger to simply waddle about the place trying to eke laughs out of us. Unfortunately, Zellweger's

shtick is barely amusing and gets tiresome very quickly. The idea of laughing at a large, buxom lass while she pratfalls her way through a horrendous film must strike a chord with some women. At the screening I attended, I sat next to four women who did not laugh—heck, I didn't hear even a chuckle from them—throughout the entire film. Yet, they applauded at the end, as if they'd just discovered their anthem film.

(anhedonia from the planet earth)

The idea that Bridget Jones's Hollywoodization recodes the character helps to contextualize the sequel's boxoffice flop in the United States. At the same time, anhedonia's own anecdotal reading of the film and its audience seems to confirm the dominant fiscal logic of sequel productions, especially as Liz Braun points out in her "bottom line": "Hugely disappointing, but if you love the Bridget Jones idea and you love Zellweger, Firth and Grant, you'll see this sequel, be sorry you did, but still love the cast" (E2). And based on *Reason*'s global boxoffice take, what else could a sequel desire?

While film sequels construct interesting dialogic encounters with changing American values and norms, remakes plumb the depths of popular films from the past. We consider the remake of *Alfie*, not for its adequate boxoffice numbers (domestic $13.5 million), but for its reworking of gender and identity politics from the swinging sixties to the current year. Whereas sequels tend to fare better, remakes generally are riskier profit-making propositions. And although several critics and reviewers question *Alfie*'s very existence and its wrongheaded rationale as a remake of a minor classic,[1] in Steven Rea's apt analysis, the film's take on shifting gender dynamics in the twenty-first century warrants interrogation. The prevalence of hypersexualized young female desirability in mainstream media culture since the 1960s—that this *Alfie* deploys rather extensively—has frustrated second wave feminists since the 1970s.

No matter that Hollywood's willful misconstrual of women's call for sexual liberation and reproductive rights got translated onscreen as somehow indicative of third wave and postfeminist women's ultimate embrace of or capitulation to "the media's pervasive antifeminism," to borrow Leslie Heywood and Jennifer Drake's terms (43). It is the case that, as Rebecca Walker (daughter of famed mother Alice) pointed out in 1995, "Young women coming of age today wrestle with the term [feminism] because we have a very different vantage point on the word than our foremothers. . . . We fear that the identity will dictate and regulate our lives" (xxxiii). For Walker and later feminists the goal was not to reject second wave feminism altogether, but for younger women and men to reconcile or "struggle to locate themselves within some continuum of feminism" (xxxiii–xxxiv). In trying to locate the appetite of American audiences for *Alfie*—this updated "seminal Brit-flick" (Rea's terms)—we do get a sense of the filmmakers' challenge: How to transport a sixties-era, hedonistic, womanizing Cockney cad from swinging London to a multicultural, multiracial New York in 2004? Changing the film's optics from black-and-white film stock to color is one distinction; pairing the Brit Alfie (Jude Law) up with African American best friend Marlon (Omar Epps) is another. Desson Thomson further explains the dilemma of the film's time-space shift by making it clear that the filmmakers not only had to overcome geographic logistics of the *Alfie* character remix as "a sort of eurotrashy poseur, living in a low-rent corner of the Big Apple, dressing in retro '60s chic." But the film also necessitated that the filmmakers

> retrofit their women. In the 1960s, women on screen weren't given much in the way of independence. The female characters in the 1966 "Alfie" are pushovers, easy to abuse and boss around. . . . In this day and age . . . they've evolved into equal contenders in the romantic power game. And pulling a fast one over them is not only impossible, it's morally unacceptable for audiences. . . . But these updated, zesty women . . . feel forced into the story. . . . They're thrown together just to look cosmopolitan and you know, New York–like.   (T35)

One thing the filmmakers understood unequivocally in modernizing *Alfie* for a postmodern, multicultural, third wave feminist era was that young contemporary audiences (male and female alike) do not expect a racially homogenous cast or a dated narrative featuring patronizing sexual double standards. Although *Alfie*'s original contribution in 1966 was Alfie's shock and awe at being displaced by a younger version of himself on the whim of his much older woman lover, by this year, however, even the young women whom Alfie beds and abandons take his departure in stride, not undone by hooking up for a night or two with this shallow pretty boy. As Thomson puts it, "Sure, he's good-looking and can expect shivery response from certain members of the audience, but *Alfie* 'e ain't" (T35). Certainly Michael Caine's sixties-era Alfie ain't about to count a young black woman among his "birds" of prey for sexual gratification. But Jude Law's Alfie breaks the miscegenation taboo with his non-discriminatory sexual antics involving Lonette (Nia Long), the black girlfriend of his best black buddy Marlon. After all, interracial romances onscreen are not the shocking anomaly of past years.

Although generally panned by critics and tepidly received by audiences, *Alfie* is an important barometer of how mainstream filmmakers seek to retrofit cinematic discourse to America's changed sexual, gender, and racial identity politics, clearly with uncertain payoffs. Genre and gender matters in film seem particularly emblematic of productions generating unanticipated boxoffice consequences. Another interesting register of stubborn gender divisions is the popular reception of one enduring genre that more than others organizes its narrative economy and conventions around relative gender parity. Formerly categorized as the screwball comedy, now, when starring a male lead, audiences recognize this generic category as the gender-neutral romantic comedy; by contrast, when starring a female lead, audiences seem to buy into the limiting chick-flick genre designation. By this logic, then, *Bridget Jones: The Edge of Reason* is called a "chick-flick" by reviewers who expect it to appeal to a female audience; and *Alfie* is just as readily positioned as a romantic comedy capable of luring audiences across the gender divide. As Rick Altman reminds us, "The interpretation of generic films depends directly on the audience's generic expectations" (14). So, in this instance of unanticipated consequences, *Reason* did beat *Alfie* at the box office by substantial numbers, despite *Reason*'s frequent ghettoization or marginalization as a chick-flick.

That *Alfie*'s remake narrative foregrounds race in a contemporary vein (perhaps untenable for the sixties original) is an important discursive modification, as is its more modern representation of women. Nevertheless, audiences likely concurred with Steven Rea that *Alfie* "feels creaky and anachronistic" (W4).

Sanitize This! or, The Year Political Documentaries Mattered: *Fahrenheit 9/11* and *Control Room*

At the same time that the year's film offerings were pro forma or rather familiar in terms of big-budget, high-concept blockbusters, experimental indie films, personal documentaries, and an unfamiliar phenomenon of highly political documentaries, began proliferating as well. Most characteristic in this regard were *Fahrenheit 9/11* and *Control Room*. Impelled by what many believed to be a significant failure of mainstream news media organizations to report objectively, honestly, and thoroughly on important political news of this election year, more filmgoers than ever turned for news of current events to political documentaries (many of which were highly partisan). After more than two years of suspicion about the shaky relationship between the George W. Bush administration's rush to war with Iraq and credible facts to justify the same, the mainstream news media began to own up to their complicity in ginning up public support for America's new military strategy of deadly "preemptive strikes" against sovereign nations merely suspected of terrorist links to 9/11. Whereas many left-leaning citizens questioned the administration's motives for war with Iraq and its equally questionable facts justifying the 2003 invasion from the beginning, it was not until high-profile news disclosures from key mainstream media outlets and other sources surfaced that public consumption for political documentary films reached its fever pitch.

No doubt that American mainstream news' too-little, too-late coverage of so-called "events on the ground" in Iraq frustrated citizens' demands to know about the consequences of the nation's unprecedented preemptive strike on a sovereign nation (in this case, a nation the United States had supported during the Iran-Iraq war of the 1980s). Thus it was in late April that Americans learned of their military's physically and sexually abusive treatment of Iraqi prisoners at the Abu Ghraib prison. One month later came the devastating admission by the *New York Times* of its reliance upon flawed and pro-government sources to help promote the Bush administration's unfounded assertion that Saddam Hussein possessed unregulated stockpiles of weapons of mass destruction (WMD) targeted at the United States. These stories and many others did little to assure Americans that their trust in the government and in its apparent mainstream media mouthpieces, as some believed them to be, was misplaced (Hoskins 46).[2] It is precisely these and other abrogations of journalistic responsibility and integrity that the films under consideration here address.

In no way is my analysis of the potent political documentaries meant to be comprehensive. Nonetheless, the two I consider here are powerfully representative of the major debates and ideological stances that characterized America's political culture of the moment. While Michael Moore's *Fahrenheit 9/11* stands alone in terms of its radical alteration of the political documentary's boxoffice fortunes and the genre's competitive positioning in the feature-length film category, Jehane Noujaim's *Control Room*, Danny Schecter's *WMD: Weapons of Mass Deception*, Nicholas Perry and Harry Thomason's *The Hunting of the President*, Joseph Mealey and Michael Shoob's *Bush's Brain*, and Michael Wilson's *Michael Moore Hates America* are representative. Each of these titles except the last features investigative journalism targeting some of the most volatile and divisive issues of the political moment and largely from a left-leaning point of view. Although I do not address all these films, I do want to stress that as counter-narratives to what many scholars and social critics consider mainstream news media's apparent capitulation to self-serving corporate business agendas and far-right Republican politics (see Chomsky; Hoskins; Kerbel), these documentaries have a different information dissemination imperative. By and large, they not only challenge the so-called "CNN Effect" and the "Fox News Effect," but help audiences understand why these terms matter in a presidential election year.

In his book *Televising War: From Vietnam to Iraq*, Andrew Hoskins situates the matter of dominant media goals and prerogatives thus: "How events come to be defined as 'news' in the first place is part of a long-standing debate, or rather assumption, about the criteria that effect journalistic selections and reselections, in other words the existence of 'news values' or 'newsworthiness'" (45). He continues:

> In times of war and other catastrophes, time is of more consequence than in the coverage of other events, as audience responses to real-time images, and the action or inaction of politicians and military leaders in turn, may save or end lives. So, the impact of the immediacy of television has been taken very seriously, with numerous studies identifying the medium's reflexivity, that is to say, its ability to feed into and shape the event being covered by news programming—the so-called 'CNN effect.'   (46)

It is the case that providing more extensive coverage of the Bush administration's 2003 declaration of war on Iraq and its aftermath outside the corporate "media monopoly" (in Ben Bagdikian's terms) is a key motive of *Fahrenheit 9/11* and *Control Room*, the products of activist filmmakers. It is widely agreed that cable TV's liveness and immediacy became incalculable assets in the government's lead up to the "Gulf War 2.0," or "Operation Iraqi Freedom," as the Bush administration named it.

Frustrated and exasperated by this unholy alliance, Michael Moore produced *Fahrenheit 9/11* to contest what he considered right-wing and right-leaning ideologues' control and influence strategies in U.S. politics, media industries, and mainstream news outlets, as well as their usurpation of American democratic structures for the purpose of profitable war mongering after 9/11. Moore stated as much in his 18 June "Dateline NBC" interview with Matt Lauer. Discussing the Walt Disney Company's move to pull *Fahrenheit* from distribution, Lauer suggested a defense of that decision: "You know what? They paid you? The checks cleared and they can look at

Michael Moore with a U.S. soldier in Washington, D.C., where Moore canvasses politicians on Capitol Hill to ask if any of their sons are risking their lives in service to the nation, in the award-winning *Fahrenheit 9/11* (Michael Moore, Fellowship Adventure Group). Photofest.

it and say, you know what? This is not the kind of movie we want to distribute right now. Maybe it's too political. Maybe it won't attract a wide enough audience. It's their right." Moore retorted:

> It's their right. Except here's the difference. It's not government censorship. It's censorship by a corporation. And we're at a point now, Matt, where we have fewer and fewer companies owning all our media. I mean here we are at NBC, which just bought Universal, which is owned by GE. As you have fewer and fewer voices in a democracy, in a free society, it's not good to limit the number of voices. . . . You know I've been sitting here for like the last twenty minutes thinking, man, if he would have only asked Bush administration officials these kinds of hard questions in the weeks leading up to the war, and then when the war started, maybe there wouldn't be a war. Because the American people, once given the truth, you know the old saying from Abraham Lincoln, give the people the facts and the Republic will be safe.
>
> ("Moore Defends")

Moore also confessed that titling his film *Fahrenheit 9/11* was a deliberate signifier of the film's incendiary nature; that it is an attack on George W. Bush and his family; that he himself is not a Democrat and that he rails against a party he says is "weak-kneed" and "wimpy" for not standing up to the Republicans; that he hoped *Fahrenheit* would motivate the electorate to turn out and vote in larger numbers; and that his film is art first and not a political film. His performance with Lauer was classic Moore, combative and compelling all at once. By challenging Lauer and other big media detractors, Moore embraced the controversy to promote his film within a marketing economy that exceeds far beyond what advertising and trailers could yield. Understanding the rhetorical dynamics of *Fahrenheit*, with Moore as its unabashed cinéma-vérité provocateur (to invoke Erik Barnouw), it is evident why the documentary captured a sizable measure of the filmgoing audience eager for his subjective oppositional message and earned a staggering $119 million in the United States alone. Capturing the year's political zeitgeist is Moore's emphatic remark to Lauer: "I'm at a point where I don't trust the mainstream media. I'm like most Americans at this point. We don't trust [you]" ("Moore Defends"). This sentiment clearly suffuses many other documentaries this year.

For *Control Room* and *WMD*, the filmmakers opted for more traditional documentary representational approaches and aesthetics to convey crucial if little disclosed facts and contexts regarding the second Iraq War. Egyptian American writer-director Jehane Noujaim's *Control Room* employs techniques of direct cinema to countermand politicians' and U.S. media's demonization of al-Jazeera, the Arab world's most popular news network, and to present a balanced perspective of the organization, its executives and journalists. That Moore's provocative cinéma vérité and Noujaim's observational documentary employ different cinematic modalities reveals much about each filmmaker's critical stance on the issues at hand. Noujaim opted for the fly-on-the-wall witness to history, with the filmmaker herself mostly absent from the onscreen narratives. She does mix a bit of that fly-on-the-wall technique with cinéma vérité's "charge of mediation with enthusiasm" in order to dramatizethe filmmaker's "intelligence and sensibility" (Winston 52). And despite the fact that such documentary conventions and modalities create shifting styles and perspectives, *Fahrenheit 9/11* and *Control Room* each deploy naturalism, realism, and reflexivity to illuminate "the real world of externally verifiable data" (55) aimed at their ideal receivers— their politically minded audiences. Still, *Control Room* is quite apart from *Fahrenheit*.

Before culling a few important and memorable messages from *Control Room* that resonated with its audiences, let us note briefly some telling observations from *Los Angeles Times* reporter John Horn, whose article "Public Keeping Its Cool Over Election Effect of 'Fahrenheit'" reflects the newspaper's poll of audience attitudes about the Michael Moore film.

Published on 23 July 2004, Horn's article appears only one month after *Fahrenheit*'s release, yet it strikes a confident tone in its assertion that despite the film's record-setting boxoffice numbers, it is significant that *Fahrenheit*'s polemical message appealed primarily to a Democratic Party base, with few converts among Republicans and Independents. On balance, then, when judged against Moore's own admission that the text was absolutely anti-Bush with a clear-cut imperative to influence the outcome of the November election, the fact that Bush was the ultimate victor vindicates Horn and the *Los Angeles Times'* poll. Consideration of whether the film became a rallying point for energizing outraged Republicans and other conservatives (so called "Conserva-Dems" included), or how much the mismanagement of Democratic nominee John Kerry's campaign helped to push Bush over the finish line, is outside the scope of this essay. Nonetheless, it is important to recognize the role of political documentaries in the maelstrom of America's fraught and extremely divisive realpolitik, a role whose ultimate consequences would be felt in the next presidential election cycle following Kerry's invitation to little-known Illinois state senator Barack Obama to be the keynote speaker at the Democratic National Convention.

Although *Fahrenheit 9/11* constructs an effective reset of industry expectations for documentary filmmaking profitability and political influence this year, Noujaim's *Control Room* seems to capture the hearts and minds of progressive-minded audiences seeking reliable information about the Bush administration's Iraq War and the U.S. mainstream media's complicity therein. What Noujaim does with *Control Room* is gain an informed perspective on the eve of the war from both U.S. and Arab media professionals. In an interview, Noujaim asserts that *Control Room* is not her personal act of protesting the war in Iraq:

> I didn't feel educated enough to go out there and protest. . . . I definitely wasn't for the war, but to make a film about the politics of war versus no war, like something Michael Moore would do, it's something you make if you really feel sure about all those questions. I would say it was a way to find out what was going on for myself, and I wanted to be around people who are very motivated to think about it.   (Chandra)

For interviewer Mridu Chandra, *Control Room*, which expresses Noujaim's even-handed approach to covering al-Jazeera's coverage of the impending war, was welcome: "Interestingly enough," Chandra says to Noujaim, "you didn't end up taking sides with Al Jazeera" ("In Conversation"). Chandra's realization, in this instance, is a result of her interview with Noujaim herself, and it comports with what nearly all the film's posters on IMDb either specify or indicate. According to most IMDB user reviewers, this film is a must-see documentary text with an objectivity that puts most American media coverage of al-Jazeera and the march to war with Iraq to shame. An IMDb poster, Ryan, whose 2 April review is entitled "The most important film of 2004," observes: "It is Noujaim's serene accomplishment to give you in two hours what no media outlet did during the war: something resembling 'the truth.'" *Control Room* posters on IMDb also draw contrasts between Noujaim's and Moore's documentaries with more favorable remarks for *Control Room*'s balance.

One of *Control Room*'s central contributions this year was disabusing Americans of the conviction that al-Jazeera is a mouthpiece for Saddam Hussein, al-Qaeda, and all manner of radical Islamist voices, when in fact some Arab leaders banned it altogether. As Noujaim herself said of al-Jazeera, "If they're hated by everybody, there has to be something interesting going on there. . . . There were very different stories being told about the same subject. We forget how perspective means everything. . . . I wanted to make a film about this issue of perspective" (Chandra). As the title indicates, *Control Room* anchors its discursive focus from inside a news operation, and in this case it is the al-Jazeera news network in Doha, Qatar. Noujaim has discussed how her documentary film came to fruition despite having no funding, no professional film workers and collaborators. She also reveals that interns on the production were enticed to join her in Egypt for the shoot and editing because she offered, in lieu of payment, her family home as a source of free food, lodging, and access to the beautiful beaches of Egypt (Chandra).

Another important perspective *Control Room* provides is on the interaction between senior al-Jazeera journalist Hassan Ibrahim and U.S. Central Command (Cent-Com) press officer Lt. Josh Rushing. Ibrahim and Rushing get into a heated discussion about why the United States is in Iraq. The unedited conversation proceeded thus:

Rushing: We believe Iraq has weapons of mass destructions and a willingness to use them against us . . .

Ibrahim: When?

Rushing: What do you mean, when?

Ibrahim: When did they use them against you?

Rushing: That they have the will to use them against us?

Ibrahim: When? I mean, do you think Sadd—[crosstalk] Saddam will threaten the U.S. with weapons of mass destruction?

Rushing: Yes!

Ibrahim: When? That's news to me. I'm sorry. Now this is news to me.

Rushing: Okay—

Ibrahim: When did Saddam threaten the U.S. with weapons of mass destruction?

Rushing: Oh, I see. I'm sorry. I misunderstood your question. We believe he had the will to give the forces, to use against us, and—well, go ahead.

Ibrahim: I'm just conveying to you what people are saying, they are saying that the U.S. is inventing a purpose as it goes along. In the beginning it was weapons of mass destruction, and then the whole thing transformed into removing Saddam from power.

Rushing: So, why do they think we're doing it? What do they think our motives are?

Ibrahim: No one knows. People think you're—

Rushing: Really?

Ibrahim: People think you're there basically to control the oil of Iraq, control the Iraqi foreign politics. To control the region.

Rushing: I won't back down off of my point when we talk about our intent in this—in what we're doing. We're not here to occupy an Arab land. We're not here to take their oil. We're not here to—to kill Arabs or take mosques, or any of the other myriad of reasons.

The candor and intractability that is palpable in each man's utterance captures well the larger differences existing between al-Jazeera's and Cent-Com's perspectives on the war. By letting the principals in the documentary speak for themselves and at length, coupled with the use of long takes and unobtrusive or straightforward editing, Noujaim constructs *Control Room* as a realist narrative probing the crisis of war so that audiences might discover some truth rather than more propaganda. After all, Noujaim confesses that she and her inexperienced team had to learn Final Cut Pro and edited the footage on six computers they set up downstairs in her family's Sinai home (Chandra). Telling an important story surely trumped *Control Room*'s competent if not impressive production values.

Among the most powerful stories and images in the film are those centering on the U.S. military's so-called accidental killings of an al-

Jazeera journalist and others not embedded with U.S. troops, which *Control Room* features utilizing al-Jazeera's footage of the events up to the moment of deadly impact, and the bloody carnage of noncombatant Iraqi men, women, and children who became innocent victims of the U.S. military's targeted and errant "surgical strikes." Indeed, it was al-Jazeera's refusal to sanitize its visible evidence of the war's dead and dying on both sides of the conflict that led to their being demonized by the Bush administration and the Western media. Andrew Hoskins explains the vestiges of the 1991 Gulf War's sanitizing imperatives that continued to exert pressures on media coverage of Operation Iraqi Freedom, which *Fahrenheit 9/11* and *Control Room* engage. Although Hoskins's discussion concerns media sanitizing efforts in effect during the first Gulf War, it remains pertinent to our look at political documentaries circulating this year. Consider, for example, Hoskins's remarks about Britain's newspaper the *Guardian* and its willingness to challenge this de facto strain of media censorship:

> The *Guardian*'s publication of graphic and disturbing photographs deliberately challenges the mediated social memory of a highly sanitized war of 1991. The main critique assembled through the accounts of the photographers and journalists in this newspaper, however, is the Pentagon and the system of reporting that prevented horrific scenes of some of those killed in 1991 from being reported at the same time. These contrast the role of the (independent) photographer and journalist as witness and as documenter of the 'real' Gulf War against the contrived and highly sanitized version produced through pool reporting. They demonstrate (by their long-standing omission) just how effectively the media-managed images of 1991 have been retained in the collective memory of the war.
>
> (44)

Control Room and other such documentaries clearly address this major element of war reportage, wherein the government and the mainstream media outlets struggle to control the flow of images from active battlefields.

Most significant in Moore's and Noujaim's important revelations about media industry practices are their concerns about the extent to which show business has swallowed up the news business. In *Staging the Real*, Richard Kilborn has made an important study of how the entertainment values and conventions of reality TV are permeating all manner of televisual discourse, which absolutely informs these filmmakers' concern about news media's increasing infotainment strategies. As Kilborn sees it, "Factual programme makers are nowadays not so much concerned with the observational chronicling of events as the staging and shaping of events for viewer consumption. . . . It became increasingly apparent that producers' principal concern was to win viewers over to a world that television itself was creating" (73). He adds, "The fear is, of course, that the entertainment imperative will continue to impose such a baleful influence that . . . any residual hopes that television will be able to exert a 'civilizing influence' will be lost" (87). In response, political documentary films of the sort we have explored thus far have, indeed, gone far to provide vital and vibrant news and information so crucial to American civil society during an important presidential election year. It is also important to mention that despite the preponderance of left-leaning political documentaries, there were also right-leaning political documentaries, such as Michael Wilson's *Michael Moore Hates America*.

Biopics and Gratuitous Troublemaking: *Alexander*, *Ray*, and *The Aviator*

This year film audiences were also drawn to a crop of blockbuster biopics that included such historic figures as Howard Hughes (*The Aviator*), Alfred Kinsey (*Kinsey*), Ray Charles (*Ray*), and Alexander the Great (*Alexander*), to choose four. A reliable and profitable genre historically for the film industry, the biopic, as George F. Custen notes in *Bio/Pics: How Hollywood Constructed Public History*, "was a known commodity almost from film's beginning. Further, it had many variants—hagiography, psychological biography, autobiography—and was embroiled in the same controversies about truth, accuracy, and interpretation as its literary predecessors" (6). Biopics of the hagiography variety are less tenable with twenty-first-century filmgoers than in past years, as cinematic treatments of these individuals' lives make clear. Hagiographies, saintly celebrations or sanitized versions of the complex lives of public personalities, could not withstand what I call the scrutiny of "the hyper-gaze," particularly where contemporary fan culture, pervasive computing's on-demand information databases, and the era's jaded view of any claims to personal perfection are concerned. Celebrity and political scandals mentioned above are striking cases in point.

Still, there is an ongoing fascination with the reputed accomplishments of historic personalities in cinematic productions since, as Custen remarks, "most viewers, at least in part, see history through the lens of the film biography" (2). When we consider, for example, the cases of *The Aviator*, *Alexander*, and *Ray* we recognize easily the narrative stress placed on these great men's foibles, in varying degrees, as major plot points and thematic foci. This is particularly true of Oliver Stone's auteurism in directing *Alexander*. Martin Scorsese's direction of *The Aviator* shares a similar approach to the construction of a young Howard Hughes's life story. Taylor Hackford's and Bill Condon's even-handed treatments of *Ray* and *Kinsey*, respectively, convey these men's stories with a believable realism that keeps historical distortions to a minimum, to borrow Custen's ideas (7). One dominant narrative thread running through these biopics is the incendiary nature of sexuality in the lives of these formidable figures and the necessity for the director to maintain an R rating by simultaneously exploiting and reining in this vital element. Unburdened by such restrictive morality clauses as those imposed by the Breen Office in 1946 when Warner Bros. banished homosexual references from its Cole Porter biopic *Night and Day*, for instance, Stone's *Alexander* not only engages the youthful warrior's bisexuality, but does not shy away from Alexander's historically affirmed homosexual relationship with his boyhood friend and contemporaneous confidant Hephaistion. In his review of *Alexander*, William Booth writes, "Stone reportedly was asked by the studio and his producer to tone down some of the violence of battle and some of the man-man sexual innuendo."

Hackford rounds out his unsanitized filmic portraiture of music legend Ray Charles by including scenes of his notorious womanizing. He does not, however, permit this feature to overwhelm the film's larger message of musical genius and personal triumph over physical disability and virulent racial segregation and institutional racism. Indeed, all these biopics share a similar imperative—the imperative that studio head Darryl F. Zanuck calls a "rooting interest" for the audience (qtd. in Custen 18). For filmgoers this year, it seems that only a part of Zanuck's formulation for successful biopics resonates with and remains relevant to fans of this popular genre. Custen cogently describes Zanuck's rooting interest imperative in this way: "Ironically, while Zanuck opted for portraying the genius as having a normal home life and love of family and children, the viewer was meant to treat the achievements of genius with reverence" (19). As the nation's cult of celebrity, its penchant for reality television, and boxoffice returns of *Ray*, *Alexander*, and *The Aviator* all make abundantly clear, contemporary audiences have no compunction about rooting for flawed geniuses, particularly when the flaw involves imperfect personal lives.

While *Los Angeles Times* film critic Kenneth Turan was exuberant in his review of another biopic that year, *Kinsey*, his review of *The Aviator* was less enthusiastic. He was not surprised in the latter to find Scorsese's familiar "show-off," self-pleasing direction, though the film's other limitations were less expected. In this instance, Turan applauds Scorsese's restraint because, "in 'Aviator' he's put all his technique, energy and style at the service of a story we can't look away from, at least initially" ("Wing"). For these biopics, all the critics made a point of singling out the lead actors' exceptional portrayals of these great men despite their having been unlikely choices for the hefty roles. A. O. Scott's special accolades for comedian Jamie Foxx as Ray Charles are apt: "What makes 'Ray' such a satisfying picture, in spite of some shortcomings and compromises, is Mr. Foxx's inventive, intuitive, and supremely intelligent performance." Scott continues, "'Ray,' while not a great movie, is a very good movie about greatness, in which celebrating the achievement of one major artist becomes the occasion for the emergence of another. I'm speaking of Ray Charles and Jamie Foxx, of course, though at this point I'm not entirely sure I can tell them apart" ("Portrait"). In many respects, Scott's remarks could easily apply to these other biopics as well, especially Leonardo DiCaprio's powerful star turn as the young, charismatic Howard Hughes. Interestingly enough, Hollywood's penchant for biopics seems to privilege great man over great woman narratives as a matter of course, and certainly throughout this year's production output.[3]

Conclusion

That it was a highly polarizing political year goes without saying. Still, many of the year's films displayed quite a willingness to engage in some profitable and spectacular gratuitous troublemaking. At the same, American film audiences demonstrated their penchant for indulging their specular pleasures and political proclivities by casting their boxoffice votes both for big-budget Hollywood film extravaganzas and well-made, politically savvy independent documentaries. It is telling, nonetheless, that as the nation prepared to ratify its core democratic responsibility of ensuring peaceful electoral politics every four years, audiences this year clearly enjoyed a bit of entertainment in their political films, and a bit of politics in their entertainment spectacles.

NOTES

1. See, for example, Chocano "Alfie?"; Thomson.

2. Another important element in public distrust of the news media is the fact that the nation's most important media regulatory entity, the Federal Communications Commission (FCC), was under the directorship of Michael Powell, the son of Secretary of State Colin

Powell. At the time, this fact further eroded the nation's confidence in the electronic and print media's objectivity and veracity, given the elder Powell's public advocacy for the invasion of Iraq based on the charge, later disproven, of Iraq's possession of WMDs.

3. For a discussion of the differences between biopics of men and women, see Bingham 10–11, 23–25, 213–22.

2005

Movies, Terror, and
the American Family

KAREN BECKMAN

The first of January marked the passing of Shirley Chisholm, the first black woman to be elected to Congress, the first woman to run for the Democratic presidential nomination, and the first major-party black candidate for the U.S. presidency. As this pioneer left the stage, George W. Bush was about to commence the second term of his ill-fated presidency. Undeterred by the doubt cast on the legitimacy of his initial election, he promised energy independence, the partial privatization of Social Security, and continued vigilance in the War on Terror. The year would also require him to replace two Supreme Court justices, Sandra Day O'Connor and William H. Rehnquist.

Terror, turmoil, and turnover marked the year for the nation and its film industry, and the disasters occurring at the national level found cinematic parallels in the industrial breakups and makeups (Universal and Paramount's joint venture ends; Disney and Pixar move toward and away from each other; the Weinstein brothers depart from Disney, but Disney retains the name Miramax, derived from the Weinsteins' parents, Max and Miriam) and in the plethora of films that depict trouble in the white American family. *Junebug* foregrounds the tension between a northern art-dealer wife and her southern in-laws. Noah Baumbach's *The Squid and the Whale* dramatizes a white, middle-class, urban couple's extramarital affairs and separation through the eyes of their two boys. *Thumbsucker* addresses the troubles of another white adolescent boy who struggles with his thumbsucking habit and with the traumatic realization that his mother has professional and sexual desires. Gus Van Sant, Jim Jarmusch, and Werner Herzog shared this fascination with white American lost boys: Van Sant through *Last Days*, a sparse account of the final days of Blake, a character loosely based on Kurt Cobain; Jarmusch in *Broken Flowers* with his lost boyman, Don Johnson (Bill Murray), who goes in search of four of his former lovers to discover which of them has sent an anonymous letter informing him that he may be the father of a nineteen-year-old son; and Herzog in the documentary realm, through Timothy Treadwell's monologues about the bears he thought he was protecting, in *Grizzly Man*. These angst-ridden performances invite a certain degree of empathy, but American screens were also populated by far less appealing if equally troubled white men, men who seem to be prepubescent but aren't. Into this category we might place *Wedding Crashers*, *The 40-Year-Old Virgin*, as well as the back-from-the-television-grave cousins found in Jay Chandrasekhar's *Dukes of Hazzard*.

Other forms of masculinity also dominate the screen this year. We see the fear of and desire for racially marked masculinity in Peter Jackson's extravagant remake of *King Kong*, and the purportedly unconventional revision of traditional male types (the soldier, the cowboy, and the wanderer) and genres (the war film, the western, and the road movie) in *Jarhead*, *Brokeback Mountain*, and *Transamerica*. But in a year so concerned with masculinity, what were female directors doing?

Though there were some strong films directed by women, there was also some discouraging news on their progress within the industry. Martha Lauzen's "2005 Celluloid Ceiling Report" noted that although in the first years of the new millennium women had accounted for 11 percent of all directors working on the top 250 domestic grossing films, a record high, the figure dropped back to 7 percent this year. The number of women in executive positions had increased, but 19 percent of the top 250 films still employed no women directors, executive producers, producers, writers, cinematographers, or editors. And after twenty-five years of spectacular programming, Women in the Director's Chair organized its last festival due to lack of funds. Nevertheless, Niki Caro's *North Country* counterbalances films such as *Thumbsucker* and *The Squid and the Whale* and their tales about the damaging effects working women have on their sons' lives with a narrative about the first class-action sexual harassment lawsuit in the United States. And Sally Potter's *Yes* (a U.K. and U.S. co-production) puts romance in a global and political context, responding to the post-9/11 demonization of the Middle East in the form of a verse narrative about an impossible affair between an Irish American woman and a Lebanese man.

This year also forged a path for a different kind of documentary, described by B. Ruby Rich as "stunt" or "extreme" documentary or "docutainment," a term that includes films like *Grizzly Man*, *Enron: The Smartest Guys in the Room*, and *The March of the Penguins*, all designed for greater boxoffice success and broader audiences (Rich 110). Yet as Rich points out, "For every eager-to-please, eager-to-shock U.S. documentary celebrated in the press, . . . there is a corresponding under-the-radar documentary, shot digitally, distributed through festivals or downloads, urgently delivering information that the mainstream media can no longer carry" (110); we explore some of these films later in this essay.

In a year of scandals, revelations, and violent extremes, it was reported that since 2002 the National Security Agency had been permitted to eavesdrop on telephone calls and read personal emails inside the country without first seeking court approval. Judith Miller retired as a reporter from the *New York Times* after spending eighty-five days in prison for her refusal to reveal her source for a story about the Valerie Plame affair, in which members of the Bush administration revealed that Plame was an undercover CIA agent in retaliation for her husband's public criticism of the faulty intelligence that supported claims of Iraq's possessing weapons of mass destruction. Former FBI official W. Mark Felt revealed himself as "Deep Throat," Bob Woodward and Carl Bernstein's secret Watergate source for the *Washington Post*, reminding a nostalgic American public of a moment when independent investigative journalism still seemed possible. In this climate of distrust, some films pondered where the real security threats lie, what exactly constitutes a stranger, and who should be responsible for ensuring our safety. *Capote* and *A History of Violence* investigate the division between "us" and "them" by exploring the concept of the "stranger within," the former through *Capote*'s representation of the ordinariness of the murderers Perry Smith and Richard Hickock, and the latter through the hidden mobster past of Tom Stall, a family guy who runs a diner. This boundary between "us" and "them" was particularly under scrutiny in a year when the 9/11 Commission report criticized the Federal Aviation Administration for failing to respond to intelligence about domestic hijackings; when air marshals shot dead forty-four-year-old Rigoberto Alpizar, a U.S. citizen who suffered from bipolar disorder, had forgotten to take his medication, and was suspected of reaching for a bomb in his bag (there was no bomb); and when the trials of American soldiers for the abuse of detainees at Baghdad's Abu Ghraib prison were in full swing.

From the beginning of the war through the end of the year, more than 2,100 U.S. soldiers had died in Iraq, more than 16,000 had been wounded, and an estimated one in four veterans had returned with some kind of mental illness. The Iraq Body Count (IBC) project recorded 14,832 noncombatant Iraqi deaths this year alone (http://iraqbodycount.org/database). In addition, more than 1,200 people died in the New Orleans area following Hurricane Katrina and the inadequate response of U.S. disaster relief organizations. In contrast to the media frenzy surrounding the question of whether to disconnect Terri Schiavo from her life-support machine in

March, many of the deaths of New Orleans area residents, including racially motivated vigilante murders, failed to reach our television screens (see Thompson, "Katrina's").

The costs of Katrina and a subsequent hurricane, Rita, can be measured primarily in barrels of oil. As the second oil-hungry Gulf War persisted, the two hurricanes reduced the U.S. energy output by 56.6 million barrels of oil (Horn 6), driving oil up to $60 per barrel in a country that had become, as its president would declare in his 2006 State of the Union speech, "seriously addicted to oil." This addiction was reflected in Stephen Gaghan's *Syriana*, as well as in *Jarhead*, which depicts the life of marines in the first Gulf War, and in Michael Tucker's documentary *Gunner Palace*, remarkable for its first-hand depiction of the chaotic lives of soldiers in the current war in Iraq but also for its rating from the Motion Picture Association of America (MPAA). After his film received an R, primarily for language, Tucker protested that it was essential that young audiences understand the situation of soldiers in the war; the rating was subsequently adjusted to PG-13. This gives *Gunner Palace* the dubious honor of being the film with the greatest number of uses of the word "fuck" and its derivatives in any film under the R rating.

Perhaps this adjustment reflected a shift within the MPAA under its new head, Dan Glickman, who took over following Jack Valenti's thirty-eight-year reign, promising to revitalize and update the organization and focus less on moral values than on the question of piracy. A study entitled "The Cost of Movie Piracy" reported: "The typical pirate is age 16–24 and male," which means that the industry's greatest threat is indistinguishable from its favorite subject: young men. Anxious about shrinking boxoffice numbers, studios began to consider how to profit from small-screen devices and mobile phones. Electronic Arts and New Line Cinema explored the possibility of using actors' images and voices in video games, and Gameloft released a mobile version of "Peter Jackson's King Kong: The Official Game of the Movie." But even as giant things began coming in ever smaller packages, the year also magnified standard Hollywood films into the IMAX format, a response to the threat posed by high-definition, flat-screen, and pay TV.

Foreign Relations

Jacqueline Goss's *How to Fix the World* and Rebecca Baron's *How Little We Know of Our Neighbours* constitute two fine examples of "under-the-radar" documentaries. Both works engage the question of how the truth of other people can be fully known, as well as how various media have been used to monitor and understand "the Other." Though Goss and

Baron's films clearly resonate with the rise in post-9/11 governmental uses of surveillance technologies—including CCTV cameras, eavesdropping devices, and the Bush administration's military and cultural imperialism in Central Asia and the Middle East—both directors displaced their engagement with these issues by focusing on historical and geographic elsewheres. Both directors also used experimental formal devices that caused viewers to reflect not only on the information being delivered, but also on the truth claims of documentary per se. While films like *Why We Fight* and *Occupation: Dreamland* may have attempted, as Jonathan Kahana argues, "to suggest, explicitly or implicitly, that traditional news sources had not provided truth about political events" (329), Goss and Baron's formally complex works made no explicit comment on the U.S. invasions of Afghanistan and Iraq, yet both use innovative documentary practices to offer viewers subtle and intelligent frames through which to consider the role that media practices have played historically as people have tried to understand, control, and "fix" the world.

At first glance, *How to Fix the World* could not be more remote from the concerns of the United States. This short video (26.5 minutes) is based on a series of interviews conducted by Alexander Romanovich Luria, a pioneering Soviet psychologist who traveled to Uzbekistan in 1931 to investigate the results of a Soviet literacy program that sent instructors from Moscow to Muslim regions of Central Asia. Yet in spite of the seeming obscurity of a North American artist-filmmaker focusing on Soviet literacy programs from 1931, *How to Fix the World* is ultimately very much a product of its own time and place. To understand the significance of an American artist making a film about cultural imperialism in Uzbekistan in the early twenty-first century, however, one needs first to look closely at the recent history of this region. The rich resources of the Ferghana valley, a site of cotton and silk production, as well, more recently, of oil and coal production, were divided among three republics under Soviet rule. After the collapse of the Soviet Union, the Soviet-era leader Islam Karimov, who had ruled from 1990, embarked on a failed economic restructuring plan, in part guided by the International Monetary Fund and the World Bank, creating situations of desperate poverty among the farming community of the Andijan region. This crisis peaked on 13 May when Karimov directed Uzbek security forces to open fire on crowds protesting both their dire poverty and the incarceration of twenty-three local businessmen who had been accused of Islamic extremism. Hundreds were killed. This local eruption of violence directly impacted the military operations of the United States in Afghanistan and Iraq. From 2001, the United States had been operating out of an air base in southeastern Uzbekistan, but from autumn of this year, in response to U.S. investigations of the May events, the Uzbek government halted this arrangement. As a former Uzbek intelligence officer explained in 2009, "Uzbekistan was, is, and will continue to be the key country in the region. It has borders with all other Central Asian states and with Afghanistan, and it makes for a good partner in security terms because it has the most powerful army in Central Asia" ("Afghan Conflict"). By making a work about the history of the Uzbek people, who rarely make headline news in the United States, Goss has given a face and a history to people who are pawns in American wars.

Unlike other documentary films made about Central Asia and the Middle East since 9/11, *How to Fix the World* focuses less on the specifics of the War on Terror than on a series of implied questions about an overlooked but significant region: How does cultural imperialism operate? What can we learn from earlier, failed models of attempts at cross-cultural understanding, education, and translation? Can we imagine better models? And finally, what role might films and filmmaking play in this imaginative project?

Goss reads aloud Luria's questions while other American voices read the various replies. Speaking as Luria, Goss asks her uneducated subjects to repeat or evaluate various questions, premises, and conclusions. When Goss asks, "There are no camels in Germany. The city of B is in Germany. Are there camels in B or not?" the voice of an elderly man replies reflectively, "Probably. Since there are large cities, there should be camels." In response to another question that requires logical deduction, another man answers firmly, "We only talk about what we have seen. We don't talk about what we have not seen."

Just as the answers taken from Luria's text challenge the interviewer's assumptions about the relation among vision, speech, and knowledge, so Goss's images require audiences to evaluate their own sense of the relation between sound and vision on the one hand and knowledge and the audiovisual text on the other. Throughout this work, Goss combines live-action footage shot in Andijan with still photographs of cotton workers in Uzbekistan taken by Max Penson between 1925 and 1945 and with Flash animation techniques. In this way, she disrupts the presumed authenticity of these images as well as the epistemological assumptions of Luria and Person.

She first troubles the truth-claims of photography, as well as our certainty that these originally black-and-white images reference only the past, by coloring the photographs' figures with garish computer-generated colors that underscore the constructed nature of the characters being presented to us: a man with a parrot becomes parrot-like himself as Goss colors him lime green; the authenticity of a traditionally dressed woman weaving a carpet is undercut by the fact that she is bright red, reminding us that, in spite of their documentary origins, these images are made, not found.

Next, color itself becomes a topic of discussion on the audio track. As interviewees are asked to describe the colors they see in the Uzbek land-scape, we hear a cacophony of voices that utter not just colors, but words describing features of the landscape and everyday life that evoke color, as well as words describing the difficulty of the task of translating vision—and specifically color—into language. We grasp verbal fragments from the com-plexly layered soundtrack—"pistachio," "lake," "air," "brown sugar," "spoiled cotton," "hard to translate," "hard to say"—and these words ren-der the once-familiar concept of color alien and strange. While Goss could have supplemented the soundtrack with live-action color images of the Uzbek landscape, she opts instead for a different kind of indexical image, one still produced, like the photograph, by the object being represented, without actually being a photograph: an animated, neon graph of the cadences of the speaking voices.

By introducing a graph of the speaker's utterances, rather than either the speaker's face or the places described, Goss reminds the digital-age viewer that the truth claims of the photograph derive not simply from the fact that the photograph's emulsion is changed by light bouncing off the photo-graphed object, but also from the way documentary images resonate with our sense of what we think an object or a person *should* look like. For documen-tary photographic images to appear true, then, they may need less to reveal factual knowledge about the unknown "Other" than to confirm what was thought about that "Other" all along. Intervening into the photograph's truth claims by juxtaposing historical, neon-colored, realist photographs with non-photographic indexical images of sound, Goss puts the mechanisms of belief under the microscope and provokes us to consider the difference between stereotype and ethnography.[1]

Flash animation, which brings the eyes and mouths of the photo-graphed workers to life, continues to trouble the documentary image. The jerky motion of these body parts that inhabit otherwise static photographic images creates an uncanny, even comic effect. But animation does more than disrupt the images' photographic realism, for the laborious process of synchronizing these animated lips with the rapid speech of the interviewees also establishes a different temporality for processing the statements Luria recorded. As Goss writes, "Producing an animation is time-consuming and involves hours of repetitive labor in one sitting. . . . Making a mouth move in sync with an audio interview gives me time to really hear subtle cadences and changes in a voice and more fully understand what that person was thinking and feeling during an interview." This statement is interesting given that Goss is, of course, not synchronizing her figures' lips to match the recorded voices of Uzbek cotton workers in the 1931, but rather the translated transcripts of those workers spoken by various American voices in English. So even as she describes the process of listening for audible signs of a person's thoughts and feelings in vocal cadences, we must remember that this labor of synchronizing the animated image with the soundtrack primarily documents both the intensity of the desire to know the other and the ultimate impossibility of doing so.

Finally, Goss blocks easy access to the Uzbek people through her use of abstract geometric shapes. Black circles, triangles, and squares, many of which are made of smaller circles, appear on the screen as we hear interviewees respond to questions about how certain shapes are similar to or different from each other. This abstraction also infiltrates the live-action images of the landscape of Uzbekistan in the form of large, black-rimmed white circles that float down the screen. But what are we to make of these abstract intrusions? They could represent the cotton that is so ubiquitous in Penson's photographs with titles like "Picked Enough!" "Field Stock," and "Cotton Picking Woman." But Goss's white circles invite associations that extend the material of cotton into the realm of education, language, and cultural invasion. A white circle in a dark blue night sky seems to signify the moon; yet as animated characters hang out of the frame and stare up at the sky through magnifying lenses, Latin letters appear one at a time on the surface of the moon, which morphs into a chalkboard-like backdrop to the project of linguistic colonization, emphasizing how alien this alphabet was to the targeted Muslim people.

Abstract circles emerge three more times in the course of the film. Green circles map out the fictionalized distances between real towns in tests of whether the participants in Luria's experiment can "solve math problems in which premises contradict experiences" (almost without exception, they can't). Then, as the voiceover says that "they gave us another new alphabet to make communication easier," a red-hued animated photographic cotton worker pours more white circles into a hole in the ground, watering them as if they were seeds, this time from the Cyrillic, not the Latin, alphabet. And in a final use of the circle, white-rimmed, brightly colored, transparent circles float like lenses over the surface of photographs that have titles like "Studying the Writing of Lenin." The lenses alter the color of the photographs as they move over them and

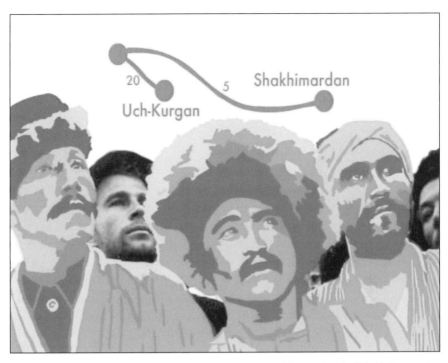

Abstracting access to the landscapes of Uzbekistan in *How to Fix the World* (Jacqueline Goss, independent production). Digital frame enlargement.

transform the Latin letters of their titles into Cyrillic ones, like a cultural translation machine.

Rebecca Baron's *How Little We Know of Our Neighbours* turns her camera on a different twentieth-century ethnographic endeavor: Great Britain's Mass Observation Project. Unlike Luria's "center to periphery" project (Moscow to the Muslim regions of the Soviet Union), Mass Observation began in response to the abdication of King Edward VII in 1936 and the sense that the press was out of touch with the feelings of the people. Anthropologist Tom Harrisson, poet Charles Madge, surrealist filmmaker Humphrey Jennings, and photographer Humphrey Spender collaborated on a project that aimed not to "fix the world" by recording the supposed improvement of people through education, but rather to record the "truth" of ordinary British people by eavesdropping on their conversations and using surreptitious photography to capture their behavior. Just as surrealist artists saw photography as a medium of psychological revelation, Mass Observation hoped that surreptitious photography could capture people's conscious and unconscious desires.

Baron traces the history of this movement, celebrating its early utopian goal of giving ordinary people a voice in the nation and mourning the movement's decline, first into a wing of the Ministry of Information and then, after the war, into a marketing research firm. Yet *How Little We Know of Our Neighbours* is important because of its complex treatment of surveillance images: the film shows us beautiful images of people unaware of being caught on film while simultaneously informing us of the current surveillance landscape (a title tells us that the average person in London is photographed three hundred times a day), and offers us a site to reflect on the ethics of photographic surveillance and on what, if anything, surreptitious images reveal—about the depicted subjects, the technologies used, and our collective epistemological fantasies about the media.

By choosing, like Goss, to consider the present through the lens of another time and space, Baron allows viewers to reflect in more complex ways on the politics and aesthetics of surveillance technologies than perhaps would be possible if they were considering these questions only in the context, for example, of the year's debates surrounding the U.S. government's unauthorized use of wiretapping. As Baron states,

> *How Little We Know of Our Neighbours* takes on these multiple desires for photography—in the case of surveillance it is about control and mastery, information and knowledge, and identification and authentication. But there's also an erotics to it—a pleasure in looking. I wanted all those things to be included so that the piece wasn't just coming to the conclusion "surveillance is bad," but also that it's tremendously pleasurable to look and those two things coexist. It's not an attempt to rectify that fact, but just to acknowledge it. (130)

How Little We Know of Our Neighbours offers neither political proscriptions nor simple visual aesthetics. Rather, by presenting viewers with a series of complex surveillance images that appear without a voiceover telling us what we should think of them, Baron forces her viewers to ask, "What can this photograph or video stream really tell me?"

Baron juxtaposes surreptitious images captured in different media. The film opens with a stream of images of contemporary British street scenes, produced not with the CCTV cameras to whose images Baron later returns, but rather with the far older technology of the camera obscura, which uses light passing through a pinhole to project—but not record—live images from the street onto a viewing surface. The fleeting images of the camera obscura are then rendered reproducible as they are recorded by Baron's digital video camera, resulting in ghostly, low-resolution traces of people act-

The complexity of surveillance, photography, and understanding in *How Little We Know of Our Neighbours* (Rebecca Baron, independent production). Digital frame enlargement.

ing without consciousness of having had their images "taken." These opening surveillance shots cause a distinct feeling of discomfort, evoking the voyeuristic and omniscient aesthetic that often sets the tone for cinematic thrillers—think of the way Alfred Hitchcock's camera creeps under the blinds to peer in at Marion Crane in the opening of *Psycho* (1960). But Baron invites this sense of suspicion only to undo it later when a more conventionally neutral or "objective" documentary shot shows children playing with the camera obscura that generates these suspicious images in a science museum. By reframing these early images within the benign context of their production, Baron causes us to reflect on how generic image conventions have the capacity to render *any* subject suspicious.

The sense of suspicion in *How Little We Know of Our Neighbours* is created in part by the grainy quality of the image, by the lack of context for the characters being watched, and also by the viewer's own awareness of participating in a transgressive, voyeuristic, and hence eroticized, power-infused gaze. Nothing makes us more aware of the erotic transgressions of the image-*makers* than Baron's use of intertitles and other forms of onscreen text (note that both Goss and Baron use printed text to make viewers question the authority of photographicallybased images). Following a surreptitious photograph of a maid sleeping in bed, a voiceover describes Edward Lenny Sanborn's secret photograph of his family's sleeping maid as Sanborn's handwritten journal entries unfold on screen ("Friday July 10. Got up at 5.45am. Saw F. in bed. Pretty. Saturday July 11. Up 5.40 and up in room. Photod [sic] F. in bed"). As viewers see the photograph of the sleeping maid while hearing this specific act of photography narrated, and also reading Sanborn's private journal, Baron invites us to participate in and reflect on how the transgressive act of looking at "stolen" images so easily morphs into projecting transgression onto, and subsequently condemning, the figures being looked at.

Baron also frames contemporary concerns about surveillance within the long history of visual surveillance technologies and the historicallycontingent anxieties that they have generated.At one point, for example, Colin Harding from the National Museum of Film and Television in Bolton, England, shows how the first Kodak cameras were marketed as "detective cameras," leaving people with the "concern that your face wasn't your own anymore." Through such moments, Baron challenges viewers to consider which of our contemporary concerns about technology will seem funny to future generations.

Images shot with Baron's digital video camera inside the British Museum feature tourists of various ages and ethnicities holding cameras in the air, setting up tripods, and peering through viewfinders. While these images emphasize the sheer ubiquity of photography and video, the context in which Baron takes them recalls a history of imperialism in which photography and film played crucial roles in providing visual evidence of the supposed barbarity of "uncivilized people" and in which power was divided between those who made documentary images and those who appeared as subjects within them. This awareness of the racialized history of image production and reception shapes how we interpret supposedly reassuring statements in the intertitles that follow, such as the one that quotes former prime minister John Major: "If you've got nothing to hide, you've got nothing to fear."

Toward the end of the film, Baron brings these more distant histories and their legacies into conversation with the live-feed images of the early twenty-first century. After a slideshow featuring stills from CCTV images of people riding on public transport, a title informs us that in 1981, the University of Sussex revived the British project of constructing an "anthropology of ourselves." Though the new project does not use surreptitious photography, recent directives, an intertitle informs us, ask participants to comment on topics such as "War in Iraq" and "Attitudes towards Americans." Americans here are cast as the questionable foreign neighbors, and Baron's film offers us one way to learn more about ourselves.

Domestic Insecurity and the Return of the Social Problem Film: *Crash* versus *Brokeback Mountain*

In a late January article entitled "Ten Years Later, the 'Kids' Are Definitely Not Alright," *Variety* critic Todd McCarthy, citing examples like *The Squid and the Whale*, Rebecca Miller's *The Ballad of Jack and Rose*, and Miranda July's *You and Me and Everyone We Know*, argued that "sexual precocity among minors jumped out as the most frequent element found in independent films this year." McCarthy begins with a simple list of the sexual transgressions of children in film: "An 11-year old boy spreads his semen over school lockers and repeats his father's filthy epithets when he blows a shot at tennis; a 16-year-old girl hangs her blood-stained sheet on the clothes line to let her father know she's lost her virginity; a 6- or 7- year old boy proposes an exchange of bodily fluids [of "poop," to be exact] in an Internet dialogue . . . ; a 15-year-old stud becomes the heartthrob of a community's older women; a 14-year-old girl drugs and binds a man twice her age with the intention of castrating him." But while McCarthy is right that we see a rise in the sexual transgressions of cinematic youths this year, this is only part of a broader increase in the depiction of sensationalized personal and interpersonal crises of various kinds. These intimate crises might be read as a collective displacement of the large-scale international and national catastrophes that come to define this decade. Though Hurricane Katrina had not yet occurred at the time the films of the year were being made, the failed attempts at disaster relief that followed in its wake simply reinforce the shortcomings of the domestic safety net with which many Americans had already become familiar after 9/11. If going to war in Afghanistan and Iraq allows Americans to project the nation's internal social and structural vulnerabilities outward onto foreign enemies through the discourse of "us" and "them," the return of the social problem film does the opposite: in a year of international conflict, it encouraged American audiences to domesticate, personalize, and even render juvenile the problems of our time. But these narratives of child sexual transgression are not all the same.

The films McCarthy identifies belong to a broader group of films that work to contain social and structural violence within personal stories.In this way, the year's films might usefully be compared with the low-budget social problem films, also known as "headline" pictures, produced by Warner Bros. in the 1930s during the Depression and the rise of fascism in Europe. But as Tino Balio writes, "In exposing gangsters, inhumane prison conditions, yellow journalism, and so forth, Warners did not meet the social problems head on; instead, the studio typically sidestepped issues by narrowing the focus of the exposé to a specific case or by resolving problems at the personal level of the protagonist rather than at the societal level" (Balio 281).

Crash and *Brokeback Mountain* both constitute contemporary "social problem" films. Like those of the 1930s, they are somewhat vague about both what the problems are and where the cause of these problems lies. In the case of *Crash*, does the "problem" lie in the fact that racial tension exists in American cities; that a middle-class African American woman has to depend for her safety on the policeman who has sexually assaulted her and gotten away with it; or that this film's narrative structure encourages us to excuse a policeman's sexual violence as well as his racist telephone abuse of an African American healthcare benefits employee because his father can't get adequate healthcare? In the case of *Brokeback Mountain*, is the "problem" that homophobia simply exists; that gay men are cast as tragic figures, depicted as almost incapable of verbal or sexual expression; that the film enacts a classic patriarchal device of pitting women against gay men by implicitly equating homosexual desire and misogyny; that this almost exclusively white film fulfills the western's fantasy of eradicating difference from the American landscape; or that, as D. A. Miller suggests, the film first casts the "Homosexual" as "a Martian," and then implicitly congratulates characters and spectators who try to discover in this alien figure "their fellow man" (Miller 53)?

This vagueness derives from the goal of harnessing the widest possible audience. If socially conscious, politically charged films run the economic risk of polarizing spectators and thus damaging boxoffice returns, these two films worked to solicit universal approval by focusing thematically on the generalized "problems" of "race and immigration" and "homosexuality" without ever taking a clear political position or even defining exactly what the social problem at hand really is. *Crash* potentially appeals to audiences for and against open borders and gated communities, just as *Brokeback Mountain* proves to be of interest to liberal heterosexual, Christian right, and gay audiences.

But the appearance of neutrality is still something of a ruse, for both films offer and withhold particular ways of thinking about the issues they address, just as both ultimately profit from a politically vacuous sensationalization of hate crimes. Whatever audiences think about *Brokeback Mountain*'s character Ennis, for example, they have no access within the world of this film to an eroticized homosexuality that is not ridden with shame and secrecy. As Miller writes, "What we are asked to 'accept' about the Homosexual is not his sexuality, but his agonized attempts to fight it—touching proof of a certain devotion to normality after all" (Miller 50). In the case of *Crash*, David Denby of the *New Yorker* finds the film "intensely moving" and "complex," but perhaps this assessment simply reveals that he hasn't thought that much about race and racism, especially when he remarks, "*Crash* is the first movie I know of to acknowledge not only that the intolerant are also human but, further, that something like white fear of black street crime, or black fear of white cops, isn't always irrational." Mick LaSalle's review of the film for the *San Francisco Chronicle* pinpoints precisely *Crash*'s tendency to reveal the already familiar to audiences, making the film's racial politics seem belated and somewhat "hackneyed": "Should it be surprising . . . that an upper-middle-class white woman (Sandra Bullock) might be a little racially insensitive in the immediate aftermath of having her SUV hijacked at gunpoint by two black youths? Is it a revelation that black citizens driving nice cars get pulled over frequently by cops, for no reason, and that some of those cops—like the one played here by Matt Dillon—may be a little twisted and racist? It's not."

Furthermore, in both films, the screenwriters attempt to justify and render neutral their characters' displays of bigoted language and behavior by claiming that the stories have roots in "real life." Writer Annie Proulx noted that her short story on which *Brokeback Mountain* was based grew out of a couple of real-life experiences, one in an upstate Wyoming bar where she encountered a young cowboy whose expression of "bitter longing" made her suspect him to be a "country gay," and another in which she overheard a "vicious rant" by a female bar owner "who was incensed that two 'homos' had come in the night before" (qtd. in Miller 52). Similarly, almost every review of *Crash* reports that Paul Haggis, the film's director and co-author of the script with Robert Moresco, had been carjacked outside his local video store ten years before writing the script, an experience that "never left him" (Peters A1). In *Crash* in particular, the film's roots in reality combine with a gritty, realist film style to produce an illusory documentary effect. Yet as A. O. Scott points out in his review of *Crash* for the *New York Times*, though these tricks of realism are tempting, they ultimately cannot sustain a belief in this view of American urban life:

The look of these movies [he places *Crash* in a category alongside *Monster's Ball, House of Sand and Fog*, and *21 Grams*] and the rough authenticity of their locations create an atmosphere of naturalism that is meant to give force to their rigorously pessimistic view of American life. The performances, often by some of the finest screen actors working today, have the tense texture and sober discipline that we associate with realism. But to classify these movies as realistic would be misleading, as the stories they tell are, in nearly every respect, preposterous, and they tend to be governed less by the spirit of observation than by superstition.

At the premiere of *Crash* in my hometown of Philadelphia, a screening attended by both Haggis and Matt Dillon, I happily observed the healthy skepticism recommended by Scott among my fellow spectators. During the post-screening question-and-answer session, an elderly African American gentleman stood up and asked Haggis whether he thought this was how things really were, because, he declared proudly, it's certainly not how they are in Philadelphia. His comments were met first by resounding affirmatives from an audience clearly weary of the media's attempt to sensationalize daily life in multiracial urban spaces through gimmicks like the recent nickname of "Killadelphia"; and then by conciliatory comments from Dillon, who tried to suggest that the gentleman's question probably simply reflected the difference between Los Angeles and Philadelphia. In Los Angeles, however, Haggis interjected that things really are "like this."

In addition to the sensationalism internal to the films themselves, *Brokeback Mountain* and *Crash* also participated in the media spectacle that cast these two films, and by extension "homosexuality" and "race," as competitors in the Academy Awards. Proulx only fanned this spectacle in an article she wrote after the awards ceremony for the *Guardian*. Though acknowledging the possibility that she could be writing a "Sour Grapes Rant," Proulx casts "*Trash*—excuse me—*Crash*" as the selection of the "conservative heffalump academy" whose sense of what the world is really like is profoundly outdated: "Next year," she suggests, "we can look to the awards for controversial themes on the punishment of adulterers with a branding iron in the shape of the letter A, runaway slaves, and the debate over free silver." What Proulx doesn't see is that, because *Brokeback Mountain* fails even to hint at the possibility of a nontragic, sexualized homosexuality, it belongs with, rather than stands as an alternative to, the "controversial" but ultimately outdated themes she lists. This is not to say that homosexual hate crimes no longer exist—of course they do—but to ask how stories like these might be told differently, and whether there are also different—and better—stories to tell.

Different Families: *The Squid and the Whale* and *Me and You and Everyone We Know*

Different stories and modes of storytelling are not hard to find; nor are they located somewhere in another decade, or a future volume: they exist right here, right now, and I conclude by briefly discussing two of them: Noah Baumbach's *The Squid and the Whale*, which won awards for best dramatic direction and screenplay at Sundance, and Miranda July's first feature film, *Me and You and Everyone We Know*, which played alongside the works of Rebecca Baron and Jacqueline Goss at the last Women in the Director's Chair conference but also won the Caméra d'Or at the Cannes Film Festival.

The Squid and the Whale is loosely based on Baumbach's own experience of his parents' divorce. The nuclear family has four members, and the film is marked by remarkably strong acting in all four roles. The father, Bernard (Jeff Daniels), is an arrogant English literature professor and writer whose publication career is floundering as part of a more generalized mid-life crisis. By contrast, the life and career of the mother, Joan (Laura Linney), is positively blossoming. In the midst of her extramarital affair with her son's tennis coach, Ivan (William Baldwin), Joan's own writing takes off, leading to a prestigious publication that galls Bernard, who had, until this point, considered himself the superior writer and intellectual in the relationship. The younger son, Frank (a k a "Peanut," played by Owen Kline), seems relieved to find in Ivan a different, less intellectual, and less demanding kind of father figure, and he mirrors his mother's newfound transgressive freedom by spreading his semen on school lockers and library books and indulging in a drinking binge that leaves him unconscious. His older and deeply pubescent brother, Walt (Jesse Eisenberg), takes his father's side and joins him in dismissing with mimetic condescension everything from his mother's infidelity and writing to "philistines" like Ivan, "minor Dickens," and the constraints of "commitment" on a young male intellectual.

The film's concern with the question of cultural capital and its production constitutes the primary way in which the narrative extends beyond the realm of the family into a broader terrain. In particular, the film encourages viewers to consider what authorship means within the contemporary American context in a number of ways. The personal relationship between Bernard and Joan allegorizes the rise of the independent woman writer, her refusal to serve as muse and housemaid to a paternalistic male "genius," and the subsequent crisis for the abandoned writer. Bernard and Walt's dismissal of "minor" literature offers a backdrop for a consideration of how modern cultural products should be valued, in which traditions they participate, and how they will be remembered. If a "philistine" is, as Bernard tells Frank, "a guy who doesn't care about interesting books or films" (to which Frank responds, "Then I'm a philistine!"), what criteria do we use, the film seems to ask, to establish what "interesting" now means? The film emphasizes the vulnerability of the undisputed "great work" and "great artist" not only through its enjoyment of Joan's literary breakthrough, or the way it makes fun of Walt's inherited cultural certainties, but also through his plagiarizing of Pink Floyd's song "Hey You," which he claims to have written himself. If his theft exposes his creative pretensions, it also exposes the cultural amnesia that surrounds so much popular culture, allowing it to be constantly dispersed, cited, and remixed. We might compare Walt's plagiarism scenes with the moment after Bernard's collapse, when he quotes the last line of *Breathless* to Joan and imitates Jean-Paul Belmondo's stroking of his lips with his thumb, a gesture in *Breathless* that is itself an imitation of Humphrey Bogart. Will *The Squid and the Whale*, we may begin to wonder, take its place alongside the greats of the French New Wave, or will it too be dismissed as "minor"? How, the film seems to ask, is cultural memory best transmitted from one generation to another, and how does that memory take on a life of its own? This, perhaps, is one of the broader implications of the film's examination of how parents influence their children.

In many ways, *The Squid and the Whale* adopts a psychoanalytic approach to the depicted family dynamics, in that it implicitly diagnoses the sources of behaviors that are marked as abnormal within the context of the narrative, and explicitly represents this approach through the character of the psychologist who is assigned to Walt. Frank's budding and unusual sexual expressions are considered, like his drinking, to signal his deep emotional distress. By contrast, Miranda July tends to eschew this causal and normative paradigm in her depiction of the evolving relationships within a twenty-first-century family. Like *Crash, Me and You and Everyone We Know* weaves together the lives of various strangers, including Richard, a shoe salesman whose wife, Pam, leaves him for another man. Though Pam and Richard's was a biracial relationship, July includes this fact in her fictional world without overdramatizing it. Pam's departure does not seem to have been caused by the impossibility of interracial love, as would have been the case in a melodramatic social problem film. Similarly, the couple's two boys, Peter, fourteen, and Robby, six, aren't happy when their parents separate, when Richard forgets to pick Robby up from school, or when there's no food except cereal in the house for dinner, but neither are they structurally

The touching oddities of normal children (Miles Thompson and Brandon Ratcliffe) in *Me and You and Everyone We Know* (Miranda July, IFC). Digital frame enlargement.

undone as the children in *The Squid and the Whale* almost are by the fact that their mother has an erotic life, or that their experience of the word "family" has to evolve.

The emerging sexuality of Peter and Robby, like that of their fifteen-year-old friends Heather and Rebecca, is seen as weird, yes, but never pathological or potentially deadly. July treats such oddities much more playfully than Baumbach, and without a clear sense of what the ideal, normal family or child would look like. Though we might suspect that some of the odd behaviors we witness have roots in family trauma, this itself seems normal. July creates a world in which people will at times act strangely, no matter how happy or unhappy the specific context, a world in which the best possible relationships adapt in response to the ordinary strangeness of life. As fixed ideas of the nuclear, normal family recede into the background, and as each character is revealed to possess some kind of mundane pathological potential, July opens a space in which teenage experiments and interpersonal blunders of all sorts abound to our great delight.

The girls, Heather and Rebecca, offer Peter a "jimmy ha-ha" (fellatio) on three conditions: first, he has to be blindfolded; second, he has to evaluate which of them performs better; and third, he has to tell them when he's going to "scooge." The resolution of this scenario is purely comic and anticlimactic in the best possible way. Peter "scooges," but mutters that he couldn't tell the difference between them; and as the girls leave his home, happy in their friendship and equality, we see July's gentle refusal of the heterosexual teen narrative that necessarily turns young female friends into enemies when they find themselves ranked in the eyes of their male objects of desire. Heather and Rebecca also flirt with an older man, Andrew, who flirts back by leaving signs of sexual instruction for them in his window. They decide to approach his door and plan to lose their virginity with him together so that they can "get it over with." In a different kind of film, this scenario would lead to an inevitably tragic and instructive end, but in *Me and You and Everyone We Know*, July again takes the comic path, one that delights in the wonderful weirdness of the everyday sexual encounters that suffuse the world we inhabit. On seeing the girls approach his door, Andrew, terrified, flings himself on the floor under his window; the girls ring his doorbell, full of bravado, but then run away together, laughing at their moment of newfound boldness. Meanwhile, as Peter experiences the delights of Heather and Rebecca, his six-year-old brother Robby uses cut and paste as well as other creative keyboard skills to get involved in an erotic online chat with an older woman, the contemporary art curator who will eventually exhibit the work of Christine, a video and performance artist played by July and with whom Robby's father, Richard, will eventually fall in love. Robby's erotic messages seem typical of a six-year-old. He sends her the message))<>((and explains to his brother that this means "I want to poop back and forth. I'll poop into her butthole then she'll poop it back into my butthole, back and forth . . . and we'll keep doing it back and forth with the same poop. Forever." More surprising to us than Robby's fantasy, perhaps, is the fact that the museum director, dressed in black and extremely stern in person, tells Robby online that she can't stop thinking about "the poop" and that she wants to meet in person. Yet because there is no "normal" relationship in the world of this film, July shows us that we shouldn't be surprised. As with the earlier intergenerational encounter between Andrew and the teenage girls, the meeting between Robby and the curator ends in a sweetly comic way. When the two realize that they are each other's blind dates, the middle-aged woman gives Robby a gentle kiss on his cheek and walks away smiling, having shared, without moral condemnation, her secret anal desires.

It is not only in the realm of childhood sexuality and family structures that July resists the normative, sensational imperative of the realist social problem film, but also in the way she introduces the function of images at the film's opening. By casting her primary protagonist, Christine, as a video and performance artist, July inserts a self-reflexive space about media into the narrative thread of the film. In the opening shot, we see the silhouette of two heads looking out over a glorious ocean sunset—a classically romantic image of the perfect couple. As we hear the sound of waves lapping on the shore, a female voiceover says slowly, "If you really love me, then let's make a vow, right here, together, right now. OK?" A deeper voice responds, "O.K." But then the image dissolves into television static as the camera pans out to reveal Christine, who is holding a microphone and working with a video camera to dub these lines, both of which are spoken by her, over a photographic image. As the nondiegetic camera scans over various snapshots, including the one of the perfect sunset that opened the film, we realize that we have just been witnessing not an intimate scene on a beach but this video artist's single-handed construction of an audio-visual romance.

Though the opening scenes of *Crash* and *Me and You and Everyone We Know* are in some ways alike—both begin with voiceovers that establish an intimate relationship between the character speaking and the audience— the differences become immediately apparent. While *Crash* asserts its relation to reality through the confiding tone of the opening voice, through the truth claims of Haggis, and through the film's gritty documentary aesthetic, *Me and You and Everyone We Know* activates our responses to the opening vocal and visual intimacy only to expose the catalysts for our emotional investments as representations, fictions, fakes . . . or art. In doing so, July asks us not to consider whether the world of the film is accurate, but rather how film might enable us to imagine the world differently. Similarly, though both films note that contemporary life lacks touch, in *Crash* this leads to the frenzied collisions and violent penetrations of characters who go smashing into each other "just to feel something," while July again gives the problem a comic, "make-do" frame. When an elderly man whom Christine takes care of asks Richard, the shoe clerk, to help him on with his shoe, Richard replies earnestly, "No, we don't touch the foot anymore. We will *never* touch the foot with our hands." But as the old man looks disappointed, Richard offers, "I'll tell you what I can do . . . I can press it to see if it fits." With the muted optimism of one of Samuel Beckett's characters, Christine encourages, "Yeah. Do that."

It's not that July conjures up a world without problems, for her characters too can be lonely, depressed, confused, betrayed, and even dying, but these characters are not fixed in stereotypical roles. They search for magic even in the absence of it; some men may be interested in pubescent girls, but this fact alone does not make them monsters—indeed, one such man is a good friend of the film's hero; girls are not innocent victims, but rather playful participants who, though not quite in control of what they are doing, are not helpless either; they are simply interested in exploring where the limits of their own control lies. In July, interracial families, intergenerational friendships, child sexuality, and broken relationships exist, but these things are just part of a landscape that also contains multimedia artists, magical pink stickers, goldfish riding on the top of cars, photo frames that utter "I love you" when pressed (to save people energy), and many other quirky wonders. Such things led *Newsweek*'s David Ansen to observe, "Jim Jarmusch had it from the start. So did Gus Van Sant. So, it seems, does Miranda July. It's an original way of looking at the world. A sensibility unmistakably their own. A singular style." So perhaps when Dan Glickman has solved the piracy conundrum, he can turn his attention to another problem: why a wonderful film like *Me and You and Everyone We Know* still has to be rated R "for disturbing sexual content involving children."

NOTE

1. Tom Gunning makes the important observation that "it would be foolish to identify the indexical with the photographic; most indexical information is not recorded by photography. Long before digital media were introduced, medical instruments and other instruments of measurement, indexical instruments *par excellence*—such as devices for reading pulse rate, temperature, heart rate, and the like, or speedometers, wind gauges and barometers—all converted their information into numbers" (24–25).

2006

Movies and Crisis

NIGEL MORRIS

Those Americans concerned about human contribution to global warming had ample opportunity this year to reflect upon carbon emissions. January began with Sydney, Australia, experiencing record temperatures while the Atlantic's worst hurricane season expired. December ended with the Met Office reporting England's warmest year since records began in 1659. Geopolitical implications of climate change loomed large when Russia blocked Ukraine's midwinter gas supplies during a price dispute. The Chinese river dolphin's extinction, following intense industrialization along the Yangtze, underlined anthropogenic environmental impact.

Despite massive protests in the United States and abroad, the Iraq War continued. U.S. bombing killed Abu Musab al-Zarqawi, leader of al-Qaeda in Iraq, and seven aides. With Iraq becoming an Islamic state, Iran and Syria recognized its government, reopened diplomacy, and sought a peace conference. Former president Saddam Hussein and two associates were hanged after Iraqi court convictions for crimes against humanity.

Car bombs and suicide bombings killed and maimed hundreds of civilians and soldiers among other attacks in Iraq and Afghanistan, and bombings caused multiple deaths elsewhere. The FBI arrested suspects plotting to bomb Chicago's Sears Tower and targets in Miami. Authorities banned liquids and gels from airline baggage when London police unearthed a conspiracy to down transatlantic flights. Notwithstanding rumors of U.S. or NATO involvement, Pakistan claimed responsibility for eighty fatalities in Bajaur during an assault on a suspected al-Qaeda and Taliban training school.

Three-quarters of the International Atomic Energy Agency voted to refer Iran's nuclear program to the U.N. Security Council. Iran proceeded to enrich uranium while denying IAEA inspection. Subsequent plans to enrich uranium in a jointly owned Russian facility collapsed when Iran declined to transfer all development activity abroad. The U.N. met North Korea's claims to have tested nuclear weaponry with sanctions. North Korea had already test-fired missiles to coincide with the U.S. Independence Day launch of the space shuttle *Discovery*.

Israeli prime minister Ariel Sharon suffered a massive stroke and was formally removed from office after four months comatose. The Islamist organization Hamas, officially a terrorist group according to the United States, the European Union, and Israel, won Palestinian Legislative Council elections by a landslide. Israel invaded Lebanon in retaliation for the Lebanese-based Hezbollah's killing and kidnapping of Israeli soldiers. Hezbollah declared a war that lasted a month until a U.N. ceasefire. The pope ignited demonstrations in Moslem countries by quoting a fourteenth-century criticism of Islam in a lecture. Iranian president Mahmoud Ahmadinejad, uncompromisingly opposed to Israel, sponsored a conference in Tehran that advocated Holocaust denial.

Subprime mortgage losses joined falling house prices and increasing defaults by borrowers, precipitating a crisis that threatened to result in bank failures and recession. More prominent in the news was Illinois senator Barack Obama's emergence as a potential White House candidate, although he had yet to declare. Also on the domestic front, alleged irregularities in news reports about inconsistencies in President George W. Bush's military record during the Vietnam War prompted CBS News to terminate anchorman Dan Rather. Cockpit recordings were released from United Flight 93, which had crashed in a Pennsylvania field during the 9/11 attacks in 2001. Bush signed the Military Commissions Act to counter a Supreme Court ruling that had deemed procedures for trying Guantanamo Bay detainees illegal. The Democrats gained control of both the House of Representatives and the Senate in midterm elections. Secretary of Defense Donald Rumsfeld resigned soon after, and Nancy Pelosi became the first female Speaker of the House, the closest any woman has reached in succession to the presidency.

New HD DVD and Blu-ray disc formats, along with the increasing popularity of large, flat-screen, high-definition TVs and surround speakers, made home cinema a reality, at least for wealthy consumers. Enhanced spectacle for domestic viewers accords with commercial logic whereby nontheatrical and video rentals have long provided more profit than theatrical exhibition (Wasko 125). Near-theatrical reception conditions for lower budget, independent, and foreign-language films offered potentially greater recognition than limited art-house release.

That category includes *Little Miss Sunshine*, in which a troubled family drives westward to California. This mordant but eventually positive satire on the American Dream (a sleazy compere croons "America the Beautiful" to the sexualized contestants in a child beauty pageant) champions cooperation over individualism, excessive ambition, and competition, challenging dominant values including conformist notions of femininity.

Spike Lee reconfirmed his mainstream status with *Inside Man*, a retro-1970s-style thriller, without abandoning politics. Class, race, and gender raise the tension as black detectives pursue bank raiders wearing hooded jumpsuits and facemasks. These accouterments not only hide identity, including color, render criminals and innocent citizens indistinguishable, and echo uniformed and sensory-deprived Guantanamo prisoners—the film explicitly evokes human rights—as well as the "hoodie" street fashion originating in black culture; they also recall Claude Rains's 1933 portrayal of H. G. Wells's *Invisible Man*—furthermore alluding to Ralph Ellison's similarly named novel of 1952. A high-level corruption conspiracy emerges, represented by an amoral fixer, pointedly named Miss White (Jodie Foster). As well as SWAT police whose uniforms and procedures bring to mind U.S. Army house raids in Iraq, one telling detail is an officer's immediate assumption that a bearded, turbaned Sikh is a terrorist.

Dreamgirls also vibrantly addresses race and gender in a musical that chronicles 1960s social history: black music's mainstream acceptance, the Detroit riots, payola scandals. What might once have been marginalized as a "race movie" refers in its title not only to Diana Ross and the Supremes ("Dinah Jones and the Dreams") but also to Martin Luther King Jr.'s "I have a dream" speech and the American Dream—celebrated through A-list black performers (Beyoncé Knowles, Jamie Foxx, Eddie Murphy, Danny Glover) who have starred in lavish, critically successful, commercial productions.

Crises of Representation: Metaphor and Memorial in *United 93* and *World Trade Center*

Claiming even closer adherence to recent history, Paul Greengrass's *United 93* and Oliver Stone's *World Trade Center*, major studios' first explicit representations of 9/11, were bound to be contentious. Los Angeles audience members yelled "Too soon" at *United 93*'s trailer, which a New York theater withdrew after complaints. Both directors are unapologetically political, advocating positions that invariably (and often intentionally) generate controversy. Conservative critics anticipated anti-Bush, even anti-American, sentiments in the films but were persuaded by human dramas that fed debate while avoiding direct engagement (Usborne 32). The films' significance cannot be overstated. These glimpses into personal experience, leaving the historical metanarrative to others, broke what was in danger of becoming taboo for fear of upsetting an unspoken, possibly illusory, consensus.

United 93 reconstructs one of the four airliner hijackings and government reactions based on false assumptions that negotiations would ensue between the hijackers and civilian officials on the ground. Delayed takeoff enabled Flight 93's passengers to learn of the Manhattan and Pentagon attacks. Trapped in a suicide mission, they retaliated. Whether they fought to regain control of the aircraft or to intentionally crash it and minimize deaths on the ground is unknowable, but their action, resulting in the deaths of everyone aboard, surely saved Washington from further assault. In effect, as Bush, Greengrass, and others all acknowledged, they mounted the nation's first response to the day's atrocities.

The movie's timing raised commercial and ethical considerations. Many involved asked: when was the right time if not now? That controversy set the agenda was not necessarily a cynical ploy, although Hollywood publicists undoubtedly valued such coverage. From the start 9/11 was always a media event—for those on the ground in New York and near the Pentagon and for viewers around the world witnessing live coverage on television. Flight 93's story had already been dramatized twice on TV. Greengrass sensed hypocrisy in newspapers and broadcasters picking over the events while accusing Hollywood of profiteering (Williams 43).

Numerous factors stoked the controversy. Conspiracy theories had filled the knowledge vacuum. Yet, Greengrass insisted, the truth is more disturbing than comforting allegations that military fighters shot down the plane: "[A] small group of people hijacked a religion, hijacked four airplanes and had an entire civilian and military system break down inside about an hour and if those passengers had not got up out of their seats the plane without a doubt would have hit the Capitol and flattened it" (qtd. in Baughan 59).

Beyond disputed facts, sensitivity to victims' loved ones and the potential emotional impact caused more general concern. Fears of exploitation, both political and commercial, were legitimate. The Pentagon specifically commissioned filmmakers after 9/11 to brainstorm security risks and devise solutions to minimize those risks, while the Bush administration endorsed patriotic militaristic movies as part of a larger response (Hoberman, "Unquiet" 20). Memorialization necessarily sought a suitable tone, between heroic portrayal and unadorned facts. Fallout was inevitable: Bush's 2002 speeches had appropriated, as a rallying cry for invading Iraq, the phrase "Let's roll!"—overheard in flight communications as Flight 93's passengers prepared their counterattack. "They said a prayer," he added, and "drove the plane into the ground to serve something greater than themselves." Bush was photographed alongside the widow of Todd Beamer, believed to have uttered the phrase—which in the film is delivered as a tense whisper, easily missed.

Many New Yorkers reportedly resented shots of the attacks on the Twin Towers in *Flight 93*, whose occupants were victims rather than heroes (Wapshott). The implication in TV dramatizations that only some of the film's passengers were heroes divided their families. So did disproportionate media attention to those who made phone calls or whose relatives gave interviews. Commentators wondered about Greengrass, a British director, telling the story, which producer Tim Bevan thought promoted "objectivity" and "non-sentimentality" (Williams 43). For his part, Greengrass meticulously interviewed every passenger's family to win support. One mother commented after a screening: "Now everyone else has felt what I felt. . . . All of a sudden I'm not alone" (Brooks 33).

Hybridizing fictional reconstruction with documentary style and truth claims produces inherent ambiguities. *United 93* reopened debates related to TV. John Corner once argued that drama-documentary "play[s] off the strong presence in television schedules of mainstream documentary," prompting expectations of greater accuracy than audiences tolerated in movies such as *JFK* (1991) and *Malcolm X* (1993), associated with entertainment (93–94). However, documentary reemerged afterward as a cinematic genre, often with political intent. This background informs questions about *United 93*'s purpose. The film neither explains the terrorists' motivation nor assigns blame for official unpreparedness. Greengrass's initial treatment pitched its subject as "the perfect metaphor of our times." The onboard dilemma, as for Western powers subsequently, was "strike back and risk destruction, or hope for the best and risk destruction? And then . . . the passengers vote, whilst in the cockpit there are only prayers and suicidal devotion" (Greengrass 33).

United 93 reconstructs its event scrupulously, with civilian and military aviation officials playing themselves and airline personnel portraying the crew. Air traffic control chief Ben Sliney, having initially been brought in a consultant, plays a central role and acknowledged in an interview how his performance dramatizes thoughts and emotions that were internalized in reality (Williams 44). While details of in-flight events are speculation, verified facts remain unaltered, from flight recorder information, passengers' phone calls, and the 9/11 Commission report. Passengers, unnamed, many onscreen only fleetingly, are individually modeled on their actual counterparts, with costume, habits, and likely reactions drawn from interviews with relatives and friends.

The action unfolds in "real-time," filmed documentary-style, utilizing improvised overlapping dialogue during extensive takes—up to an hour—with multiple cameras started and reloaded separately to maximize coverage. After departure the plane is represented only internally, encouraging identification with its occupants' claustrophobia and helplessness. Flight crew, travelers, and filmmakers were sealed into a real fuselage mechanically rigged to simulate pitching and tilting as the terrorist pilot sought to hinder and disorient retaliating passengers. Despite percussive underscoring, which evokes a heightened heartbeat and distant explosions, authenticity is implied by hand-held cinematography, naturalistic lighting, focus shifts, and jump cuts. This style belies considerable crafting. The camera seemingly chances upon the terrorists amid airport crowds. Sometimes selective focus isolates them; this suggests character psychology but also that their narrative is one among complex interacting forces. Unsuspecting passengers are individuated through seemingly inconsequential attention and overheard conversations and cellphone calls. Such techniques, including zooms and pans that underline the terrorists' nervousness and intensify foreboding, together with uncertainty as to which passengers, and how many, are terrorists, turn the mundane awaiting and boarding of a plane into sustained drama. The filmmakers also keep unauthenticated material offscreen. By shooting close and jostling the camera or interposing obstructions while rapidly intercutting, the film leaves contentious events undecided—whether passengers gained control, for instance, or who crashed the aircraft, intentionally or not.

The cameras' ostensibly random "hosepiping," as if unsure where significance lies, implies restricted narration, and hence, paradoxically, alternative possible outcomes. Yet prioritizing telling over the already-known tale makes remembrance the primary rationale. As a passenger's sibling gratefully explains in a DVD extra: "Many . . . passengers' voices will just evaporate, if it isn't for the tenacity of the families . . . and for a storyteller to keep it alive."

Despite suggesting objectively recorded history, the material is shaped for essayistic, not just aesthetic reasons. A terrorist secreting a knife foreshadows a passenger concealing a fire extinguisher to use as a cudgel. Another terrorist phoning "I love you" to his girlfriend parallels similar actions by passengers conscious of their fate. Terrorists' impatience about delaying their cockpit assault prefigures the buildup to the passengers' retaliation. A slogan on a freight container—"GOD BLESS AMERICA"

United 93's documentary aesthetic (Paul Greengrass, Universal) includes a glimpse of the World Trade Center in the background. Digital frame enlargement.

alongside the flag—implicates religion in patriotism, politics, and commerce and anticipates imagery and values that informed popular and official responses. A passenger crossing himself and praying for deliverance mirrors the terrorists' repeated prayers. The film's dedication "to the memory of all those who lost their lives on September 11, 2001" logically embraces the terrorists as well, of whom three of the four on Flight 93 were uneducated and suggestible—"terrifyingly devout. But . . . blind too—to humanity, to decency, to pity" (Greengrass 33)—arguably, therefore, themselves tragically duped by circumstances.

World Trade Center's aesthetic is closer to soap opera's heightened emotion or movie-of-the-week melodrama on big-screen scale. This is not necessarily to denigrate it, although repeated use of slow motion and an unyielding string score do no favors in relation to events of such magnitude, both globally and personally. Emphasis on relationships, talk, and suffering is motivated by the two main characters' immobility, buried under Ground Zero, reduced literally to talking heads, and tension experienced by their waiting families. It contrasts with bustling action, exuberant camerawork, and increasingly frantic editing in the first twenty-four minutes, which slide from a police procedural documenting an average morning to horror and bewilderment inside the concourse before the collapse. Stone's movie complements *United 93*'s objectivity with personal accounts, locating meaning in shared experience. The protagonists, Port Authority police officers McLoughlin (Nicolas Cage) and Jimeno (Michael Peña), trapped while helping to evacuate the Trade Center, are typical—as is the courage of rescuers who risk themselves to aid them. Eighteenth and nineteenth of only twenty who escaped the rubble, the officers incarnate the statistics presented in the film's closing captions. What's more, they personify New York, introduced in a kinetic city symphony montage as patrol members commute during a perfect dawn: a sequence echoed somberly with trains and ferries deserted the next morning and smoke shadowing the streets strewn with ash, debris, and paper streets. The cleanup begins—a new day, a new world order, as the protagonists, the only patrol members who survive, start painful journeys toward recovery.

More problematic is one rescuer's story. Accountant Dave Karnes (Michael Shannon) has his head shaven, dons a uniform, declares himself a marine, journeys to Ground Zero, and vows to reenlist—"They're gonna need some good men out there to avenge this." Captions that he served twice in Iraq associate the outrages with Saddam, a Bush administration ploy. The real Karnes reportedly "was wary of the film" (Dalton). As portrayed, his behavior and attitude might in other contexts appear fanatical, indeed insane. He grimaces strangely before announcing, "This country is at war." He insists, "God gave me a gift to be able to help people. To defend our country. I feel him calling on me now for this mission." When he visits his pastor the Bible sits open at Revelations. Karnes delivers oracular utterances: "It's like God made a curtain with the smoke, shielding us from what we're not yet ready to see." Wild-eyed, staring, robotic, he introduces himself as Staff Sergeant Karnes to another rescuer. Asked, "You got something a little shorter?" he replies: "Staff Sergeant."

Such portrayal of the most fully proactive character, who by saving the officers satisfies real-life and narrative definitions of heroism, complicates tone and attitude. His religious patriotism and thirst for vengeance parallel the terrorists, who—apart from a minor character calling them "bastards"—remain absent and unmentioned. Perhaps this is Stone's uncharacteristically subtle point. In the guise of non-judgment, voicing competing positions and presenting events supposedly neutrally, he incorporates, without endorsing, the Bush administration's response. In contrast to rugged individualism—nevertheless effective within the narrative's bounds—the film honors community. McLoughlin's epilogue observes merely that rescuers acted "because it was the right thing to do."

Christianity, as sustaining faith rather than excuse for warmongering, provides the movie's symbolism. McLoughlin, convinced he is dying, asserts, "I am gonna see some place better" and recites the Lord's Prayer. The officers describe as "hell" their semi-conscious paralysis, isolated in near darkness, choking dust, and toxic fumes; parched; surrounded by licking flames; guilt-racked and anxious about domestic relationships; overlooked by a comrade's corpse, whose pistol, heated by embers, in a sequence of truly Satanic cruelty shoots bullets at them. Overhead light promises salvation. Stone presents Jimeno's vision of Christ literally, although editing relates it logically to penetrating daylight or glare from rescuers' flashlights.

Stone's parable of suffering and resurrection avoids the rhetoric of jihad and crusade even if Karnes is reborn as savior, then warrior. A subplot involves an alcoholic redeemed by remembering his paramedic training. Sunshine, applause, and community during the postscript, with Jimeno embracing his daughter, unborn during the attacks, celebrate lives rebuilt and continuity. The aperture through which McLoughlin, in a coffin-like stretcher, returns into dazzling light resembles a grave. Explanations and political consequences remain unexplored beyond acknowledgment of unpreparedness—even the first plane hitting the towers appears obliquely as a shadow. Nevertheless, there may be implied commentary on the president's slow response in McLoughlin's ability, despite personal doubts about his popularity, to lead; he knows each patrol member's name, notwithstanding its ad hoc constitution, and demands reports immediately after their burial. Courage for survival extends beyond that shown when McLoughlin, Jimeno, and their lost colleagues volunteered to enter the buildings. Ultimately it expresses the spirit of the city, reclaimed from political cooptation.

Crises of Patriotism: The Story behind the Glory in *Flags of Our Fathers* and *Letters from Iwo Jima*

Flags of Our Fathers and *Letters from Iwo Jima*, a diptych of opposing perspectives on one of the decisive and most bloody World War II battles, resonate with parallels between now and 1945. This year, like then, a reelected president, having weathered the aftermath of suicidal aircraft attacks and cemented overseas alliances, was embroiled in controversy concerning civil rights for incarcerating individuals allegedly on the basis of ethnicity (rather than proven terrorist or espionage intent) and unpopular, expensive campaigns in two theaters of war. Troops encountered fanatical opposition that routinely adopted suicide tactics during attrition over barren, rocky, inhospitable, yet strategically important territory. Enemy forces entrenched in labyrinthine caves made combat particularly difficult.

Now 9/11 had punctured postmodernism's façade. Smaller, cheaper cameras, proliferating TV channels, and Internet sites exponentially ramped up the ubiquity of mediations. Naive employment of camera phones revealed U.S. and Allied abuse of security detainees and again exposed the horrors of the Real, despite obfuscation by patriotic slogans and imagery. Central to these, the War on Terror in effect posited the enemy as an abstraction; it could last as long as politically expedient by shifting the shape of the threat.

Flags' historical perspective aptly highlights the power, and sometimes unintended effects, of signs and representations as it portrays the repercussions on several servicemen involved in a casual incident that became an internationally recognized icon of patriotic unity and endeavor. Although directed by prominent Hollywood Republican Clint Eastwood, the movie steers far from uncritically endorsing militarism. Continuing memorialization of World War II veterans in *Saving Private Ryan* (1997) by well-known Democrat Steven Spielberg (Eastwood's co-producer), it invites contrast of the just war concept with recent campaigns and respectfully embodies memories from a passing generation of veterans whose opposition to the Vietnam War had displaced their suffering and achievements for over thirty years.

Instead of relegating the story to the past, flashback narration and dramatized interviews with ex-combatants suggest continuity and contrast with recent events. "Our fathers'" flags, the title hints, carry different connotations from "ours." These strategies acknowledge reflection and commentary: a subjective, personal, and relative dimension to witnessing. From official truth promulgated through combined accident and propaganda, survivors reclaim their stories and those of comrades, perished or traumatized in battle or through entanglement in a fundraising campaign that cared as little for individuals as any military operation sacrificing cannon fodder for an objective. Furthermore, the decision to film a complementary narrative in Japanese—a bold project for American mainstream cinema—and from the former enemies' perspective, indicates humanism, tolerance, forgiveness, and desire to understand. These contrast with many current politicians' and most media's routine demonization of Islam, and its conflation with Islamists as an undifferentiated mass unless personified by Osama bin Laden or, more confusedly, Saddam.

Within hours of the World Trade Center collapse, Thomas E. Franklin took his photograph, "Ground Zero Spirit." Although the American flag hangs at half-mast, the diagonal pole and the uniformity of three helmeted firefighters, concentrating as one, recalls Joe Rosenthal's image of the Iwo Jima flag-raising (1945), history's most reproduced photograph. Within days, Bush and his staff sported flag lapel pins, reviving a symbol the Nixon administration had appropriated to differentiate themselves from Vietnam protestors.

"Every jackass thinks he knows what war is," asserts *Flags'* opening— voiced by an actor playing Rosenthal (who died this year)—"especially those that have never been in one. They like things nice and simple. Good and evil. Heroes and villains. And there's always plenty of those. Most of the time they are *not* who we think they are." It is hard not to infer censure of Bush, whose military record had been besmirched by scandal since before his reelection. Claiming "the right picture . . . can win or lose a war," Rosenthal stresses the arbitrariness of his snapshot, shown circulating while (as again this year) "the country was becoming bankrupt . . . cynical, tired of the war." Suddenly a Roosevelt aide declares: "We may have found it!" A movie that uses available lighting for present-day interviews, and lights and composes full-color scenes in 1940s America to resemble Norman Rockwell's idealized *Saturday Evening Post* covers—contrasted with graininess and gruesome chaos in the Robert Capa–influenced combat sequences, nearly monochrome except flames and blood—demonstrates acute consciousness of questions of representation. Almost immediately a disconcertingly stagey battle on Mount Suribachi is revealed as the surviving flag raisers' reenactment in a cheering stadium, until fireworks motivate a flashback to battlefield horror. Eastwood acknowledges that history is told, truth mediatized, for specific purposes. End credits show documentary photographs and formal portraits of the actual heroes, demonstrating the movie's authenticity while stressing that it is dramatization.

Epic, computer-generated, aerial shots of the fleet and from atop Suribachi deliver the spectacle promised by a major war movie. They stress the campaign's scale and importance, hence enormous expense, motivating the propaganda for which Rosenthal's image became the trademark and which exploited the flag raisers as reluctant heroes. That the flotilla is unstoppable when a serviceman disappears overboard emphasizes how easily, randomly, and inexorably lives are destroyed, forgotten if not chronicled, despite individualist and heroic rhetoric that nurtures the values driving the war effort.

Flags of Our Fathers (Clint Eastwood, DreamWorks SKG): the decisive moment. Digital frame enlargement.

The film's heart is a dramatization of the flag-raising. Yet this is ephemeral, insignificant at the time for participants and a chance conjunction of time, place, light, framing, and composition for Rosenthal, who swung his camera and clicked without preparation. It was anything but a defiant gesture, a victory seized under heavy fire against overwhelming odds—the myth newspapers created; rather, the action occupied a lull during fighting, which had already lasted four days and continued for a month, killing three of the six flag raisers and eventually seven thousand Americans and twenty-two thousand Japanese. The picture in fact captured a second flag-raising by marines laying a telephone cable to the summit, replacing a flag that Colonel Johnson decided to preserve for the Marine Corps after the secretary of the navy claimed it as a souvenir. That the initial flag-raising also was photographed, and that Rosenthal acknowledged posing a portrait of the second flag-raising patrol, unaware that his improvised shot was the one transmitted worldwide, sustained allegations of staging. These aspersions—compounded with naiveté concerning visual media and confusion over one dead flag raiser's identity resulting from the duplicated events—intensified pressure on the survivors, feted in a national tour

to support the Seventh Bond Drive to finance the war, despite their awareness of disparity between what they were lauded for and their incommuni-
cable battle experiences.

Those recollections, and personal consequences of the publicity
machine, inform the movie. Naval medic "Doc" Bradley (Ryan Phillippe),
who repeatedly risked himself to treat injuries, keeps to himself memories
of his marine buddy's tortured and mutilated body. Rene Gagner's (Jesse
Bradford) girlfriend (Melanie Lynskey) exploits newfound celebrity as
hero's sweetheart, amid suggestions that he never fired his weapon. Native
American Ira Hayes (Adam Beach) struggles with alcoholism, racism, loss of
his beloved sergeant, and desire to rejoin his unit, while publicists insist on
his adhering to false attribution of another flag raiser's identity. A cynical
Treasury Department official's glib assertion, "What you guys must have
seen over there. I saw it in the newsreels. Jeez, that was a fight and a half!"
before changing the subject parallels President Harry S. Truman's attitude;
their lack of comprehension represents all of America's while their
loquacity contrasts with stoicism, tears, and repressed anger among the
band of brothers who share an unspoken bond.

Against Bush's simplistic certainties, *Flags'* screenwriter Paul Haggis had
been determined in *Crash* (2005) to retain balance, to understand, and to
defer judgment in presenting situations invariably more complex than
appearances suggest. *Letters*, a counterpart to *Flags* that Haggis co-wrote
with Japanese American Iris Yamashita, neither seeks to explain Japanese
aggression nor blames all Japanese servicemen for atrocities. It portrays
common decency among its principal characters, trapped by circumstances
they ultimately cannot control. U.S. guards who, instead of being contrasted heroically, execute prisoners casually, simultaneously disobeying
orders and ignoring conventions intended to uphold higher values: conduct
as culpable as any merciless code. Rather than asserting moral equivalence,
this again stresses warfare's human cost. *Letters* begins with shots of the
Japanese memorial on Suribachi that echo the final, post-credits shot of
Flags. Similarity between the films' melancholy piano scores underlines
respect for those on both sides coerced into battle.

Whereas in *Flags* the enemy is concealed in tunnels so that the ground
itself appears to spit fiery venom, for Japanese soldiers in *Letters* the invading Americans, while far from invisible, are distant, equally faceless, de-
humanized. Reverse-shots from gunners' positions in *Letters* match shots in
Flags of artillery emerging from foxholes, while battle sequences and images
of the U.S. fleet differ only slightly. Emphasizing correspondences, the Rising Sun, momentarily limp, repeatedly resembles the Stars and Stripes.

Low-angles and martial music confer respect upon Japanese combatants. General Kuribayashi's (Ken Watanabe) fruitless appeal to superiors in *Letters* parallels the U.S. commander arguing for resources in *Flags*. Horrific violence matches that witnessed by Americans, although much is self-inflicted, according to the "Death before Dishonor" *bushido* code. One scene, nevertheless, shows infantryman Saigo (Kazunari Ninimiya), who shares with Kuribayashi the film's central point of view, witness a U.S. soldier brutally beaten and bayoneted. Surrender by low-ranking Japanese is presented sympathetically as realist, rather than cowardly, in the context of failed command structures—even as admirable in that Saigo, the one survivor shown, promised to return to his family.

Despite such radical decentering, this Hollywood war movie judges Japanese characters by contemporary Western standards, notwithstanding their enmity. Good officers lead by example; are thoughtful, inspiring, compassionate, animal-loving. Bad ones are zealous, sadistic martinets. This mirrors how *Flags* sets the obnoxious, albeit triumphantly successful, Treasury Department publicist against its modest heroes. Kuribayashi, esteemed for fairness and paternalistic concern as well as military prowess, admires America, where he has lived; but he defends his homeland in compliance with internationally recognized martial honor, as he once vowed he would when answering a hypothetical question at an American tribute to him, prompting his host's response: "Spoken like a true soldier."

Some of Kuribayashi's letters accompany flashbacks to happier times—his stay in America, not his Japanese life, although he loves his family—and several originate in America in addition to dispatches from Iwo Jima. His futile defense of the strategically essential island is calculated to delay inevitable assault on the mainland. When wounded, death by his own hand, using a pistol presented at the American dinner, results from personal conflict as much as adherence to military ceremonial (he leads the final desperate attack rather than staying to commit ritual suicide as honor dictates). He, the commander, tells Saigo, the lowest ranked soldier: "I promised myself to fight until death for my family, but the thought of my family makes it difficult to keep that promise."

Key scenes intercut the suffering of a fatally wounded U.S. marine, Sam (Lucas Elliot), with Kuribayashi's American trip and blackly comic, insanely cruel narratives showing Japanese extreme patriotism. Kuribayashi's aide, Nishi (Tsuyoshi Ihara)—an Olympic equestrian who has also visited America and consorted with Hollywood stars—orders a subaltern to treat Sam's injuries. This affront to protocol, initially resisted because of the belief that Americans would not do the same, prompts Nishi's response: "Have you ever met one?" Conversing with Sam, translating for his men—then, after Sam's death, translating a letter from Sam's mother that urges, "Always do what is right because it is right"—Nishi makes his soldiers and the viewer aware of situations and sentiments shared on both sides, including respect for motherhood. Curiously, the phrase—which Nishi repeats when, blinded, he orders a retreat, before ritualistically shooting himself—unemphatically states one definition of a just war, thereby ambiguating all the codes, military and maternal, American and Japanese, by which characters live. (Curiously, too, McLoughlin's epilogue to *World Trade Center* celebrates how rescuers acted "because it was the right thing to do"—a call to duty that lacks specificity.)

Letters looks back before the battle (only one central character survives), whereas *Flags* looks forward to its effects on veterans. *Flags* dramatizes survivors' memories; *Letters* resurrects the dead through their written testimony. (*Flags* too restores lost comrades, shown perishing in a series of flashbacks, by visualizing Bradley's deathbed memory of them frolicking in the sea during a respite.) In *Letters*, the flag-raising is absent—either inevitable to, or unnoticed by, the Japanese. Saigo finally looks directly to the camera—the Other humanized and embodiment of life and continuity. U.S. troops protect themselves and others because life is sacred; Japanese suicide culture contradicts this, as do more recent suicide bombers, Robert Burgoyne points out.[1] Tellingly, Eastwood "does not . . . ironise or call into question Japan's civilian beliefs the way he did with his own side" (Bradshaw), presumably because the matter is long settled—unlike manipulation of once-revered images and ideals for current political gain.

Crises of Identity: Smoke and Mirrors in *The Prestige* and *The Illusionist*

The gap between presentation and reality looms wider still in *The Prestige* and *The Illusionist*. Both are, unusually, tales of stage conjurers. While space, sorcery, wizardry, and superhero fantasies imagine paranormal abilities, movies rarely feature theatrical magic. Cinema, pioneered by magicians during the 1890s–1900s, when both films are set, *is* illusion. As Houdini learned by losing a fortune, onscreen tricks lack the mystery accompanying unmediated performance (although TV's rhetoric of liveness later supported magic). The return this year of movies fascinated with both the exploitation and exposure of diversion and trickery—and that they overcame the risk of undercutting each other's popularity and distribution strategies—suggests that they spoke to contemporary concerns.

Christopher Nolan distills Christopher Priest's science-fiction, Gothic horror, and supernatural novel *The Prestige* (1995); Neil Burger's *The Illusionist* elaborates Steven Millhauser's short story "Eisenheim the Illusionist" (1990), replicating its magic realist uncertainty, ambiguity, and fantastic occurrences. Both favor handheld camerawork and natural lighting to convey period settings in a spontaneous, current style. *The Prestige* exhibits blockbuster values in its casting, contemporary naturalistic performances, "high concept" aesthetic (see Wyatt), and spectacular effects. *The Illusionist* pastiches Eastern European art cinematography, digitally manipulated to imitate a color process developed by the Lumières in 1903. Golden-tinted painterly exteriors and chiaroscuro close-ups, screaming "quality cinema" (although without the restraint formerly associated with costume drama), complement stylized performances and middle-European accents to emphasize artificiality commensurate with illusionism. Anachronistic early cinematic devices enhance this: grainy, juddering sepia images accompany the shakily focused credits, shadowy vignettes frame certain subjects, and iris transitions abound. These signify narrative uncertainty—anything not witnessed by Inspector Uhl (Paul Giamatti), the focalizing consciousness. *The Prestige* adopts Victorian painter John Atkinson Grimshaw's green and yellow palette to evoke its urban setting (Holben 70). In both, location shooting grounds illusionism and self-reflexivity (including deployment of lanterns and projectors in *The Illusionist*) in realism, to naturalize, and function as a foil for, fantasy.

The Illusionist, a mystery concerning loss, secret texts, rivalry, doppelgängers, and suicide, and *The Prestige*, fitting this description with serial killings added, contain apparent murders and resurrections involving individuals framed for crimes they did not commit. Each revisits an identity-threatening world of alterity, horror, illusion, disguise, retribution, and seemingly self-destructive obsession. Each toys with film as technological spectacle, optical illusion, scientific instrument, art, and entertainment commodity. In both, ambiguities, puns, parallelisms, symbolism, unreliable and excessively self-conscious narration, and shifting chronology foreground textuality while enhancing suspense.

Against scientific progress and technological triumphalism, Romanticism's Gothic underside revealed uncontainable sexual impulses and morbid attraction to violence. The visible world became a cipher, as in illusions; these tease perceptions and exploit paranormal imagery or esoteric knowledge while the mind struggles for answers. As in Gothic, these films manifest duality in patterns of doubling and secret texts. Encoded diaries advance *The Prestige*; so too in *The Illusionist* do secret instructions for tricks and a locket intricately conceal a portrait. Their narrative enigmas do not merely reveal but flaunt clues. Yet motivations remain uncertain and identity is radically destabilized.

Horrific implications evade notice. In *The Prestige* obsession with stage magic kills 105 characters: 101 in agonizing suicides, avoidable 100 times had relevant knowledge been available. Burials alive, betrayals, and double-crossings occur, with deliberate crippling, self-mutilation, and apparent murder leading to false conviction and execution, and an incredible but chilling paranormal denouement. *The Illusionist*, lighter, more subdued, foregrounds romance and discounts supernaturalism it outwardly suggests, but embodies a powerful, understated, sinister, political subtext, entailing autocratic power, secret machinations in a corrupt police state, deep social prejudices, and popular ignorance and superstition.

Dismemberment and discorporation suggest the self's lack of integrity or boundaries, reinforced in both films through doppelgängers in stage illusions and the wider narratives. Rival magicians in *The Prestige* become mutual nemeses. Doubling accompanies splitting, the self apparently divided. Alfred Borden (Christian Bale), generally rational, self-controlled, driven, is boozing near the start when arguing over a knot. Years later, he appears drunkenly boorish in a scene that precipitates his wife's (Rebecca Hall) self-destruction. *The Illusionist*'s framing flashback literally narrates verbally through Uhl. He and Eisenheim (Edward Norton), counterparts, strive to outwit each other. Uhl, an amateur magician, is interested as much in illusions as in upholding what he knows is an unjust regime. As in *The Prestige*, where plot twists appear through the eyes of the albeit skeptical, knowledgeable magicians being duped, rather than through those of the perpetrators, the spectator of *The Illusionist* identifies with an onscreen observer as correspondences emerge between fascination with magic and criminal investigation, in turn linking magic with both science and darker, unsettling forces. Eisenheim and Uhl, implicated in high-level political intrigues of the Austro-Hungarian Empire, become complicit, thanks to Eisenheim's ingenuity, in the villainous Crown Prince Leopold's (Rufus Sewell) downfall. During a montage that enables reassessment of previous understanding, Uhl appreciates Eisenheim's audacity, having been educated and liberated by it. Eisenheim and Leopold too are counterparts, rivals for the Duchess Sophie (Jessica Biel). Their hazardous power game of personal bluffing during magic shows escalates into competition for public influence. Eisenheim's parallels with Uhl and Leopold are accentuated visually, the dark-haired, bearded characters of similar age being suspicious, formal, and repressed in each other's company.

Borden's constant companion in *The Prestige*, his ingénieur Fallon (also Christian Bale), visually mirrors him. Borden and his rival Robert Angier (Hugh Jackman) also are counterparts. Crosscutting repeatedly enhances parallels. Angier employs a violent drunkard as his onstage double and seethes while this impostor accepts his applause. Borden eventually kills Angier, who thought he had effected the perfect crime: his staged murder leading to his rival's execution. Both films broach the morality of framing characters for crimes not committed, although disposition and past behavior (and Leopold's failure to deny guilt) indicate capability, even willingness, while narrative convention suggests, for as long as duplicity remains concealed, that justice has been achieved.

Perceived originality might account for these films' simultaneity, fascination, and success; recalling his attraction to *The Illusionist*, Norton commented, "I really can't think of the last good magic movie." This fails to explain how they overcame incompatibility between cinema as illusion and illusion as content. Neither can one ignore the appeal in recent years on TV of, among others, David Blaine (who helped conceive *The Illusionist*) and David Copperfield (consultant on *The Prestige*), nor Susanna Clarke's hugely promoted novel *Jonathan Strange and Mr Norrell* (2004), another narrative of adversarial nineteenth-century magicians. Duplicitous and excessively limited narration provides hermeneutic pleasure, as does questioning the boundaries of what is acceptable as real. Beside interactive and immersive digital entertainment, audiences still crave shared wonder and ritual, being told a story, not feeling entirely in control, including trickery within the security of narrative closure. *The Prestige* and *The Illusionist* succeed other "smart cinema" (Sconce) that self-consciously heightens these pleasures, extending at least as far as *The Sting* (1973).

Costume dramas traditionally evince nostalgia; *The Illusionist* and *The Prestige*, despite artifice, spectacle, and bracketing of serious history, resonate with contemporary interests and anxieties. Eisenheim reconstructs real-life illusionist Robert-Houdin's "Mysterious Orange Tree." Circling the plant, rather than adopting Eisenheim's audience's view, the movie offers one of those "spectacles of comparison" that challenge spectators to spot discrepancies between live action and CGI within a shot (North 2). Conversely, Eisenheim's apocryphal childhood encounter with a magician utilizes "obvious" pro-filmic and studiously crude CGI or matte effects: a frog, supposedly produced from thin air, is concealed behind Eisenheim by camera placement; a levitating flute lacks perspective, rotational movement, and parallax. Not merely contrasts with Eisenheim's stagecraft, these distract from the narratively—not just visually—misleading main illusion. Anachronistic overhead wires in the railroad station at the end intrude extradiegetic reality and—if noticed—heighten playfulness and illusoriness as Uhl, with the spectator, experiences revelation. Similarly, despite melodramatic and distracting lightning effects, illusions in *The Prestige*, including the "New Transported Man" on which the plot hinges, utilize modest jump cuts, a technique originating with Méliès in the 1890s.

Such ambiguity and deception match advertisers', marketers', spin doctors', and politicians' slippery language and abuse of evidence, abetted by postmodern notions of relativism. If the most audacious illusionism of recent years conjured weapons of mass destruction, defeat of authoritarian leadership in *The Illusionist* may offer some compensatory satisfaction. Its plot implicating a crown prince in his younger consort's apparent death, and the cult of idolatry thus provoked, parallels allegations surrounding a more recent popular princess. That *The Prestige* includes bitter rivalry between real-life "Wizard of Menlo Park" Thomas Edison and the visionary Nikola Tesla (David Bowie), purportedly the engineer of Angier's greatest illusion, accords with further conspiracy theories and urban legends such as belief that Edison's light bulb still works, indicting built-in obsolescence and throwaway culture. Subjects misrecognize their mutually sustaining economic and ideological relationship with capitalism, science, and technology, exacerbating uncertainties about identity further complicated by organ transplantation (the first face transplant occurred while these films were being made) and prospective human cloning (announced two years previously).

Cages and victimization (a sustained image system in *The Prestige*) and state oppression (*The Illusionist*) chime with the surveillance society that, moreover, appropriates potential identity theft and anti-terrorism measures to advocate ceding the self to the state, as in routine biometric screening and U.S. and U.K. government plans for compulsory identity cards. Identity is precarious, negotiated constantly between the socially constructed self and its manifold others. Loss of selfhood and integrity are genuine concerns when agencies monitor Internet, telephone, and text communications, and trace movements through security and traffic cameras and bank card transactions. Meanwhile the Internet, promising to show everything, steals secrets, financial details, privacy, and leisure time, worries parents, infects records with viruses, externalizes personal tastes and interests to sell them back, and offers alternate identities, second lives, and meetings with others' avatars. E-mail correspondents on another continent seem closer than colleagues down the corridor. Cell phones transform relationships with society, work, and leisure. DNA screening maps physical identity but offers no insight "experientially or psychologically" (Warner 374), while demographics, medicine, forensic science, and marketing counterintuitively group populations, supplanting traditional categories such as nation, region, class, religion, and occupation.

The events of 9/11 and afterward graphically foreground mirroring, doubling, shadowing, and projection as functions of identity—as also do these movies. Grimly spectacular collision between the immediate, material, and secular with its timeless, fundamentalist, and spiritual Other, as advanced technology brought apocalyptic clouds and flames out of daylight sky, augured an incontrovertible return of the Real, as well as nightmarish fantasies, to confront postmodernism and digital simulacra. TV's clarity, immediacy, and compulsive repetition replaced the familiar with the horror of multiple murders and suicidal obsession, or empathetic projection into the awareness of victims; it raised to consciousness fearsome anti-Western forces. Foreign policy, a Frankenstein monster turning against its maker, was gestated through centuries of conflict, too often hidden and repressed. "War on Terror" conveyed Gothic terminology into normality. Events provided imagery—and, despite hoaxes, reasons to trust again in indexicality—to fill out the phrase's vacuity. Masked captors beheaded hostages on camera. "Suicide bombers project[ed] themselves into eternity by enshrining their last hours in ritual videos: turning themselves into lasting ghosts" (Warner 336). Allegations and revelations concerned "extraordinary rendition," incarceration without trial, systematic abuse, and torture in Guantanamo Bay and Abu Ghraib. As Philip Gourevitch and Errol Morris ask, "If you fight terror with terror, how can you tell which is which?" (10).

Something jars when the best-funded, idealistic, and efficiently organized forces—self-proclaimed "good guys," the innocent wronged party, upholders of civilization—fulfill their enemies' characterization of them as the Great Satan and fundamentalism mirrors fundamentalism. Gothic always expresses unease by imagining opposites within superficial appearance, yet as fantasy it is easily dismissed, ignored, or denigrated. These social facts are accompanied by resurgent Creationism and retreat into supernatural explanations ("the Rapture") for climate change and terrorism. Homeland security blurs innocence with guilt, a binary collapse represented in these films when Leopold and Borden appear justly punished for crimes they did not—but easily could—commit.

Crisis Interventions: Inner World, Outer World in *Inland Empire* and *An Inconvenient Truth*

A final pairing of movies exemplifies contrasting responses to such pressures and contradictions—dramatization of psychic confusion in one and democratic engagement in the other. *Inland Empire* premiered at Venice Film Festival, where director David Lynch accepted a lifetime achievement award. Resembling his previous feature, *Mulholland Dr.* (2001)—which shares cast members, a Hollywood setting presented as both glamorous industry and sleazy underbelly of broken dreams, a fractured protagonist whose alter egos (dark versus blond) may or may not be imaginary, and an unresolved, cryptic plot that repeatedly splits and convolutes—the movie is a summation of Lynch's career. Expanded from experiments on his subscription website, self-funded, shot by the director on outmoded standard-quality digital video, and distributed personally in the United States, where just four theaters screened it after Lynch rearranged his deal with Canal Plus to avoid editorial interference, this is large-scale, star-studded, artisanal filmmaking.

Delirious and free-associative, *Inland Empire* defies classification and explication. The title card resembles a studio ident, associating the movie with the industry of which it is equally a part and an aberration: the first of uncountable categories collapses. The graphic emphasizes light—whether a searchlight into dark recesses, seeking meaning, or a projector beam, averring meaning, is unclear. Sound follows, disjunctively as a close-up gramophone needle hisses with either applause or surface noise masking an announcement: "Axxonn—the longest running radio play in history." However, this is film, not radio, and live radio is not usually associated with 78 rpm discs—although both radio and recording studios previously existed on Hollywood and Vine, where the final act begins with one of Laura Dern's characters, fatally stabbed, vomiting blood over Dorothy Lamour's commemorative star on the Sidewalk of Fame. Dern's character, a movie celebrity who merges with the roles she is playing, appears herself to have followed a sign reading "AXX^{O}N$_N$" into interconnecting alternative worlds. Perhaps this relates to Lamour "starring" in a novel, Matilda Bailey's *Dorothy Lamour and the Haunted Lighthouse* (1947), one of an illustrated series in which "the heroine has the same name and appearance as [a] famous actress but has no connection . . . it is as though the famous actress has stepped into an alternate reality in which she is an ordinary person"; in hers, Lamour bizarrely enough works as secretary to a lighthouse keeper—a further resonance with the title card—and "hears strange sounds at night.

She discovers a hidden room and a secret passageway and single-handedly solves a jewel heist" (White).

The uncertainty yet richness of intertextual and internal correspondences in the opening seconds of a 180-minute movie demonstrate the impossibility and undesirability of fixing explanations. As Lynch told filmmaker Mike Figgis: "A great poet might articulate abstractions with words but cinema does it with pictures flowing together in sequences" (18). His protagonist disappears like Alice into a hole that is a whole. Portals like wormholes riddle the text, linking scenes allusively and elusively. Absence of scene selection on the DVD version stresses continuity and fluidity. Cheap video allows a continuously evolving, semi-improvised script to produce a cinematic equivalent of surrealist automatic writing, while deployment of stars and professional facilities results in a feature-film version of avant-garde experimentation, classics of which it resembles in its dreamlike structure and unsettling, haunting visions, from Luis Buñuel and Salvador Dali's *Un Chien Andalou* (1929) to Maya Deren's *Meshes of the Afternoon* (1943). Hardly commercial in any usual sense, *Inland Empire* exemplifies the diversity and force of vision still possible thanks to international co-production, an established auteur name, inexpensive techniques, domestic sell-through, and an unbounded text that originates in form on the Internet and continues to proliferate there in interpretations posted by fans.

A characteristic shared with other films already discussed from this year is the way *Inland Empire* involves doubling and incorporates defining others. (So, too, does Martin Scorsese's *The Departed*: its main characters are alter egos sharing a symbolic father and the same woman's bed, in an America in which organized crime and law enforcement are indistinguishable.) *Inland Empire* constitutes independent cinema with a Hollywood setting and, in part, production values. It embraces American entertainment and European art cinema, with scenes shot and set in Lodz, Poland's film capital that boasts its own sidewalk of stars, although Lynch does not allude to this. Wealth and poverty, gentility and violence, beauty and obscenity rub together. Mind and body, self and other, performance and identity, reality and imagination blur. Identity involves similarity—identification *with*—as much as individuality. Meaning, made rather than extracted, requires both consciously analytic activity and willingness to surrender.

Whether Lynch is pursuing his unconscious or commenting on contemporary media's confusion of image and reality remains a moot point. Less ambiguous is *An Inconvenient Truth*, which continued a trend of critically and commercially successful documentaries. Reaching this year's U.S. boxoffice top quartile, it also created impact worldwide, despite being a wake-up call to America, the largest contributor to climate change. It became the third highest grossing documentary ever on general release in North America after *Fahrenheit 9/11* (2004) and *March of the Penguins* (2005).

Before *An Inconvenient Truth*, former vice president Al Gore presented his "slide show"—his description—a thousand times, advancing arguments developed during thirty years of campaigning to cultivate political will, among leaders and voters alike, to take responsibility. Upgraded for the movie, Gore's presentation was recorded before live audiences on a set constructed for multi-camera shooting. The rockumentary-like format is a staged tour as much as a vehicle for Gore's message. His ever-present laptop computer, center stage on set, and on which Gore constantly works while traveling, links lecture sequences with personal and political autobiography. The phenomenon of Gore's mission leavens scientific facts with human interest and narrative continuity.

Gore introduces himself: "I used to be the next President of the United States of America." The film's success, owing much to Gore's dignity, humor, and authority, rallied widespread antipathy to Bush's policies and style. Overseas audiences took comfort that Bush's dismissal of green issues, willfully oafish yet apparently (and, to outsiders, terrifyingly) grounded in religious conviction, was not universal within the United States. Gore recalls the ignorance of one of his schoolteachers who, he jokes to cheers and applause, "went on to become science advisor in the current administration."

Apparent simplicity belies the sophistication of Gore's rhetoric and filmmaker Davis Guggenheim's weaving together of materials. Both combine forcefully to supply Aristotle's three elements of persuasion. Gore's articulate, confident charm, citing of experts ("My friend Carl Sagan"), quotations (e.g., Mark Twain and Sir Winston Churchill), and overt appeal to moral obligations establish *ethos*. Data, charts, and the evidence of before-and-after photographs meet demands of *logos*. *Pathos* operates through inclusion of Gore's controversial presidential defeat after an inconclusive recount, making him the indefatigable underdog, and through formative events such as his son's near-fatal accident and his sister's death from lung cancer in the context of his family farming tobacco; images of human devastation in recent storms; and animations both humorous (a "Futurama" clip) and poignant (a polar bear attempting to mount a disintegrating ice floe). These coalesce in a still of New Orleans plumed by smoke. Gore never overtly blames global warming for Hurricane Katrina, response to which was Bush's most visible domestic failure, but he does note increasing storm incidence. However, when he describes it as "something new for America,"

An Inconvenient Truth (Davis Guggenheim, Lawrence Bender Productions): "How in God's name could that happen here?" Digital frame enlargement.

asking, "How in God's name could that happen here?" parallels with 9/11 are unmistakable. Focusing next on the election fiasco, the movie challenges Bush's entire agenda, not just his foreign policy. Gore looks down from a superior perspective in a still intercut with Bush beginning his presidency. Denials by Presidents Ronald Reagan and George H. W. Bush and Senator James Inhofe, followed by Gore's choice of the World Trade Center Memorial site to illustrate rising sea levels, and his question, "Is it possible we should prepare for other threats besides terrorists?" indicate that hullabaloo surrounding this film concerns more than climate science.

Intellectual montages incorporating Gore, at various ages, looking down from inside aircraft, effectively imply a godlike position. Bestowing authority, contextualizing his career, implying an omniscient overview, these relate to photographs of Earth—*Apollo 8*'s "Earthrise" (1968), which, Gore claims, initiated modern environmentalism, and an *Apollo 17* shot (1972), which Gore calls "the most commonly reproduced photograph in all of history." Although impossible to ascertain whether the accolade belongs to this or Rosenthal's Iwo Jima flag-raising, the space images recognize our planet's beauty, its fragility, and human accountability toward it.

Gore, in dark blazer and blue shirt against the deep blue set and the blackness of space, occupies the firmament, harmonizing visually and asserting identity with the planet. An almost monochrome tracking shot twice follows Gore striding backstage toward the auditorium, unmistakably recalling presidential candidate John F. Kennedy in *Primary* (1960); shots in cars similarly recollect the Drew Associates' documentary, although Guggenheim and Gore's closeness contrasts with direct cinema's objectivity. Indeed, the last shot of Gore, a black-and-white still silhouette before a satellite image of a hurricane, both echoes George Tames's photograph "John F. Kennedy in the Oval Office: The Loneliest Job" (1961) and confers an aura. Before the main title, a close-up of Gore working holds TV images in the background; his voiceover comments that, for any party's politicians, "the moral imperative to make big changes is irrepressible," just as Old Glory, flying over New Orleans floodwaters, materializes behind him.

Gore's construction as elder statesman, prophet, visionary, leader— younger adults dominate his audiences—emphasizes didacticism. Nevertheless, through infectious enthusiasm for science, he represents his audience, proselytizing what he considers self-evident rather than condescending. Proclaiming itself "carbon neutral," the production throws down challenges and suggestions to the audience during the end credits. "Ultimately," Gore insists, "this is not so much a political issue as a moral issue." However, opposition remains mainly political, not least because, Guggenheim has commented, "smart journalists" have to provide "balance." Superficially one of the least interesting aesthetically and formalistically, this may be one of the year's most important movies.

ACKNOWLEDGMENTS

The author gratefully acknowledges the University of Lincoln Undergraduate Research Opportunities Scheme for research assistance by Emma Samia Howard.

NOTE

1. Sincere thanks to Professor Burgoyne for generously sharing draft chapters from *Film Nation: Hollywood Looks at U.S. History*.

2007

Movies and the Art of Living Dangerously

DINA SMITH

Exhausted after playing tennis on their new Christmas Wii game consoles, a few Americans stayed in to celebrate the New Year, logging on, for the first time, to YouTube. Forget Yahtzee and Scrabble: the video interactive website, recently acquired by Google, contained inventive narrative shorts and video clips, providing a double click to media fun. Indeed, many that night must have clinked champagne glasses and shamelessly watched the YouTube sensation: the cell phone video capture of Saddam Hussein's execution, by hanging, that had been uploaded onto the site the day before. "Should old acquaintance be forgot" had become an ironic turn of phrase that evening, as, during the height of the war, many watched the gruesome death of Iraq's former leader.

Days later President George W. Bush announced a surge of U.S. troops to Iraq—"I've committed more than 20,000 additional American troops to Iraq"—making the total 170,000, at a time when 70 percent of Americans opposed sending more troops ("Timeline"). By year's end, 899 American troops, hundreds of contractors, and thousands of Iraqi civilians had died, making it the deadliest year since the 2003 invasion ("Timeline"). In addition, in May the *New York Times* reported that between "100,000 and 300,000 barrels a day of Iraq's declared oil production over the past four years has been siphoned off through corruption or smuggling," leading many to believe that this had indeed been an "oil war" (Glanz). Adding to the year's corruption, the security firm Blackwater faced charges of the indiscriminate killings of Iraqi civilians, requiring the U.S. House of Representatives, in October, to pass a bill making all private contractors subject to prosecution in U.S. courts, ending four years of legal immunity (Broder). A week later a Philadelphia law firm filed suit against Blackwater U.S.A. for its "senseless slaying" and "lengthy pattern of egregious misconduct in Iraq," suggesting that Blackwater had in effect become a mercenary fighting force in the region, one financed by the U.S. government ("Iraqi"). By

year's end, with approval ratings at 32 percent, George W. Bush's administration, like the war, reeked of failure ("Presidential").

Against this backdrop of violence and American swagger, Hollywood
saw the resurgence of that most American of genres, the western. There
were the real westerns, the spirited and successful remake of *3:10 to Yuma*
and the poetic and introspective *The Assassination of Jesse James by the Coward
Robert Ford*. Then there were the disguised westerns, *There Will Be Blood* and
No Country for Old Men. Nevertheless, all these films possessed paternal
anxieties: a father emasculated in front of his son, trying to regain his
respect (*Yuma*); an outlaw prodigy Oedipally obsessed with his gunfighter
hero, portrayed as the ultimate father (*Jesse James*); an oil man pursuing the
frontiers of capital only to abandon his adopted son, inevitably left to die
alone (*Blood*); and a third-generation lawman who sees the border reconfigured, changed since his father's days, impotent to invoke justice (*No
Country*). These films all configure an emasculated and/or deranged cowboy
hero, laying bare the way in which the "western [had historically] served
as one of the principal displacement mechanisms in a culture obsessed with
the inevitable encroachments on its gradually diminishing space" (Ray 75).
A genre embedded in a mythology of American exceptionalism, the western had moved beyond simple revision and started to impose upon itself,
suffering from an Oedipal crisis that gets narrativized in stories about impo-
tence, failure, and dying fathers. Given their critical, if not box office, success, the films act as displaced allegories for a failed war and administration
(one film literally focuses on oil-as-capital), narratively signaling the end of
American empirebuilding, if not the western itself. Thus, not even the western could mediate us out of this mess, especially since the self-styled "cowboy president" seemed intent on creating foreign policy based upon the
most reactionary of colonial westerns.

Seemingly inured or completely oblivious to the war and to a shifting
ideology of nation, a record number of Americans bought homes, spurred
on by subprime mortgages, 80 percent of which were adjustable rate mortgages. By this year, the credit and housing boom started to feel the pinch of
rising interest rates, leading to the inevitable financial crisis the following
year. In the wake of the decade's housing boom, the United States witnessed the biggest baby boom since 1957 with over 43 million births
reported by the National Center for Health Statistics (Jayson). As a tabloid
rejoinder, Julia Roberts, Naomi Watts, Selma Hayek, and a host of celebrities showed off their "baby bumps," which became as fashionable as a
Hermès Birkin bag. As in the 1950s with its famed Dr. Spock books, this
new baby culture produced a publishing frenzy in child-rearing texts,

notably the bestseller *The Dangerous Book for Boys*, a how-to manual on how to make such things as flawless paper airplanes, the perfect tree house, and a functioning go-cart (Iggulden). The book signaled yet another return to a rustic mythos, touting individual gumption as the core to a proper manhood. With encyclopedic sections devoted to dinosaurs, insects, and the Seven Wonders of the Ancient World, the book was nostalgic for an imaginative boyhood before it had been colonized by electronic technologies like Xbox and the Internet (Brown 287–89).

Hollywood, too, waged a battle against new colonizing technologies in the year's writers' strike, in which more than 12,000 radio, television, and screenwriters, members of the Writers Guild of America (WGA), united for a three-month strike against producers (AMPTP). At the center of the WGA strike was the unprotected usage of new media, the new platforms and technologies of sharing and accessing media content: interactive channels, like video-on-demand, Internet protocol television (IPTV), Internet streaming and downloading, wireless and smart phone downloading, and any future online distribution methods that illegitimately profited off writers' stories. These new interactive or "convergence" technologies were thought to replace standard television and movie theater venues, and, like VHS and DVD sales before them, needed to account for writer's compensations and residuals (Safrath 118). Although the AMPTP continued to deny that new media presented a viable market, a spokesperson for Paramount let the cat out of the bag when he admitted, "There is a revenue being created today [by new media]. It's not a lot, but we're not losin[g] money" (Safrath 120). As this Paramount gaffe illustrated, producers were investing in and acknowledging the changing infrastructure yet delaying outlay and shortchanging labor for as long as possible in order to see how consumption patterns and the industry would shift. The WGA strike goals came down to acknowledging a present and foreseeing a future that producers wished to avoid.

Clearly, this was a new year of living dangerously, of the past reckoning with its more mediated present. Old genres, like the western and, as we will see, the Disney princess film, recycled and adapted to face a changing American audience and an increasingly imbricated media landscape. And newly touted genres, such as the "bromance," offered unique entry points into sublimated cultural anxieties—How long will this boom last? How has boy culture changed in this decade of war? This was a year brimming with cynicism and irony, like the boxoffice hit *Juno*, a film seemingly devoid of computer references (Juno uses the *Penny Saver* instead of Craigslist to navigate classified ads) yet was presold via the Internet. Media convergences framed much of Hollywood discourses and entered into their narratives, like a series of competing windows that bridge the fantastic with the real.

Juno; or, "The Devil Made Me Do It"

A twenty-first-century story tailor-made for Hollywood: a suburban Catholic girl, after a brief stint as a secretary, moves to Minneapolis to begin a life with her long-lost Internet boyfriend. Eventually she writes advertising copy for Twin Cities radio stations while dreaming of escaping to Hollywood, or, if all else fails, to a strip joint. Along the way, she creates a series of fictional identities via the blogosphere, finally constructing the popular "Pussy Ranch" blog that chronicles her brief stint as an exotic dancer. Extending the dissociative move, somewhere in between blogging and stripping, our girl travels west, like Kerouac before her, and, lingering at a few stoplights in Cody, Wyoming, our heroine, "Brook Busey," reinvents herself into "Diablo Cody," screenwriter of the year.

Eventually the "Pussy Ranch" blog catches the attention of a porn-surfing book agent, Mark Novick, who signs her to script a memoir, *Candy Girl: A Year in the Life of an Unlikely Stripper* (2005), a smashing success. While on a promotion junket, her easy, provocative banter woos the host and audience of "The Late Show with David Letterman." So begins her beautifully scripted move from book culture to media culture, as YouTube fixates on her salacious talk show and media interviews. Her agent subsequently encourages her to write a screenplay, whose main character, Juno, is, as we will see, yet another veiled version of the sharp-tongued, precocious writer.

So big was the industry buzz regarding her script and forthcoming film that critics admitted that they were sick of *Juno* before it had even been released. The writer eclipsed the director, Jason Reitman, becoming one of Hollywood's most marketable stories, judging by the number of media spots devoted to her before and during *Juno*'s release. This story of the Internet phenom-turned-screenwriter is perfectly pitched for a Hollywood besieged by the Internet, the common thread of screenwriters' grievances. Here the WGA accepts the "illegitimate" writer into its legitimate ranks, thereby punctuating the possibilities for collaboration between new and old medium. On 7 November, two days after the strike began, Cody published a photo of herself standing in front of that old stalwart, Paramount Studios, wearing go-go style boots and baby heart-shaped pink sunglasses and brandishing a WGA strike placard (Thompson "Diablo"). The WGA strike had found its postergirl. In this "striking" composition, Cody's stance

Screenwriter Diablo Cody's *Juno* (Jason Reitman, Fox Searchlight) balances between old and new generations, between the traditional Writers Guild of America and the edgy new media. Smith Collection.

is akin to a baseball batter's: no outs allowed—the WGA will hit a home run. A month later, two weeks ahead of schedule, Fox Searchlight released *Juno*, financed for $7 million; in New York and L.A. alone, the film grossed a half-million by week's end. Two months later, as the writers' strike ended, *Juno* had earned close to $125 million, becoming a breakout success for not only Diablo Cody but also director Reitman and the lead, Ellen Page ("Juno"). Cody had hit it out of the park. Her victory had echoed the WGA's.

As this prelude to coming attractions indicates, *Juno*, as a character and film, cannot be read outside of "Diablo Cody," so imbricated were the scripting of self and film/character. In review after review, the "colorful," "outspoken" Cody is not so unlike the "quirky" and "unconventional" dialogue-driven movie and sharp-tongued, iconoclastic title character (Hiscock). Indeed, what distinguishes *Juno* from standard Hollywood fare was the fresh, character-driven screenplay with its snappy dialogue that evoked 1930s screwball comedy or film noir. As James Naremore describes the players in classic film noir: "They have a gift for repartee, and their longer speeches have a distinctive cadence and rhetorical flair" (87). *Juno* self-consciously draws on the long melodramatic and film noir tradition that revolves around the enigma of the title female characters— *Stella Dallas*, *Laura*, *Gilda*, and *Mildred Pierce*. What will become of her? Was she the good or the bad girl? Did she or didn't she?

During the first five minutes of *Juno*, we realize that Juno did indeed "do it." After drinking her weight in "Sunny D" orange drink, teenage Juno walks into a neighborhood drugstore and takes her third over-the-counter pregnancy test and heads to the bathroom, peeing on the stick, in one of the films many disarmingly intimate moments. Waving it before the store clerk, played by the brilliantly dry Raine Wilson of "The Office" fame, she discovers that, yep, her "eggo is prego." When he asks, "What's the prognosis, fertile Myrtle?" she admits that the "the pink '+' sign is so unholy." In verbal riposte after riposte, the store clerk mocks Juno's desire to avoid the unavoidable. Nodding toward the pregnancy stick, he tells her: "That ain't no Etch-a-Sketch. This is one doodle than can't be undid, home skillet." Her body, like a sketch, will thus follow a seven-month script outline, starting with the film's intertitle "Autumn" and ending in "Summer," a narrative that gestates, in trimester fashion, along with its central character.

Though a fairly conventional plot—follow the pregnant woman through the course of her pregnancy, in which the narrative resolution is the birth of the child—*Juno*'s dialogue and its attention to intimately sketched characters bear the signature of "Best Original Screenplay." Knowing in its allusions to genre and methodic detail to character construction ("Diablo"), *Juno* reworks a narrative cliché into a film that renders teenagers ironically respectable, as something more than tits-and-ass-loving, bong-smoking, mall-shopping leeches of American culture.

Juno discovers that she's pregnant and doesn't punish her wimpy boyfriend, Paulie Bleeker (Michael Cera). In fact, when confronting him, she creates a mise-en-scène, a staging, in his front yard, of their first night together, when Paulie "went live." Smoking a fake pipe, sitting on a Barkalounger with tacky disposed furnishings, the same furnishings on which these teenagers "lost it," connecting teenage sex with disposability, Juno MacGuff bluntly and publicly tells her errant paramour, who's about ready to go for a run with his cross-country team, that she's pregnant. The film thus saves us from some horrible high school hallway confrontation in front of lockers. Instead, we are presented with a young woman who creates her own tableau for telling her fallen tale. And, as she is in control of the telling, so too we come to understand through an earlier flashback that Juno was "on top," the one who initiated sex with Bleeker, approaching him sitting on that soon-to-be-bereft lounger and even leaving her panties behind as a souvenir.

Ellen Page constructs a character who is playing confident. Juno displaces her anxiety about what's happening underneath her own shorts onto a comment about how nice Bleeker's gold running shorts are: "Your shorts are especially golden." To which he responds, "My mom uses color-safe bleach." They discuss the pregnancy; Juno says she'll "nip it in the bud before it gets worse." They awkwardly admit that pregnancy usually "turns into a baby," and Bleeker, in wimp-fashion, foretells that this "typically happens when our moms and teachers get pregnant." In a nutshell, the golden fleece isn't that golden—the first unprotected sex can turn teenagers into moms and teachers.

The scene mixes Juno's seeming precociousness with Bleeker's naïveté, betraying that teenagers don't really know who they are yet. Such a sense of identity/conversational confusion, in which confidence mixes with the "hell, if I know?" tone, occurs more palpably later in the film when, faced with her father's critique about "being that kind of girl," Juno confesses: "I don't really know what kind of girl I am." And, indeed, the indeterminacy of these characters, how they will interact and what they say to each other, defies the simple "bundle of traits" model of Hollywood character development. We don't really know what kind of girl Juno is, as she is a more complicated, richly developed character over the course of this film than is Hollywood's norm.

For instance, we think our punk rock girl will "nip it in the bud," reminiscent of that other girl-centered, point-of-view-driven teen picture, *Fast Times at Ridgemont High* (1982). In the earlier film, main character Stacy has a bad one-afternoon stand and goes it alone to an abortion clinic and has the procedure offscreen. The scene renders abortion as a naturalized part of teenage girls' experiences. Directed by Amy Heckerling, the film has become arguably the most progressive U.S. teen film, shot from a girl's point-of view. Much more cynical, Juno seems a character suited to follow in Stacy's shoes, a twenty-first-century teenage version of Heckerling's fable. However, when Juno goes to the abortion clinic, named "Women Now," ironically evoking Shakespeare's "Now is the winter of our discontent," the narrative moves in a different direction.

Critics lambasted the regressive politics of Juno going to term, not opting for an abortion. And, if we place it alongside *The Waitress* and *Knocked Up*, the other pregnancy narratives of the year, the film does appear as a flight from 1970s, post–*Roe v. Wade* feminist politics. However, I would argue that one must see this film as a remaking of *Fast Times* from Diablo Cody's point of view, namely the product of Catholic high school culture. Almost everyone who has been to a Catholic high school has experienced the story of the "pregnant girl who goes to term." That story has not, before *Juno*, been told without becoming a morality tale. It is not the moral placards of sin and judgment that turn her off to abortion when Juno goes to

Women Now, but the notion that her baby has fingernails (granted, this scene hearkens to the discourse of the pro-life movement that often reduces the complexity of pregnancy to the corporeal details of the fetus). Juno enters the Women Now waiting room, and all she can hear are the amplified diegetic sounds of women's fingers scratching, scraping, and tapping. Fingernails are organic matter that is decomposing, representing circularity. Redeemed from melodramatic excess, the Women Now scene is only six minutes long. It's crucial, it's in there, but we as an audience must move on and realize that in 2006 the teenage birthrate rose 3 percent, reversing a fourteen-year decline (Stein). The moment Juno runs out of the clinic in the first weeks of her pregnancy, she embraces the film's seven-month narrative. And this is the narrative of many teenage girls, made famous by 2008 headlines of teenage Gloucester girls making a pregnancy pact.[1]

The film constructs a loving Midwestern family tableau, a distinctively lower-middle-class vision. Juno's father is a heating/cooling guy and her stepmother, Bren, is a nail technician with her own salon; the latter springs into action once Juno confesses that she's pregnant and plans to carry the child to term for adoption. Readying the prenatal vitamins, Bren declares to the film's little fertility goddess: "Well, you are a little Viking. First things first, let's get you healthy" and, of course, "prenatal vitamins do incredible things for your nails." And, her dad's comedic response: "Who knew Paulie Bleeker had it in him?"

Full of knickknacks and scrapbooks and other comfortable trappings of mid-century suburbia, Juno MacGuff's home world is the antithesis to the film's other home, that of the Lorings. Found in a *Penny Saver* advertisement, they are the "baby-starved wingnuts" who wish to adopt Juno's "precious blessing from Jesus in this garbage," as Bren sums up the situation. The Lorings act as the dysfunctional doppelgänger to the MacGuff family. Theirs is a world of McMansions, a home filled with Pottery Barn, antiseptic decorations and expensively framed photographs with the couple in choreographed action poses. From Juno's point of view, the mise-en-scène of the Lorings' home is one of collapsing interiors, where Mark Loring has his tiny, hidden band room (a vestige of his punk rock youth) and Vanessa has her perfectly organized tray of expensive perfumes tucked away in the bathroom. The home's cold décor and isolated rooms punctuate the suggestion that this "happy" yuppie couple is in fact slowly separating.

If Huck Finn traveled down the river only to realize the value of home, then Juno travels to the Lorings' with the lonely stretch of highway between these two worlds acting as a river that transports her home. After leaving their divided abode, she parks in front of her own, picks a blooming crocus, first sign of spring, and circles the bloom across her rounded stomach. The narrative is about ready to come full circle, as Juno cycles back home again. In voiceover, she confesses: "I never realized how much I like being home unless I've been somewhere really different for a while." Yearning for a stability that seems fleeting when her body gets puffier and puffier each day and prom comes and goes without her, Juno eventually asks the film's big questions in one of its most touching scenes. Standing in the kitchen after leaving the soon-to-be-divorced Lorings, she wants to know whether "two people can stay happy together forever," to which her father admits that it's not easy and he's happy with Bren. "Find the person who loves you for exactly *what* you are: good mood, bad mood, ugly, pretty," he advises. "The right person is still going to think the sun shines out of your ass" no matter what.

This exchange crystallizes the narrative's fable that is ultimately a tome to home. We are always in a state of becoming, as Juno is throughout this narrative. Chance and the world act upon us, and we react back. Who one appears to be, ugly or pretty, is not important; it's the self known, the reliable what, that is important. Though the seasons may change, Paulie Bleeker's cross-country team always cuts a reliable swath through the mise-en-scène, an apt visual motif for the film's focus on a narrative of becoming that connects yesterday with today and tomorrow. So as she gives birth to the baby, allowing the now single Vanessa Loring to adopt him (Vanessa possesses a similar adaptive constancy), Juno returns to Paulie Bleeker, now in love with the boy who never stared at her stomach when she was pregnant, who instead met her eye-to-eye. Though no Dorothy, and pregnancy is surely not Oz, Juno in fact returns to where she began. She and Paulie sit in his front yard, play their guitars, constructing yet another performative tableau, closer but the same.

Judd Apatow and the "Bromance"

In an embedded scene in *Superbad*, the two main characters, friends Evan (Michael Cera again) and Seth (Jonah Hill), hang out in Evan's bedroom after school. While hefty Seth plunders skinny Evan's wardrobe looking for an outfit to wear to a high school graduation party, the one party to which these nerds have been unlikely invited, Evan sits in the corner playing a video game. As the two boys discuss Seth's limited fashion options in a closet filled with Baby Gap size clothes, Evan comments on his frustration with the video game: "You know I have to kill these guys because you don't negotiate with terrorists, with terrorism. . . . God, these fuckin' terrorists multiply like bunnies. . . . Where did I leave the M-16?" Eventually, the game's pulsing gun sounds subside, as Evan puts down the control, complaining, "Why do they make that if you can't even win? Then why I am I fuckin' playing?" The camera cuts to a point-of-view screen shot of the game, wherein a lone police/military officer fires futilely at a building filled with unseen terrorists. Game over.

The game is a veiled reference to the first-person shooter video games made popular in late 1990s, and, more specifically, to the World War II game *Call of Duty*, which released its fourth version, *Modern Warfare*, the year "Apatown" (the term for the writer, director, producer collective led by Judd Apatow of *The 40-Year-Old Virgin* fame) took over Hollywood. With a plot that crosscuts between storylines and utilizes flashbacks from individual soldier's perspectives, *Modern Warfare* transplanted its fighting to the contemporary milieu, specifically the "terrorist-ridden" Middle East. Evan thus enters into a fantastical Middle East war zone in this different rendering of an after-school special. These scenes remind us that such games, calibrated for high school boys, are the perfect recruitment tool and work beautifully when paired with the elaborately produced, video game–inspired army commercials screened in theaters before movie previews. This is cross-media product placement at its cinematic best. Evan's audible frustration while playing this war game acts as a meta-commentary on the futility of an Iraq war. To repeat his question, "Why do they make that [war] if you can't even win?"

Within the veneer of a high school nerd film that focuses on three boys in their last few weeks of high school before they ship off to college, *Superbad* references the U.S.'s military escalation through the film's prolific allusions to battle and brotherhood. The film is a reminder that, though there is no draft, boys encounter the virtual presence of war each and every day in their homes. As a generic feast, the film cites from a series of war/buddy films, from *Star Wars* and *Platoon* to *Forrest Gump*. The boys' desperate and hilarious attempts to make it to a party and "save each other" remind us that the most intimate of buddy movies tends to be staged against the backdrop of battle (later in the film, Seth carries a passed-out Evan out of a party, walking for miles home in an homage to the classic war trope of a soldier carrying an injured man to safety). Their third friend, Fogell in his "McLovin" persona (akin to an avatar), actually enters into a first-person shooter situation during the movie's parallel narrative. Trying to purchase alcohol for the cohort, Fogell-as-McLovin finds himself in the midst of a convenience store robbery, after which police officers Slater and Michaels take him under their wing, giving him a circuitous ride to the party. So as Evan and Seth encounter one pedestrian obstacle after another on their way to Jules's, McLovin is fantastically sutured to Officers Slater and Michaels. The latter live out a game-style evening, shooting guns and taking part in car chases, all of which emerges as a night of high jinks.

While Evan, Seth, and Fogell spend much of the film worrying about college and getting laid, reminiscing about earlier "dick operations," men a few months older than they are heading off to war, with record numbers dying by year's end. Thus, the fallen in this film (Seth gets run over twice by a car in the film and Fogell gets punched out while trying fretfully to buy alcohol) allude to many war dead whose unseen coffins fly in daily to Dover Air Force base (Kerley and Heussner). As spectators witness their struggles to make it to a party and find a girlfriend for the summer, the film constructs a tale of male bonding against seemingly insurmountable obstacles, one that bespeaks a desire for an intimacy with those "other" boys fighting elsewhere. The latter can only be rendered through memes and State of the Union addresses, less real than video game figures.

If war creates love between men, then the film also inversely traces the outlines of the "love is war" metaphor. Seth and Evan are in love, as, cueing title for a future Apatow film, Seth later admits to Evan: "I love you, man." While the plot focuses on three very different nerds (proof that nerds come in all shapes and sizes) trying to buy alcohol and make it to a senior party, the more central narrative is that of Seth and Evan reconciling themselves to their eventual separation, as Evan plans to go off to Dartmouth, leaving Seth behind, like a fallen marine, to attend the local university. Evan's inevitable departure fuels Seth's own frenetic desire to find a girlfriend or lose his virginity, whichever comes first, over the course of this torturous picaresque night, alluding to Martin Scorsese's *After Hours* (1985). A graduation party at gorgeous classmate Jules's house becomes the battleground for proving his heteronormative might, with the hopes of finding a female substitute for Evan. Though the initial quest is to walk in the door with loads of booze, impress the party's women, and score some action, as the narrative progresses the holy grail changes shape, becoming that moment when Seth can physically embrace Evan and confess his love.

Friends since eight, enrolling in the same classes by day and attending sleepovers at each other's homes most nights, Evan and Seth's onscreen relationship typifies the twenty-first-century "bromance," a new genre that has elicited mixed critical response. According to one critic, "The bromance formula mixes poignant character-driven and feelings-based relationship drama with raunchy humor," emerging as R-rated male melodramas (Walker). For others, they are a male-centric variation of the romantic comedy (move over Nora Ephron), which favor the "bawdy bonds between

In *Superbad* (Greg Mottola, Columbia), the bromance of two nerds tests their masculinity and discovers their friendship. Digital frame enlargement.

men over heterosexual romance" (Walker). From these descriptions, the bromance has encroached upon and appropriated traditional women's genres and has raised the ire of a few feminist critics. In an editorial in the *Guardian*, Sady Doyle reductively laments that in these films "men seem to love each other primarily because they aren't women."

The various definitions and responses to these films suggest the inherent instability of generic categories or any homology (narrative formula) that tries to contain and confront the contradictions of the historical and cultural present. As a pastiche of melodrama, romantic comedy, buddy/war films, with a twinge of road movie, the bromance illustrates Timothy Corrigan's notion that "genre seems invariably to overdetermine, mimic, repeat, and shuffle its structures so excessively that what is most designated is a contemporary history that insists it cannot be ritualized according to a single transhistorical pattern" (138). The bromance challenges not only genre's codified borders but, as it does so, also navigates and negotiates that other liminal terrain, "the treacherous middle stretch of the modern homosocial continuum," or the spectrum of same-sex interactions between men (Sedgwick 88). The bonds between men are as nimble and unstable as the contours of genre. Nerd boys like Evan, Seth, and Fogell need each other in the emotional desert of high school. And yet, as Eve Sedgwick has argued, "intense homosocial desire is at once compulsory and the most prohibited of bonds" (187). One public display of affection too many between these boys may elicit a "homosexual panic," the fear that arises in a homophobic culture when straight men's love for each other could be confused for that other desire that dare not speak its name. Such panic is usually accompanied by homophobic and misogynistic displacement, which *Superbad* hilariously illustrates when Seth, after waking up and finding himself cozily sleeping alongside Evan, declares, "Your mom has big tits," and then races out of the house.

The film ironically illustrates the continuum of such male bonds, as it narrates the Seth/Evan relationship as one of confrontation, acceptance, and then separation. The film's early misogyny and homophobia—Seth's relentless references to sexual conquest and calling Fogell "Fagell"—eventually disappear as they meet up with their respective crush objects at the mall. *Superbad*'s ending is a *Dr. Zhivago* moment, when the boys depart with their prospective girlfriends: Evan to buy a new comforter for college (a Seth substitute) and Seth to help Jules pick out makeup (Seth openly confesses to wearing makeup during those awkward acne years, ameliorating the film's earlier gender divide). In a shot-reverse-shot from the boys' point of view, they look wistfully at each other as Seth rides down the escalator, moving farther and farther from Evan. This lingering shot stresses both their literal and figurative separation. Perhaps things will never be the same when women are involved, and such may be the case in a heteronormative culture that discourages such profound forms of male intimacy. The film nevertheless leaves us with a utopic longing for a future in which Evan and Seth can be close to each other as well as women.

In the other major Apatow film of the year, *Knocked Up*, the bromance takes a more misogynistic turn. The film focuses on the problematic male bonds of late-twenty- and thirty-year-old men. With a split narrative and point of view dividing male and female characters, the film focuses on the inexplicable one-night stand between Allison Scott (a gorgeous *Hollywood E!* producer) and Ben Stone (a ragamuffin, unemployed stoner); the proverbial had-too-many drinks engenders a pregnancy, the most regressive pregnancy narrative of the year. Of course, the couple meet in a bar, ignoring Officer Michaels's paternal advice to Fogell/McLovin in *Superbad*: "You don't want to meet a chick at a bar, man. . . . You gotta go to other places. You gotta go to spin class, a farmer's market, a pumpkin patch, given the time of year. Just somewhere social, nonthreatening." *Knocked Up* presents the nightclub as the threat, a threat to single, successful women everywhere.

Though they barely know each other, in the blink of an eye Allison decides to follow through and have a baby with Ben, even though it may jeopardize her emerging career. The narrative's (and Allison's) refusal to imagine abortion as an alternative bespeaks the film's favoring a male point of view. Though the parallel narratives come together, the film tends to focus more on Ben's obstacles in facing romantic commitment and father-hood. Allison's primary narrative function is to redeem Ben from his slacker bromance ways. She enables Ben to enter into heteronormative culture, one ineluctably tied to capitalist production and reproduction. As Allison delivers their baby, Ben is delivered into corporate cubicle culture, isolated from his male friends.

Allison and her sister, Debbie, are cast as shrews, harping on the men in their lives for not buying into bourgeois bliss (the women are associated with commodities—shopping, giving elaborate parties, and circulating themselves in nightclubs). Meanwhile, Ben and Debbie's husband, Pete (Paul Rudd), stand in contrast to this female culture that attempts to con-tain them. With a stable of children and a constantly complaining wife, Pete sneaks off to play fantasy baseball with a group of men every week and starts to spend more time with Ben, even taking a trip with him to Las Vegas. Yet the film suggests that Pete has been so thoroughly domesticated that there's no going back. For instance, in a scene in a Vegas hotel room, Pete counts the number and variety of chairs in the room and notes the brilliant fabric choices. It's just a matter of time before Pete's back ensconced in home, ordered around by Debbie, and turned into a veritable ottoman. Instead of resolving his misery, the film renders him as resigned to his fate. In all of the film's funny episodes brims a desire to break out of the yuppie emasculating, suburban fantasy. The fact that this fantasy is exclusive to women, something they perpetrate on men, represents a back-lash against feminist ideals.

Inexplicably, *New Yorker* film critic Richard Brody listed *Knocked Up* as the eighth best film of the decade, a list that included films by Godard and Sembene, among other cinematic greats. Celebrating a new kind of comedy, Brody declares: "Judd Apatow discovered, or rediscovered, the trick of the great silent clowns—to put funny people on screen—and to make it per-sonal." And *Knocked Up* is a more personal and more cynical bromance than *Superbad*. With its unlikable female characters, *Knocked Up*'s misogyny limns a collective frustration with a new baby boom culture and a new bread-winner ethic, one that resonates differently from that of the 1950s–1960s. It's never an option for Ben to become his baby's caregiver, with the prospect of having baby playdates with other fathers. This is a figuration of male bonding not available in our cultural discourse of child-raising. Instead, the expectation is that he must get a job as good as if not better than Allison's in order to be a proper father/husband/breadwinner. Few films of the decade have ventured to offer such a cynical appraisal of marriage, illustrating a gender divide that is still economically motivated. *Knocked Up* is prescient in many ways, predicting a bourgeois bubble that would burst the following year, accompanied by skyrocketing unemployment rates, and, by 2010, a record low in contemporary U.S birthrates. From such a vantage point, we cannot help but think that Ben should have kept his "dick in a box," to reference a popular "Saturday Night Live" skit circulating the web in 2007–2008, rather than enter into a domestic fantasy that, like *Modern Warfare*, was impossible to win in the film's terms.

The Fantastical Real: *Enchanted* and *Lars and the Real Girl*

As with every year, the year's cinema was given over to illusions, or what Karl Rove has euphemistically referred to as "creating new realities." A beater car turned into a celestial robot (*Transformers*); a country rat turned into a Parisian chef (*Ratatouille*); and Steve Buscemi turned into a romantic leading man (*Interview*). Indeed, the cinema has always had a tendency toward exploring not only physical reality but also the "realms of history and fantasy" (Kracauer 176), and many filmmakers, like Méliès and his heir Disney, have "rendered dreams and visions with the aids of settings that are [by design] anything but realistic" (178). With advances in editing, mobile camerawork, and special effects alongside a narrative causality that invites the spectator into a seamless fictional world, Hollywood endeavors to make the fantastic real. In fact, one of the primary goals of conventional narrative cinema is to transform the reality of a flat, two-dimensional screen into the illusion of a three-dimensional space in which the spectator is encouraged to enter and participate vis-à-vis an identification with a central character who motivates the story. We are not supposed to notice the cuts between shots, the transition between scenes, the elision of space and time in a two-hour movie that imagines a week or a winter of its characters' lives. As the theater lights darken and the projector flickers on, we are to forget those popcorn-munching people sitting around us, leaving "real" time and our physical bodies, and enter into the cinematic window that beckons us toward another, more fantastic reality—one in which the hero diffuses the bomb, the girl gets the guy, and all live happily ever after in the fade to black.

Of course, a number of films have parodied such closure and the way in which the cinematic apparatus lulls us into its world: Buster Keaton's *Sherlock, Jr.* pierces the closing, happily-ever-after fade into black by questioning what was "made in the fade," as Patricia Mellencamp has argued;

Woody Allen has a movie character step out of the film and interact with his audience in *The Purple Rose of Cairo*, reversing the fantasy of inter-subjective projection; and *Total Recall* satirizes the causal, character-driven Hollywood narrative by having its main character, who may be suffering from a delusion, get the girl and save the world at the end, all that a movie could ask for. Similarly, melding "fictional" and "real" worlds, one of Disney's top-grossing films of the year, *Enchanted*, adapts the princess film for an audience of older girls inured to the happy lull of the Disney formula and reflexively projects the formula onto a consumerist everyday.

Enchanted begins with an animated rendering of Cinderella's castle. Along with Mickey, the castle denotes the Disney brand. Its silhouette graces the center of the Disney Pictures logo, and the bricks-and-mortar version of the castle forms the spatial center of the company's theme parks. As the company's promotional copy describes it: "Cinderella Castle is the iconic fairy-tale fortress that serves as the gateway to Fantasyland in the Magic Kingdom theme park. It is not only one of the central icons of Walt Disney World Resort, but its romantic beauty has also come to represent all of the Walt Disney Company. . . . Step inside Cinderella Castle and it's like you are walking into a fairytale come true" (Cinderella). The Castle-as-logo, like Mickey Mouse, "absolutely transcends the relationship to specific com-modities leaving only its visual consumption as a sign, which grants the consumer not only all of Disneyland and Walt Disney Enterprises, but all of popular culture [that is similarly thematized]" (Willis 56). The castle as sign narrates its own becoming, that which it signifies: a Disney picture that promises a happy ending.

The film begins with an animated starlit sky and the "When You Wish upon a Star" theme. Then, magically, fireworks ignite against this sky, whereupon the camera reframes to discover the eponymous castle, ablaze in cascading light with the "Walt Disney Pictures" logo in the foreground. Such an aural/visual mix is a gesture toward the theme park's evening fire-works performance and presents us with a series of packages that open up the Disney corporate brand. From this static, copyright tableau, the cam-era reanimates and tracks through one of the castle's windows and dis-covers a book, a pop-up book, of course, that motivates us into the film's animated world. According to Susan Willis, Disney constructs its con-sumers into "active theme builders and logo collectors—not narrators but instruments of the narration" (58). The opening sequence illustrates how the Disney apparatus frames and continues to reframe *Enchanted*'s narra-tive landscape, and the way in which we are positioned as "instruments of that narration."

Leaving the Castle, we transition from the book's storyboards to a typical, Technicolor Disney landscape, an animated world with chirping birds and talking rodents who provide acoustic harmony to a besotted princess who is in love with the prince she hasn't met. This is the familiar "Disney princess" formula: the desire for a rescuing prince who liberates the girl from her isolated domestic tower. Only minutes before her rescue, our princess, Giselle, has been fabricating a "dummy" prince made out of gathered material. With help from her fauna friends, she's all but finished with her faux love; all that is missing is a mouth and then, winkingly, the film introduces the song of "True Love's Kiss" sung by approaching Prince Edward (yet, as the film later reminds us, princes aren't supposed to speak, just rescue and kiss). His singing thus fills in the mouth and here we have the gobbledygook of Disney romance.

The film's cloying opening sequence is itself a self-contained narrative: a near-fatal fall of a princess attempting to flee a marauding monster who is rescued and kissed by "her" longing prince. After the rescue, Prince Edward brings her to his castle where a wedding is forthcoming—the made in the fade. Yet the film challenges its own closure, opening a window onto another narrative and leaving the castle again. Alluding to *Snow White* and *Cinderella*, Prince Edward's stepmother, in disguise as an old hag, is jealous of Giselle and lures her to a waterfall for a last wedding wish. Giselle duly notes that all her wishes have come true, yet she nevertheless stands before the waterfall, and, signaling the end of such tales, wishes "and they both lived happily ever aft . . ." The hag then pushes her in, and Giselle falls into the abyss of her own desires. So much for happily ever afters.

This moment undoubtedly resonates with the generations of girls who, bewitched by Disney movies, stood before suburban mall fountains and chucked their pennies in, all the while dreaming of becoming "a princess who finds her prince charming." Instead of a prince, the only wish to come true was a piece of Sbarro pizza within the lush surroundings of the food court. Giselle's wish leads to a similarly (dis)enchanted future, as she spirals into the "real" of New York City. Through an interstitial real/fantastical landscape, she takes corporeal form (as Amy Adams). Moving through a dark winding landscape between fantasy and real realms, Giselle eventually becomes real by being figuratively shat out of the Disney romantic fantasy, emerging from a manhole cover above the city's sewers into one the dirtiest intersections in the universe: Times Square. This is the logical birth canal from the womb of Disney. Yet, what is Times Square now but a version of New York Disney, albeit one that Giselle will have to get used to?

And so we are presented with *Enchanted*'s real life that fuses the Disney princess formula with a conventional romantic comedy, literally so, as elements of the formula invade the core narrative of Giselle's meeting a divorced divorce lawyer who's a single dad (Patrick Dempsey). The film's continual irony mocks the Disney princess formula: What would happen if a princess called New York's voluminous rodents to help clean house? What could be more annoying than having a sew-happy princess using one's house as the fabric for her dresses? How silly to break into musical song with other Central Park loonies? And, playing off *Pretty Woman* (1990), imagine if our princess substituted the fairy godmother for a day of credit card purchases with her soon-to-be stepdaughter?

The Disney animated formula continually acts as an unconscious that slips through the narrative's cracks, especially through the intermixing of animated and corporeal characters. Although the film purports to mock its origins in the Disney fantasy, hence its many allusions to Alice's falling in and out of the rabbit hole (four entrances and exits through the beloved sewer), the film collapses its worlds, suggesting how the Disney fantasy anchors the twin narratives. The film's coerced happy ending, in which all disguised princes and princesses romantically unite, illustrates a remixing of various Disney-inspired narratives for an irony-driven twenty-first-century audience. These are the same tropes updated for contemporary audiences.

Enchanted tells us that the Disney formula can work in real life, which is what Disney has always been selling. Giselle ends up living happily ever after with her New York prince, creating her own dress clothing line at the end. In an interesting tie-in, in 2010 Disney Enterprises would partner with a bridal fashion design company to make knock-off Disney princess wedding gowns in order "to fulfill the dreams of brides everywhere who long to feel like a Disney princess" ("Alfred"). The Disney Fairytale Weddings collection aspires "to capture every girl's fantasy of feeling like a princess on her wedding day, while being inspired by the magic and identity of each Disney Princess" ("Alfred"). The promotional copy individuates the seven gowns along with their respective princess muse. Each possesses a unique identity; nevertheless, as a Disney executive informs us, the brand makes "gowns accessible to all brides at a broad retail distribution and affordable prices" ("Alfred"). The collection reminds us that, as Anne Friedberg and Charles Eckerdt have argued, the movies are extensions of shop store windows, selling the fabric of the princess formula for only $599.

While Disney continually insists that fantasies are potential, another film from the year has a dramatically different take on the relationship between fantasy and reality. The little indie film *Lars and the Real Girl* focuses on how "reality is a production of fantasies," to quote French film-maker Chris Marker. In its stark mise-en-scène and exploration of madness as a way of seeing anew, *Lars and the Real Girl*'s narrative pathologizes and yet embraces its title character's "delusional disorder." In a stark upper Mid-west location, Lars lives in a converted garage space adjacent to his brother and sister-in-law's large farmhouse. The cold, gray sepia landscape punctu-ates not only that it's winter's beginning but also the isolated frozen world in which Lars exists, entombed in the knowledge that his mother died dur-ing his childbirth, after which his father became a shadow to depression. We are to assume that, aside from a few years of boy bonding with this brother, who quickly went off to college and abandoned him, Lars has led a solitary life. He's the man in a cubicle, literally so: he works in a cubicle, at an anonymous company, where he avoids as much human interaction as possible, and then every evening he returns to the tiny room where he stares into emptiness. The film suggests that this is a perfectly acceptable reality (Lars is obedient, polite, and, for the most part, invisible). He fears any intimacy that might lead to abandonment. Even the touch of another causes Lars pain.

Yet his sister-in-law intrudes upon this world. Pregnant and wanting connection with the uncle to her soon-to-be child, Karin continually pesters Lars to enter into their home that has been partially willed to Lars. And, whether or not she realizes it, Karin motivates Lars's emotional migra-tion. Her pregnancy restages the trauma of his own birth/loss, one that he literally carries with him: he wears, as a scarf, a birth blanket his mother knitted for him. A vestige of his mother's touch, the blanket acts as an ex-pressive prop throughout the film: he gives it to Karin when she sits out-side in the cold (thereby embracing her but also signaling his concern over her pregnancy); later, during their courtship, he folds it over the lap of his delusional love, Bianca; and, as he conquers his fears of abandonment, he eventually relinquishes the blanket.

In the film's second scene, set in the repeatedly figured small-town church, Lars hears a sermon that motivates his desire for human connec-tion: "Love another. That, my friends, is the one true Lord. Love is God in action." Afterward, riffing off the sermon, an older townswoman, Mrs. Gruener, discovering Lars has no girlfriend and is not gay, advises Lars to "not leave it too long. It's not good for you." After this humorous scene, we realize that Lars has listened intently and will become an ever-faithful servant to the Lord. He does so by visiting the "Real Doll" website (intro-duced to him by his pervy officemate) and purchases a life-size, ana-tomically correct doll, Bianca, that's "flexible" as well as "half Brazilian,

As the doll Bianca assimilates into the community, Lars rediscovers his own lost ability to interact with others in *Lars and the Real Girl* (Craig Gillespie, MGM). Digital frame enlargement.

half Danish." Indeed, he constructs an elaborate biography: Bianca is disabled and in need of a wheelchair (so that she can be portable); she was raised by nuns and is "on leave now so she can experience the world"; she is shy, sexually naive, and religious, preferring to sleep in a guestroom in the house. As the town's doctor later explains, such a delusion "can be a communication, a way of working something out." Since Lars projects pieces of his own history onto Bianca (her parents died when she was young, he tells us, but she "never felt sorry for herself"), we begin to understand the complex nature of Lars's delusion. As Bianca sits in a wheelchair unable to move, Lars too has been left emotionally debilitated.

With Bianca, the socially dysfunctional Lars plays pretend and in the process learns how to communicate with others and be in and of the world. He does so by letting her venture forth and be accepted by the community. Hilariously, the entire town begins to share in the delusion, playing along with Lars initially but eventually forming their own attachment to Bianca. Bianca volunteers at the hospital in the children's cancer ward (children love dolls), works part-time at a mall dress shop, and gets a salon makeover under the guidance of the townswomen. She's even elected to the P.T.A. By film's end, the busty, Brazilian sex doll has turned into a regular Plains woman, wearing prairie skirts and bad Norwegian sweaters and attending Sunday church services.

With lingering shots of Bianca's emotionless silicone face, the film continually reminds us that she is "just a doll." Inevitably, Lars will leave her, restaging his own mother's death on his terms, burying Bianca on the eve of Karin's delivery. On one hand, these close-ups help divert us to the other love interest in the film, Lars's endearingly quirky co-worker, Margo, the ostensible "real girl" of the film's title, as reviewers have noted. Yet Margo is also fairly loopy: she forms close attachments to the stuffed animals that litter her cubicle's coves and wears ridiculous moose-patterned sweaters. As a character sketch of small-town life, the film reminds us that almost everyone can find themselves on a page of the *Diagnostic and Statistical Manual of Mental Disorders*. As Mrs. Gruener tells a gathering of the church's elders: "Sally, your cousin puts dresses on his cats. Hazel, your nephew gave all of his money to a UFO club. Ernie, everyone knows your first wife was a klepto [and that's] why she's buried in a pair of my earrings. These things happen. Lars is a good boy," to which everyone nods.

At film's end, Bianca is as real as she is perceived, and perhaps more so as she ignites Lars's great social adventure akin to that of literary history's most inspiring delusional hero, Don Quixote. In one scene, Lars reads parts of Cervantes to Bianca, specifically the passages that describe Quixote's imaginary love, Dulcinea: "And so he solaced himself with pacing up and down the little meadow, and writing and carving on the bark of the trees and on the fine sand a multitude of verses all in harmony with his sadness, and some in praise of Dulcinea." We then become aware that *Lars and the Real Girl* is a revision of *Don Quixote*. The film carves our hero's sadness in the isolated transitional shots between scenes, in images of a stark north woods or an orphaned snowfield. As Quixote constructs a knight of himself and romantic consort out of a farm girl/prostitute, so too does Lars emerge from his lonely garage to become the perfect suitor for a sex doll turned real girl.

Like Quixote, what Lars most desired was "having another hermit there to confess him and receive consolation from." And it is through a series of confessions to his doctor, Gus, Karin, Margo, and others in the town, all those who eventually share in his delusion, that Lars leaves solitude behind. When Karin tells Lars that everyone has taken a fancy to Bianca and cared for her mostly out of love for him, Lars possesses the knowledge that he will never be abandoned again. Bianca thus offers him a window onto human companionship. Unlike Quixote, who dies tragically when others play cruel practical jokes mocking his delusion, Lars survives, yet his survival demands Bianca's departure. In that way, Lars is both Quixote and his conspiring friend, Sancho, who breaks Quixote's fantasy, leading him inevitably to die facing the real. As Sancho, Lars presents himself with a silent, dying Bianca, breaking his own spell. Yet instead of falling, like Quixote, into a consuming melancholia, Lars embraces the town, a place inhabited by fellow loonies. At the end of the film, during her funeral, mother's baby blanket gone, Lars wears the sweater Bianca had worn during their romantic outings, a pink Nordic number, of course, as well as a whimsical carnation boutonniere. Bianca had come north "so she [could] experience the world." As she is buried in memory, in the same big box in which she had been shipped, Lars takes a little of Bianca with him, as he too has experienced the world. The film ends with him taking a walk with Margo, his ever-sheepish smile still present but no longer afraid to hold someone's hand. We can only hope that Lars may discover more giants to joust, that there's still a little insanity in the north woods to inspire life's romantic fictions.

NOTE

1. During the summer of 2008, American news outlets descended on Gloucester, Massachusetts, when officials released the story that eighteen Gloucester High School girls, some as young as fourteen years old, had made a pregnancy pact with the hopes of raising their children together. School officials blamed popular films such as *Knocked Up* and *Juno*, which, they argued, romanticized unplanned pregnancies.

2008

Movies and a Hollywood Too Big to Fail

THOMAS SCHATZ

The defining event of the year was of course the economic recession, which began in the United States with the collapse of several mammoth Wall Street firms and quickly became a global crisis. But while the recession devastated the American economy and left many major industries in chaos, it had remarkably little effect on the movie industry— or on the dominant Hollywood powers, anyway. Hollywood enjoyed a record boxoffice year both at home and abroad, grossing $9.8 billion domestically and $28.1 billion worldwide, and for the first time ever all six major studios—Paramount, Warner Bros., Disney, Twentieth Century–Fox, Columbia, and Universal—took in over $1 billion in both the domestic and foreign markets. Whereas Wall Street giants like AIG and Goldman Sachs were saddled with "toxic assets" and required federal assistance to survive, the studios continued to thrive due to the relative health of their parent conglomerates and the worldwide appeal of high-cost, high-yield block-busters like *The Dark Knight*, *Iron Man*, *WALL-E*, and *Quantum of Solace*. Washington's rationale for bailing out the Wall Street giants (after Lehman Brothers declared bankruptcy in September) was that they were "too big to fail"—perhaps a specious argument in Wall Street's case, but an uncannily apt description of the Hollywood majors and their signature blockbusters. In terms of both the global marketing-and-distribution operations of the major studios and the sheer size and sizzle of their spectacular tentpole mega-films, Hollywood indeed had become too big to fail.

But while the major studios and the mainstream movie industry surged, the independent film sector continued its rapid, seemingly inex-orable decline. The economic recession in no way caused this decline, which began much earlier, but it certainly accelerated the downward spiral for both the conglomerate-owned indie-film divisions (New Line, Fox Searchlight et al.) and for the scores of genuine independents. These com-panies still supplied the bulk of theatrical releases and enjoyed occasional hits; indeed, the year began with an Academy Award ceremony dominated by two indie-division films, *No Country for Old Men* (2007) and *There Will Be Blood* (2007), and it ended with the release of *Slumdog Millionaire*, an even bigger critical, commercial, and Oscar-winning success. But the independent and art-cinema ethos that had been so crucial to American filmmaking since the 1990s was increasingly undercut by "commercial" imperatives that now seemed to pervade and shape every phase of the industry.

This essay charts these developments and assesses the key films and filmmaking trends of the year, relying heavily on press accounts and box-office data—the latter indicating a film's popular appeal as well as its commercial value. Critical reception is also gauged, particularly the response (and attendant discourse) of leading print critics like Manohla Dargis and A. O. Scott of the *New York Times* and David Denby and Anthony Lane of the *New Yorker*. They may be a vanishing breed, but these top critics still set the terms and tone of critical discussion on American film, and their writing is especially useful when dealing with recent (and still current) films. Just as the trade press accounts provide the first draft of film history, these critics provide the first phase of evaluation, theoretical formulation, and canon formation. I push beyond critical reception into textual analysis in a few cases, notably *The Dark Knight* and *Slumdog Millionaire*, which clearly (in my view) were the most significant films of the year in terms of popular appeal, critical response, and commercial success. The two films also warrant close attention as the most obvious instances of the dual trajectory of franchise blockbusters and indie films that has characterized Hollywood filmmaking since the onset of the modern conglomerate era.

Hollywood, Indiewood, and the Curious Case of TimeWarner

The American film industry was dominated and effectively controlled by a cartel of global media conglomerates, which owned all six major Hollywood studios along with numerous indie-film divisions.[1] The major studios released about 150 feature films and captured over three-quarters of the domestic market (the United States and Canada). The nine leading conglomerate-owned indie divisions—a k a "Indiewood"—released another 80 films, which garnered about 10 percent of the domestic market. Meanwhile, the genuine independents, which comprised another 135 companies, released nearly 400 features, some two-thirds of all theatrical releases, but captured less than 15 percent of the market. Most of this business was by two companies, Lionsgate and Summit, the only profitable independents in North America. In fact, the conglomerates' major studios and indie division, along with these two independents alone, accounted for over 95 percent of the domestic theatrical market.[2]

Thus the movie industry had coalesced into three distinct classes of producer: the major studios, focusing primarily on big-budget, wide-release films; the conglomerate-owned indie divisions, with mid-range films assured of marketing and distribution; and the genuine independents, whose low-budget films struggled to find distribution and rarely turned a profit. Of the genuine independents, only Lionsgate really qualified as a studio—earlier termed a "mini-major"—releasing nineteen films that grossed over $400 million domestically. That put Lionsgate ahead of all the conglomerate-owned indie divisions in terms of both output and income, but commercially well behind the major studios. A few other independents released an occasional mid-range film—Summit's *Twilight*, Weinstein Co.'s *The Reader*, UA's *Valkyrie*—but the vast majority of independent releases were low-budget films made for well under $10 million, usually without the benefit of a marketing budget or access to the lucrative ancillary markets (foreign, cable, home video, etc.). There were breakout Indiewood and independent hits, notably *Slumdog Millionaire* (from Fox Searchlight) and *Twilight*, but these were increasingly rare in an industry ruled by the studios' high-stakes, wide-release blockbusters.

The motion picture operations of TimeWarner, the world's leading media conglomerate, underwent significant changes that provide considerable insight into the general state of the conglomerate-controlled movie industry. The central figure here was Jeff Bewkes, who rose through the executive ranks at HBO to become CEO of TimeWarner in January. He immediately turned his attention to the movie division, which generated less than one-tenth of TimeWarner's $35 billion in revenues but attracted excessive attention—and criticism—from stockholders, Wall Street, and the press. In the first of a series of bold moves, Bewkes resolved a long-standing dispute between filmmaker Peter Jackson and New Line's founder and chief executive Robert Shaye, which had stalled TimeWarner's multi-billion-dollar *Lord of the Rings* series since 2004, when franchise auteur Jackson stopped working on a two-film "prequel" to the series based on *The Hobbit*, due to a feud with Shaye over his profit share in the *Rings* films. Bewkes settled the dispute with Jackson (in an out-of-court settlement for undisclosed terms) and reactivated the Hobbit films, with Jackson, who had moved on to other projects, attached as executive producer for a reported $40 million fee and the films to be shot in his New Zealand facility.

Bewkes's next move involved New Line and the *Rings* franchise but addressed much deeper structural and operational concerns. Moviemaking at TimeWarner was conducted by four separate entities: Warner Bros., its major studio; New Line, an indie division acquired in the mid-1990s that ascended to mini-major status with the *Rings* franchise in the early 2000s; and two other recently launched indie divisions, Warner Independent Pictures (WIP) and Picturehouse. In late January Bewkes informed Shaye and partner Michael Lynne that their contracts would not be renewed, and weeks later he announced that almost all of New Line's other 600 employees were also being fired and that the indie division was being integrated into Warner Bros. This move came, ironically enough, within days of the Oscar ceremony dominated by two indie-division films, *No Country for Old Men* and *There Will Be Blood*. Both were co-produced by Miramax (owned by Disney) and Paramount Vantage, two erstwhile indie divisions that themselves had been integrated into the conglomerate owner's major studio. In fact, the New Line purge recalled the earlier Miramax scenario, in which founders Harvey and Bob Weinstein were sacked and their once-mighty indie company was downsized and folded into the Disney studio, surviving mainly as a brand name—and a hollow one at that, as conglomerate Hollywood steadily abandoned indie-film operations. Bewkes contended that the main reasons for his moves were fiduciary responsibility to TimeWarner stockholders (to optimize profits) and his own campaign to streamline marketing and distribution operations—which he now redirected to the other indie divisions.

The leading candidate to write and direct the Hobbit films was Guillermo del Toro, whose wondrous *Pan's Labyrinth*, an Oscar contender a year earlier, was released in the United States by Picturehouse. Created in 2005 via a merger of an independent distributor, Newmarket Films, and New Line's art-film subdivision, Fine Line, Picturehouse focused on imports and art-cinema acquisitions. Besides *Pan's Labyrinth*, its recent imports included *La Vie en Rose*, a biopic of French cabaret singer Edith Piaf starring Marion Cotillard, who had just won the Oscar for Best Actress. But critical prestige and Oscar wins were not sufficient to keep Picturehouse alive. In early May, one week after announcing it had closed a four-year deal with del Toro to helm the Hobbit films, TimeWarner closed both Picturehouse and Warner Independent. Picturehouse was given several months to wrap up its current slate, while WIP was immediately shuttered and its projects moved into Warner Bros. These included *Slumdog Millionaire*, to be discussed later, but it's worth mentioning here that Warner Bros. decided the film did not merit theatrical release, deciding instead on a straight-to-DVD deal.[3]

Actually, *Slumdog Millionaire* was barely a blip on Warner Bros.' radar in May. The studio was now the only motion picture company at TimeWarner, and it was heading into a summer season of wide-release blockbusters, global marketing blitzes, and make-or-break opening weekends. The season began disastrously with *Speed Racer*, the Wachowski brothers' $120 million live-action cartoon, but soon picked up with two mid-range New Line hits, *Sex and the City* and *Journey to the Center of the Earth*. Both did excellent business during a record-setting summer whose top hits included *Iron Man*, *Indiana Jones and the Kingdom of the Crystal Skull*, *Hancock*, *WALL-E*, *Kung Fu Panda*, *The Chronicles of Narnia: Prince Caspian*, *The Incredible Hulk*, *Wanted*, *Tropic Thunder*, *The Mummy: Tomb of the Dragon Emperor*, and *Hellboy II: The Golden Army*. Warner Bros.' *The Dark Knight* was the biggest hit of the summer—and of the entire year, for that matter, grossing over one billion dollars worldwide to become the most profitable film at the box office since *Titanic* (1997). A consummate tentpole, *The Dark Knight* accounted for 30 percent of Warner's record boxoffice this year, surpassing its closest competitors, *Iron Man* and *Kingdom of the Crystal Skull*, by over $200 million in the United States alone. It was also among the top critical hits in a year when remarkably few films of any stripe, Hollywood, Indiewood, or independent, were embraced by a solid majority of America's top critics.[4]

The Dark Knight and Hollywood's Superhero Syndrome

The Dark Knight was a definitive film of the era, culminating a decade dominated by effects-driven, fantasy-oriented blockbuster franchises—*Lord of the Rings*, *Harry Potter*, *Spider-Man*, *Shrek*, *Pirates of the Caribbean* et al.—and revitalizing (along with *Iron Man*) Hollywood's comic-book superhero subgenre. *The Dark Knight* was also distinctive in terms of its financing. It was co-produced by Warner Bros. and Legendary Pictures in a long-term, multi-picture deal set up specifically to develop blockbuster franchises; its first releases were *Batman Begins* (2005) and *Superman Returns* (2006).[5] Interestingly enough in light of the recession, Legendary began as a private equity firm whose investors included AIG, Bank of America, and Columbia Capital. Thus the Warner-Legendary partnership brought Wall Street's and Hollywood's "too big to fail" entities, megabanks and media conglomerates, into direct alignment, creating assets than proved far less toxic commercially than subprime loans and credit default swaps.

After the successful Batman reboot, Warner-Legendary quickly greenlit a sequel—a remarkable reversal of fortune, considering the series' disastrous decline a decade earlier.[6] *Batman Begins* marked a clean break from the 1990s cycle and a complete reauthoring of the Batman myth, as its title suggests, with filmmaker Christopher Nolan reworking the foundation story and reimagining its style and narrative technique. A hyphenate writer-director with indie-film credentials, Nolan asserted his creative control on *Batman Begins* and established working methods that he refined on *The Dark Knight*, realizing a degree of authority that few filmmakers in the franchise blockbuster realm other than James Cameron and Peter Jackson have achieved. This included Nolan's decision to stage much of the action in "practical locations" (principally in Chicago) and to direct much of the extensive second-unit work. Nolan also relied less heavily on computer-generated effects, digital previsualization, and other high-tech gimmickry than other filmmakers working in the big-budget fantasy realm. Stylistically, the new Batman films did recall the dystopic, nightmare vision of the Tim Burton–directed Batman films, *Batman* (1989) and *Batman Returns* (1992), although Nolan's depiction of Gotham was decidedly more somber and realistic than Burton's hyper-stylized, postmodern metropolis.

After successfully reviving the franchise on his own terms, however, Nolan decided to revisit Batman's epic battle with the Joker in a film that was heavily indebted to—if not a remake of—Burton's 1989 film. The scenario for *The Dark Knight* originated in 1940 with Bob Kane and DC Comics, and in fact the Joker was among Batman's first arch-enemies. The screenplay was based on a story by David S. Goyer, who co-scripted *Batman Begins* with Nolan and envisioned two subsequent films focusing on the Joker and another key figure from the Batman mythology, Harvey Dent/Two-Face. But Nolan, who co-scripted *The Dark Knight* with his brother Jonathan, decided to condense the drama into a single film in which Dent's crusading district attorney teams with Batman against the Joker, but then is transformed into a psychotic killer. The initial alliance between Batman (Christian Bale) and Dent (Aaron Eckhart) is complicated by their mutual love interest, assistant DA Rachel Dawes (Maggie Gyllenhaal, who replaced *Batman Begins*'s Katie Holmes), and the alliance and the love story are destroyed midway through the film, when the Joker kills Rachel and grotesquely maims Dent, thereby creating Two-Face and radically changing the film's emotional and dramatic stakes. Nolan deemed Dent's transformation "the arc of the story,"[7] although *The Dark Knight* is driven from the outset by Heath Ledger's Joker—a character devoid of backstory in this iteration, who is presented from the outset as the nemesis function personified, already a master criminal and self-described "agent of chaos" bent on controlling crime in Gotham and battling Batman.

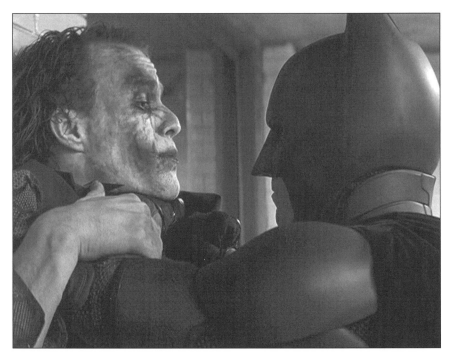

Between cynicism and moral complexity: the art of darkness in *The Dark Knight* (Christopher Nolan, Warner Bros.). Digital frame enlargement.

Thus *The Dark Knight* is essentially a three-character drama—or four, including Gotham, which emerges as a distinct character not only in the depiction of the city itself but also its citizenry, who figure prominently in the story. Or five, if we consider Batman and Bruce Wayne as separate figures, which perhaps we should. Bruce Wayne is plagued throughout by self-doubt and deep moral conundrums, and is given considerable face time, so to speak, both with Alfred (Michael Caine), more advisor than butler in this version, and also with Lucius Fox (Morgan Freeman), the chief executive and high-tech wizard at Wayne Enterprises. Both Alfred and Fox counsel Wayne as he wrestles with issues of individual responsibility, vigilante justice, and so on; but once he suits up the moral questions vanish. Batman is all business—that is, fighting crime by whatever means necessary, with no apparent qualms about torture, extradition, or the letter of the law. His key concern is of course the Joker, a figure who is permanently masked and operates only in the realm of comic-book fantasy, but who steadily coalesces into the film's most compelling, multidimensional figure. The Joker is left hanging at the end of *The Dark Knight*, both literally and figuratively, although any prospect of a sequel closed when Ledger died of an overdose of prescription drugs in January. The film was then in postproduction and Warners had just launched a massive marketing blitz keyed to Ledger's performance, including a four-minute Joker-focused trailer and a special IMAX teaser of the robbery that opens the film and introduces his character. Ledger's death added a macabre twist to the ad campaign, making him a sudden, posthumous sensation even before the film was released. He had already garnered attention and an Oscar nomination in Ang Lee's 2005 indie hit, *Brokeback Mountain*, but it was his performance as the Joker that would secure his stardom.

The Dark Knight opened in mid-July on over 4,300 screens in North America and another 4,500 screens overseas, breaking a succession of box-office records en route to a global take of just over one billion dollars. The critical reception was overwhelmingly positive, although most reviewers, and notably the leading American critics, invariably hedged due to the film's franchise status and comic-book lineage. *Variety*'s Justin Chang, for instance, praised the film as "seriously brainy pop entertainment," while Manohla Dargis in the *New York Times* wrote that "it goes darker and deeper than any Hollywood movie of its comic-book kind." David Denby of the *New Yorker* was among the film's severest and most articulate detractors, bemoaning its persistent explosions, unintelligible fight scenes, and pounding score: "In brief, Warner Bros. has continued to drain the poetry, fantasy, and comedy out of Tim Burton's original conception for *Batman* (1989), completing the job of coarsening the material into hyperviolent summer action spectacle." Denby found the film lacking in "craftsmanship" and "jammed together" without coherent shape or structure. "*The Dark Knight* is constant climax," he wrote; "it's always in a frenzy, and it goes on forever." He did cite "one startling and artful element," namely "the sinister and frightening performance of the late Heath Ledger"—a point on which critics were virtually unanimous.

Critics also were split on *The Dark Knight*'s open-ended resolution, in which the Joker is captured, Two-Face is killed, and Batman decides to assume the blame for Two-Face's killing spree, thus ensuring Dent's posthumous reputation as a crusading hero while branding himself as a social pariah. Chang and Denby typified the disparate critical response. For Chang, Nolan "bravely closes the story with both Gotham City and the narrative in tatters, making this the rare sequel that genuinely deserves another." Denby dismisses the film's ending as symptomatic of its deep cynicism, noting that the studio was "making sure, with proper calculation, to set up the next installment of the corporate franchise."

Yet another bone of contention was *The Dark Knight*'s political stance, particularly regarding 9/11 (first invoked in the film's poster art) and the Bush administration's War on Terror. This was addressed not only in reviews but also, interestingly, in editorials that began to appear within days of the film's release. Two diametrically opposed op-eds by mystery novelists written for the mainstream press—"Art of Darkness" by Jonathan Lethem in the *New York Times* and "What Bush and Batman Have in Common" by Andrew Klavan in the *Wall Street Journal*—set the tone for this debate and underscored the narrative and thematic ambivalence of the film itself. For Lethem, "a morbid incoherence was the movie's real takeaway, chaotic form its ultimate content"—a view not far from Denby's. "In its narrative gaps, its false depths leading nowhere in particular, its bogus grief over stakeless destruction and faked death," opined Lethem, "'The Dark Knight' echoes the civil discourse strained to helplessness by panic, over-reaction and cultivated grievance." Klavan, conversely, saw a film "of real moral complexity" that was, among other things, "a paean of praise to the fortitude and moral courage that has been shown by George W. Bush in this time of terror and war." He also noted wryly that the movie "was making a fortune depicting those values and necessities that the Bush administration cannot seem to articulate worth beans."

Interestingly enough, *Iron Man* had not provoked this kind of discourse two months earlier, despite a plot involving Afghani-terrorist heavies and a U.S. industrialist who is exploiting the War on Terror to make a fortune and rule the world. This generally indifferent response to *Iron Man*'s politics may have been due to its comic-book tone and playful take on the superhero genre—more Marvel Comics than DC, one might say—although its jingoistic Americanism distinguished the film from the other superhero fantasies, including *The Dark Knight*, and probably contributed to its relatively subpar performance overseas (where *Iron Man* did only half as well as both *The Dark Knight* and *Indiana Jones and the Kingdom of the Crystal Skull*). Iron Man actually had been a politicized figure since the comic-book hero first appeared in 1963, initially doing battle in Vietnam, and was revived for the Gulf War in the early 1990s. This year's movie version updated the action to Afghanistan, retaining a hip-ironic, comic-book mentality toward the war and the military-industrial complex. The blockbuster film was designed for a much wider audience, of course, which raised some troubling questions that only a few critics addressed. Denby in the *New Yorker* was amused by Robert Downey Jr.'s portrayal of Tony Stark/Iron Man, which "turns the movie into a hundred-and-eighty-five-million-dollar put-on." But he found the film's treatment of the Afghan conflict in comic-book terms "enraging"

Auteur-star Clint Eastwood returns as Walt Kowalski, a grumpy vigilante determined to protect his home and rescue his neighborhood in *Gran Torino* (Clint Eastwood, Warner Bros.). Digital frame enlargement.

and wondered whether audiences would see beyond the put-on and the juvenile geopolitics, noting quite correctly that "more Americans will see this dunderheaded fantasia on its opening weekend than have seen all the features and documentaries that have labored to show what's happening in Iraq and on the home front."[8]

Another vigilante drama that did extremely well at the box office but without invoking 9/11 or the War on Terror was Clint Eastwood's *Gran Torino*.[9] The seventy-eight-year-old icon-auteur directed and starred as a long-retired, recently widowed, guilt-ridden, and chronically ornery codger who refuses to abandon his inner-city Detroit home and becomes embroiled in the racial conflicts and gang violence that plague the economically blighted community. The setting is indeed a war zone, and one in which the protagonist takes action and ultimately prevails—albeit in ways that radically undercut our expectations of both the Eastwood persona and the comic-book heroics of vigilante fantasies like *The Dark Knight* and *Iron Man*. The specter of 9/11 shadows another of the year's offbeat hits, *Cloverfield*, a monster movie for the new millennium in which the destruction of Lower Manhattan is captured, run-and-gun, by fleeing youth on a hand-held camcorder. A savvy work of digital cinema that was propelled by viral online marketing and myriad transmedia tie-ins, *Cloverfield* repeatedly invokes the nightmare scenario, the panicked citizenry, and the ubiquitous, YouTube-ready amateur video coverage of the 9/11 attacks. And while it shares with *The Dark Knight* and *Gran Torino* a dystopian vision of the modern American metropolis, in this grim monster-on-the-rampage fantasy there is no hero, caped or otherwise, to intervene—although it's implied that the military has exterminated Manhattan (and the last two camera-wielding survivors) in order to save it.

"Cut to the Chase" and the Aesthetics of Action-Adventure: *Crystal Skull*

Along with the superhero blockbusters, another significant strain of male action-adventure films—by now, without question, Hollywood's governing meta-genre—included adventurer-hero fantasies like *Indiana Jones and the Kingdom of the Crystal Skull*, *Quantum of Solace* (the inexplicably titled new James Bond installment), *The Mummy: Tomb of the Dragon Emperor*, and *Journey to the Center of the Earth*. All were blockbuster franchise films and sizable global hits. The Indiana Jones and James Bond installments were by far the most expensive, spectacular, and successful of the lot; moreover, they shared a kinship and lineage that defined and shaped the current male-action ethos. In the late 1970s, George Lucas, Steven Spielberg, and writer Lawrence Kasdan consciously designed the Indiana Jones series to revitalize the 1960s Bond cycle starring Sean Connery, and thus formulated the definitive 1980s franchise. *Crystal Skull* was the first new series installment since 1989, when *Batman* and *Indiana Jones and the Last Crusade* were the year's top films. The two franchises repeated that feat this year, with *Crystal Skull*'s success overseas and on DVD (and the reissue of the earlier series installments) carrying it to the billion-dollar range alongside *The Dark Knight*. Significantly enough, Paramount had retired the series despite its success because of escalating costs and the crippling revenue-sharing deals with Lucas, Spielberg, and star Harrison Ford. Paramount was now willing to resume the series for two reasons: because Lucas et al. agreed to restructure their deal, and because the current global market conditions meant that the studio-distributor of a billion-dollar hit reaped several hundred million dollars in interest payments, production cost recovery, and distribution fees.[10]

Crystal Skull was not exactly a reboot, although the two-decade hiatus between installments and the series' massive influence since then made

Crystal Skull a rather unusual sequel. One astute assessment of its peculiar status was critic Terrence Rafferty's piece in the *New York Times*, "Indiana Jones and the Savior of a Lost Art"—a title that seemed to signal a pre-release puff piece, although it proved to be anything but that. Rafferty opened by lauding the "free-spirited inventiveness" of the 1980s Indiana Jones cycle—those "unabashedly preposterous movies" and exercises in "high-adventure pulp" that revitalized the "stodgy and joyless action genre," inflecting it with physical comedy, wry humor, and "vivid, intricate, ingeniously choreographed action." But certain elements of those earlier Indiana Jones films hardened into formula in the scores of action-adventure films they spawned, so that by now "the pace had to be blindingly fast; the stunts insanely elaborate; the villainy extra-villainous; the hero's attitude blithe, insouciant, almost sociopathically cool." In the process, the development of character and story were overwhelmed by sheer movement. Thus the contemporary action film is "a good deal snappier" but tends "to skimp on exposition and go straight for sensation . . . as if cutting to the chase were not a metaphor but literally the cardinal rule of filmmaking." Rafferty closed the piece with a severe swipe at both Spielberg and the industry at large: "If only everybody else in Hollywood hadn't tried to imitate him, he'd have nothing to be ashamed of at all."

Not surprisingly, Spielberg and his collaborators—including writer David Koepp, whose credits included the Jurassic Park films, *Mission: Impossible* (1996), and *Spider-Man* (2001)—imitated not only themselves but also their imitators, creating in *Crystal Skull* a film that was utterly lacking in the wit, charm, inventiveness, and energy of its forebears. The problems and the compromises are clear from the opening, a can-you-top-this set piece in which the hero survives a computer-generated atomic blast in the Nevada desert—and a scene in which both Harrison Ford's age and Spielberg's reliance on CG-spectacle are painfully evident. At age sixty-three, in fact, Ford was now several years older than Sean Connery had been when he portrayed Indy's father in the 1989 installment (Connery was fifty-nine and Ford forty-four at the time). Here Indy is the father figure, with Karen Allen (back from the first Indy flick, *Raiders of the Lost Ark* [1981]) as his long-lost love interest and Shia LaBeouf his rebellious offspring. Updating the Jones saga to the Cold War 1950s, which only seemed to reinforce its archaic, formulaic qualities, *Crystal Skull* was a predictable, by-the-numbers rehash that drew mixed reviews (especially from top critics) and tepid fan response, but was a global boxoffice hit nonetheless. The filmmakers were literally and figuratively going through the motions, which may have contributed to the film's success. And the outcome was yet another clear indication that, for a franchise of this caliber with the name-brand talent and marketing heft behind it, commercial success was virtually assured while critical reception seemed all but irrelevant.[11]

Not surprisingly, the run of summer male-action hits led to some critical grousing, but most of it was directed toward the superhero syndrome generally rather than specific films. A. O. Scott of the *New York Times*, for instance, who shared regular reviewing duties with Manohla Dargis, followed her upbeat review of *The Dark Knight* with a piece entitled, "How Many Superheroes Does It Take to Tire a Genre?" "I'm willing to grant that 'The Dark Knight' is as good as a movie of its kind can be," wrote Scott. "But that is damning with faint praise." There is only so much that "first-rate actors" and "bankable auteurs" can do with this kind of material, given the overriding requirements that were growing more rigid with every comic-book blockbuster—relentless action and CG spectacle, breathless and incoherent plotting, pounding musical scores to punctuate clockwork explosions, overwrought and overlong climactic battles, and troubled protagonists whose problems vanish when they suit up for action. But Scott ultimately acknowledged that his grousing was wishful thinking. The superhero fantasies clearly had revived and revitalized the male-action film and were now the coin of the global entertainment realm, and thus Hollywood's investment in comic-book franchises was bound to increase.

Reformulating Fantasy: *WALL-E*

Hollywood's heavy output of action-adventure fantasies was complemented by a number of G- and PG-rated hits, most of them either computer-animated films or live-action fantasies designed for family audiences, along with a smaller but growing number of films aimed at women and girls. While the young-male "quadrant" remained Hollywood's primary target market, families and females were targeted as well—and invariably with films that were equally fantastic and effects-driven. Family films included seven of the top twenty-five boxoffice hits in both the domestic and worldwide markets, and as in previous years the prime purveyors were Disney and its subsidiary, Pixar. The Disney studio's top hits included *The Chronicles of Narnia: Prince Caspian*, *Bedtime Stories*, *Bolt*, and *Beverly Hills Chihuahua*, while Pixar gave Disney its biggest commercial and critical release with *WALL-E*. Other studios were now creating family-friendly hits as well, notably Paramount with *Kung Fu Panda* and *Madagascar: Escape 2 Africa*, and Fox with *Dr. Seuss's Horton Hears a Who* and *Marley and Me*. All these underscored the value of family entertainment as a renewable resource, thanks to their library and sequel value and their unequalled licensing potential, and it also explains the studios' enormous investment in these films—*Prince Caspian*'s $225 million budget, for instance, and *WALL-E*'s $185 million price tag.

In terms of popular reception and critical prestige, *WALL-E* was without question the most significant computer-animated release of the year, and a film whose crossover appeal beyond the family audience reaffirmed Pixar's singular capacity for sophisticated storytelling and innovative technique. A post-apocalyptic romance between two robots who literally save the human race from its sedentary, technology-dependent fate, *WALL-E* skewered contemporary society's rampant commercialization, dehumanization, and toxic self-destruction. Thus it's both paradoxical and deeply ambivalent about technology, progress, and commerce—*WALL-E* is, after all, a big-budget, computer-generated, globally marketed Hollywood movie. But despite its pessimistic take on current social conditions and the fate of the planet, the story and tone are decidedly upbeat and open to a possible sequel, as well, with the human race returning to Earth at film's end after signs of organic life unexpectedly appear on our devastated planet.

WALL-E 2 is unlikely, considering Pixar's general resistance to sequels, although Disney already has transformed the film hit into a successful entertainment franchise via videogames, toys, theme park attractions, and so on. Franchising is Disney's singular strength, of course, and among the year's more intriguing developments was the mobilization of established franchises across media platforms. The year's top-selling DVDs included reissues of two animated Disney classics, *101 Dalmatians* (1961) and *Sleeping Beauty* (1959), while its original straight-to-video (and cable) productions included *The Little Mermaid—Ariel's Beginning* and *Tinker Bell*.[12] After successfully launching the *High School Musical* series on its cable channel (and its record division), Disney went with a theatrical release of *High School Musical 3: Senior Year*, which was a major worldwide hit. Disney also enjoyed crossover success with a concert film featuring its cable series and recording star, Miley Cyrus (a k a Hannah Montana).

These Disney franchises are important not only for their transmedia expansion but also their cultivation of female audiences—a market that only Disney has consistently pursued with any success, although major (and unexpected) hits like *Twilight, Sex and the City*, and *Mamma Mia!* certainly caught the other studios' attention. All three grossed over a half-billion dollars in theatrical and DVD release, making them far more profitable than Hollywood's action-adventure and animated hits due to their lower production costs, and all three were based on presold story properties and thus had solid franchise potential. They also countered Hollywood's male-action films, offering instead live-action female fantasies with a degree of verisimilitude offset by an overtly fairy-tale story and tone. All three are indebted to the traditional Hollywood melodrama—and particularly the "woman's film" with its virtuous, long-suffering female protagonist. In fact, all three employ themes of self-denial and sexual abstinence, albeit in PG-13 or R-rated films that dwell on sexual coupling—only to end "happily" enough, as seven of the eight principal female protagonists in the three films ultimately couple with an appropriate (or at least satisfactory) male counterpart.

Slumdog Millionaire and the Deepening Decline of American Independent Film

The phenomenal success of *Slumdog Millionaire* notwithstanding, the year was difficult for Indiewood and truly desperate for genuine independents. Simply stated, indie and independent films had to be more blatantly "commercial"—and thus more costly—for any real hope of success in a marketplace ruled by tentpole blockbusters and bloated star vehicles. Moreover, any equation between independent production and quality filmmaking, whether real or imagined or conjured up by marketing experts, was not in evidence. The reception by top critics of both the indie and independent films that did any business at all was remarkably weak; in fact, the top twenty-five studio releases fared better with critics than the top twenty-five films in both the indie and independent sectors. The Motion Picture Academy continued its ritual celebration of independent filmmaking, with the majority of Oscar nominations in every major category going to indie-division and independent productions. But most of these films were commercial failures, with award-season marketing campaigns adding to their losses, and all but a few of their producer-distributors were in desperate financial straits or on the brink of extinction.

A widely publicized appraisal of the independent film scene was provided by industry veteran Mark Gill in a keynote address at the Los Angeles Film Festival in June, shortly after the closing of Warner Independent Pictures and Picturehouse. In that talk, "Yes, the Sky Really Is Falling," Gill pegged the odds of commercial success for a low-budget independent film at one-tenth of one percent—a calculation he based on current market data. "The strongest of the strong will survive and in fact prosper," Gill said. "But it will feel like we just survived a medieval plague. The carnage and the stench will be overwhelming."[13]

One could hardly dispute this view, as the genuine independent sector collapsed and the Indiewood arena was decimated by closings and consolidation. As recently as 2005, thirteen of the top twenty-five distributors were conglomerate-owned indie divisions operating independently from their major studio counterparts. Now only four enjoyed even "quasi-autonomous" status—Fox Searchlight, Focus Features (owned by NBC Universal), Sony Pictures Classics, and Sony Screen Gems—while the other survivors like New Line, Miramax, and Paramount Vantage were essentially indie-film brands controlled by major studios. The surviving indies enjoyed a few critical and commercial hits, notably Fox Searchlight's *Slumdog Millionaire* and *The Wrestler*; Focus's *Milk* and *Burn After Reading*; and Sony Classics' *Rachel Getting Married* and *Frozen River*. Sony Classics continued to provide American distribution for art-cinema imports, which included the acclaimed animated features *Persepolis* and *Waltz with Bashir*.

Sony Screen Gems was the only surviving indie-film division that continued to specialize in so-called genre and exploitation films—that is, low-grade, efficiently made action and horror films, teen comedies, and urban (African American) films—which had once been the purview of companies like New Line, Dimension, and Rogue as well. Screen Gems released only six films but did reasonably well commercially. In fact, the domestic box-office returns of its top hit, the critically reviled teen horror film *Prom Night*, were roughly equal to Sony Classics' grosses on *all twenty-four* of its more prestigious releases.[14] Clearly there was still a market for genre and exploitation films, although now that demand was being met (as it had been decades earlier) by true independents. Chief among these was Lionsgate, which was in a veritable class by itself among the genuine independents in terms of both output and revenues. As usual, Lionsgate eschewed franchise blockbusters and costly star vehicles, with Oliver Stone's Bush biopic, *W.*, and Sylvester Stallone's *Rambo* its only high-profile releases. Far more profitable among its nineteen films were low-budget genre franchise entries like *Saw V*, *Transporter 3*, and Tyler Perry's urban comedies *Meet the Browns* and *The Family That Preys*. The only other successful independent company was another, far less productive genre outfit, Summit Entertainment, thanks to the success of its teen-horror hit, *Twilight*, one of five releases that accounted for 75 percent of its domestic boxoffice revenues.[15]

In terms of popular and critical reception, commercial success, and art-cinema credentials, the year's top film clearly was *Slumdog Millionaire*. It was one of only four indie films consistently embraced by top critics—along with *Milk*, *The Wrestler*, and *Rachel Getting Married*—and the only indie division release among the top fifty boxoffice films (other than New Line's mainstream releases, mentioned above). *Slumdog Millionaire*'s box office was fueled by award-season success, notably at the Oscars and BAFTA (British Academy) ceremonies. And its actual release was a major story as well—a fairy tale unto itself and a good indication of the challenges faced by indie and independent companies. *Slumdog Millionaire* was co-produced by Film4 and Celador, both British companies with strong television ties; in fact, Celador had been a major force behind the global TV phenomenon "Who Wants to Be a Millionaire?" They commissioned screenwriter Simon Beaufoy, whose credits include *The Full Monty* (1997), to adapt the award-winning novel *Q & A* by Indian writer (and diplomat) Vikas Swarup. Beaufoy's script attracted director Danny Boyle (*Trainspotting* [1997]; *28 Days Later* [2003]); after Boyle was attached, Warner Independent put up $5 million, roughly one-third of the budget, against North American distribution rights. But WIP was closed in May and the film was moved into Warner Bros., whose executives decided on a direct-to-DVD rather than a theatrical release.[16] At that point Fox Searchlight stepped in and picked up the distribution rights. After a successful run at the Telluride, Toronto, and London film festivals, Searchlight gave *Slumdog Millionaire* an extremely limited release (on ten screens) in November. The film drew rave reviews and built steadily at the box office until the Oscar nominations in January and the award ceremony in February, which propelled it to runaway hit status. The morning after the Academy Awards, the *Times* of London predicted that it might double its current worldwide box office; it did even better than that, eventually grossing $141 million in North America and $365 million worldwide.[17]

Slumdog Millionaire's success was no fluke, nor was it driven by a costly marketing campaign. On the contrary, the marketing budget (and screen count) expanded as the film performed, with word-of-mouth crucial to its success. Clearly the film was well suited to current industry conditions and struck a chord with audiences in the United States and abroad, although gauging those conditions and anticipating audience appeal had never been more difficult in the independent film realm. Mark Gill underscored those points in the keynote address mentioned above, given in June when *Slumdog Millionaire* seemed destined for DVD release. Ironically enough, Gill had been the chief executive of Warner Independent when it was launched in 2003 (he left in 2006), and in his speech he offered something of a formula for success in the dire independent realm. To wit: Spend at least $15 million on production, which would ensure the involvement of "professionals who know what they're doing to create emotional content that has a market." Develop projects with global appeal "that the whole world can embrace." Come up with "a good title" which, in turn, "should have many of the attributes that a movie needs to embody now." Gill specified five of those attributes: succinct and descriptive ("the film has to lend itself to brief encapsulation"); distinctive (a good film story that "takes the cliché and twists it"); provocative (a story with "incident, conflict, excitement . . . that hits a cultural nerve"); memorable ("avoids cotton candy" and has "the possibility of resonance"); and, finally, "not too dark" in what were "very dark times, for audiences the world over." These criteria were offered by someone with a distinguished track record in independent filmmaking whose passion for innovative, artistic work was tempered by the realities of the marketplace. These criteria also summarized the main selling points, literally and figuratively, of *Slumdog Millionaire*.

The film's costs met Gill's minimum and the project engaged seasoned professionals in all phases with the notable exception of its cast, which provided a means of cost control while enhancing the patina of realism. The star of *Slumdog Millionaire* clearly was director Danny Boyle, whose style well suited the subject and whose indie-auteur credentials were crucial to the film's popular and critical reception. The title was a brilliant high-concept stroke, encapsulating the story in a pithy paradox—social realism meets media-fueled fantasy—while forecasting its narrative trajectory and unabashed happy ending. The story itself was based on two utterly im-plausible premises: that between appearances on a nightly high-stakes quiz show, the police (in collusion with the program) would kidnap and brutally torture a contestant suspected of cheating, only to be convinced of his inno-cence and allow him to return to the live show hours later; and that the slum-kid's success on the quiz show is due to various occurrences in his life that now provide him with answers to a range of obscure questions. The premises generate a narrative that is both distinctive and provocative, in Gill's terms, giving a braided twist to multiple clichéd movie formulas—the coming-of-age story, the against-all-odds teen romance, the good brother/ bad brother gangster saga, and the rags-to-riches fairy tale set against the world's most popular and ubiquitous TV series format.

Slumdog Millionaire's most engaging feature is the deft interweaving of the three main narrative threads—the present-time police interrogation (which opens the film), the flashback reconstruction of the quiz show hours earlier, and the more complex reconstruction of the protagonist's life since his early childhood. These interwoven threads present the viewer with a "puzzle narrative" that recalls films like *Reservoir Dogs* (1992), *The Usual Suspects* (1995), and *Memento* (2000). *Slumdog Millionaire* also recalls *Citizen Kane* (1941), interestingly enough, in that a series of seemingly ran-dom questions from different interrogators (the quiz show host and the

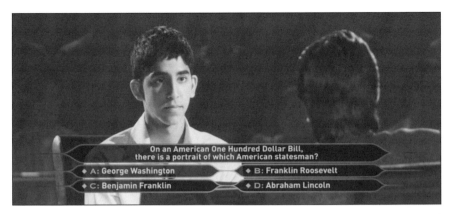

The year's biggest hit: a game-show narrative becomes part of a police investigation and the search through a traumatic past in *Slumdog Millionaire* (Danny Boyle, Celador Films). Digital frame enlargement.

police) motivate a *chronological* recollection of the protagonist's past life, which renders the complex narrative quite manageable. The readability and clear trajectories of the interwoven plot lines also allow Boyle and editor Chris Dickens to keep things moving at a rapid pace. The visual stylization of the different narratives by Boyle and cinematographer Anthony Dod Mantle are distinctive as well, with the alternating dream states of the torture sessions and the quiz show countered throughout with the semi-documentary treatment of everyday life in India, although the realist techniques (location shooting, natural lighting, mobile camera) give way at regular intervals to stylized music-video montages (usually in chase scenes) and Discovery-style travelogues.

The graphic depiction of the Mumbai slums certainly hit a cultural nerve and resonated with audiences, as did the brutal exploitation of the three orphans at the center of the story—the upstanding quiz show contestant, his ne'er-do-well brother, and the girl he loved and lost in childhood. But it's important to note that the "darker" aspects of *Slumdog Millionaire* are steadily displaced by the quiz-show and teen-romance plotlines. By the time the flashbacks end and the multiple stories converge roughly ninety minutes into the two-hour film, just in time for the deadline-driven final act to commence, the film's realist impulse is abandoned and its fairy-tale imperatives kick in. Our hero wins the quiz show—as we may have expected, considering the title—and thanks to his brother's redemptive (suicidal) sacrifice, he gets the girl as well. The lovers' reunion is celebrated in a closing dance sequence, a knowing nod to the film's Bollywood and Hollywood roots.

The critical response to *Slumdog Millionaire* was overwhelmingly positive but frequently qualified due to its fairy-tale story and narrative technique.[18] Manohla Dargis's *New York Times* review termed it "one of the most upbeat films about living in hell imaginable," but also one whose "joyfulness feels more like a filmmaker's calculation than an honest cry from the heart." Anthony Lane wrote in the *New Yorker* that the film's Dickensian impulses were overwhelmed by the "sheer fantasy" of the story, to which he willingly submitted. Kenneth Turan's review in the *Los Angeles Times* was rife with backhanded praise, deeming it "the best old-fashioned audience picture of the year, a Hollywood-style romantic melodrama that delivers major studio satisfaction in an ultra-modern way." Perhaps the most ambivalent of the positive reviews was David Edelstein's in *New York Magazine*, which pegged Boyle as "a director for whom brutality and slickness are so inextricable" who once again delivered "the kind of hyper-kinetic, every-shot-a-grabber kind of filmmaking that many attempt and few bring off."[19] Far less ambivalent in its assessment was the Motion Picture Academy. The most heavily nominated film was *The Curious Case of Benjamin Button* with thirteen, one shy of the all-time record. But the big winner was *Slumdog Millionaire*, which won eight Oscars overall.

Conclusion

Slumdog Millionaire's Oscar sweep said less perhaps about the merits of the film itself than about the quality of the competition, and also about the Academy's adamant if increasingly irrational celebration of an indie-film ethos that was facing extinction. The "Oscar snub" of *The Dark Knight*, which was not nominated for Best Picture (or Best Director), led the Academy brass to increase the number of Best Picture nominees from five to ten, although Warner Bros. seemed altogether unconcerned about the situation. *The Dark Knight*, after all, grossed more in its opening weekend ($158 million) than *Slumdog Millionaire* returned in its entire six-month run, carrying Warner Bros. to the top of the industry heap in terms of revenues and market share. In fact, the studio went on a tear in the first year of the Bewkes regime, with domestic box office alone climbing a phenomenal 20 percent over 2007—a trend that would continue for the next two years.

Despite this commercial success—and in many ways because of it—Hollywood in the late 2000s faced a deepening failure of a different sort. As the studios reaped record revenues year after year, the indie divisions had become a luxury that their parent conglomerates could not—and need not—afford. The events at TimeWarner made it painfully evident that the prospects for more adventuresome filmmakers were fading fast. Guillermo del Toro was one of many indie auteurs to seek refuge (and steady work) helming a studio franchise—a trend that accelerated after *The Dark Knight* and *Iron Man*, which made it not only cool but compulsory for the studios to attach directors with indie credentials to blockbuster franchises. Christopher Nolan and Jon Favreau brought a modicum of style and élan to those mega-productions, and they clearly won over a critical community long since resigned to Hollywood's pervasive franchise aesthetic. But there is no mistaking *The Dark Knight* and *Iron Man* for anything but what they are: well-crafted, predictable, by-the-numbers blockbusters. Indeed, they are emblematic of an industry more blatantly commercial and risk-averse than ever, an industry constitutionally resistant to innovation and independence, an industry increasingly wed to formulaic fantasies and infantile spectacles designed and dumbed down for an all-too-receptive worldwide audience.

NOTES

1. The so-called Big Six media conglomerates (and some of their key film and television holdings) included TimeWarner (Warner Bros., New Line, HBO, TBS, CNN); Disney (Walt Disney Pictures, Pixar, Miramax, ABC, ESPN); News Corp. (Twentieth Century–Fox, Fox Searchlight, Fox Broadcasting, Fox News); Viacom-CBS (Paramount Pictures, Paramount Vantage, CBS, MTV, Showtime); NBC Universal (Universal Pictures, Focus Features, NBC, USA);and Sony (Columbia TriStar, Sony Pictures Entertainment, Sony Pictures Classics, Sony Screen Gems). Note that Viacom and CBS split into two publicly traded companies in 2005, both of which remain principally owned and controlled by Sumner Redstone. Note also that Comcast in 2009 initiated a buyout of NBC Universal from its principal owner, General Electric, which is still pending.

2. The financial data throughout this essay, unless indicated otherwise, are culled from three principal sources: *The Numbers*, an online data service provided by Nash Information Services, available at http://www.the-numbers.com/; *Box Office Mojo*, available at http://www.boxofficemojo.com/; and the *Motion Picture Association of America*, whose annual reports on all phases of the film (and filmed entertainment) industry can be requested online at http://www.mpaa.org/researchStatistics.asp. According to the MPA, 606 features were released in North America this year. According to Nash, 150 companies released 635 films that sold at least 1,000 tickets. Only 13 companies captured a market share of 1 percent or more, while just 26 companies had a market share of 0.1 percent (one-tenth of one percent).

3. For a more detailed account of the Peter Jackson, New Line, Picturehouse, and Warner Independent contretemps, see my essay "New Hollywood, New Millennium." Note that del Toro left the *Hobbit* project in 2010, after working for two years in New Zealand with Jackson et al., when New Line's partner on the two-film project, MGM, failed to secure funding and firm up a start-date and schedule.

4. I rely here and throughout this essay on *Rotten Tomatoes*, the leading "aggregator" of film reviews, which can be accessed online at http://www.rottentomatoes.com/. According to Rotten Tomatoes, only *The Wrestler* [97 percent] and *WALL-E* [97 percent] had higher per-

centage of positive reviews from top critics than *The Dark Knight* [94 percent]. Also at 94 percent were *Slumdog Millionaire* and *Milk*, followed by *Iron Man* [92 percent], *The Bank Job* [90 percent], *Rachel Getting Married* [90 percent], *Frost/Nixon* [89 percent], *Forgetting Sarah Marshall* [89 percent], *Hellboy II: The Golden Army* [87 percent], and *Vicki Christina Barcelona* [82 percent].

5. On the Warner Bros.–Legendary Pictures "partnership," including the *Superman Returns* and *Batman Begins* co-financing deals, see McClintock; Kelly; and Galloway.

6. The previous *Batman* cycle included four films produced and distributed by Warner Bros. between 1989 and 1997. The commercial performance declined with each new film, leading Warner to abandon the franchise. *Batman Begins* (2005) grossed $205.3 million domestically and $372.3 million worldwide. *Superman Returns* (2006) grossed $200.1 million domestically and $391.1 million worldwide.

7. For an excellent article (cum interview) on the conception, writing, and execution of *The Dark Knight*, see Thompson *"Dark Knight."*

8. Note that *Iron Man* grossed $98.6 million in its opening weekend in the United States, and that Denby's assertion is accurate even if one includes the total worldwide gross of *The Hurt Locker* (2009), which was $48.6 million.

9. *Gran Torino* reportedly cost $33 million and returned $270 million worldwide. The *Curious Case of Benjamin Button* cost $150–160 million and returned $334 million; *Valkyrie* cost $80–90 million and returned $200 million; *Yes Man* cost $70 million and returned $224 million; *Seven Pounds* cost $55 million and returned $168 million.

10. On the restructured deal, see Eller.

11. According to *Rotten Tomatoes*, 61 percent of top critics responded favorably to *The Kingdom of the Crystal Skull*. The film grossed $317 million domestically and $787 million worldwide.

12. The reissues both returned about $40 million; meanwhile, *Ariel's Beginning* returned $38 million and *Tinker Bell*, a spinoff of *Peter Pan* (1953), generated revenues of $52 million.

13. Mark Gill, CEO of the Film Department, delivered the keynote address at the L.A. Film Festival Financing Conference on 21 June 2008. The full text of his talk can be found on Anne Thompson's *Variety*-sponsored film blog.

14. *Prom Night* grossed $43.8 million in the domestic market, with Sony Screen Gems taking in a total of $186 million overall fromits six releases. Sony Pictures Classics's top release was *Rachel Getting Married*, which grossed $10.3 million domestically. SPC's total domestic gross in twenty-four releases was $41.6 million.

15. Summit Entertainment grossed $232.7 million on six releases; *Twilight* alone grossed $176.9 million.

16. See Goldstein.

17. See Ayres, Mostrous, and Teeman. On the development and production of the film, see also Argy. According to Nash Information Services (see note 2), *Slumdog Millionaire*'s domestic release was expanded to 169 screens in early December and built to about 600 screens in January, when the Oscar nominations propelled its release to 1,600 screens. After its Oscars sweep in late February, the release was expanded to just under 3,000 screens.

18. According to *Rotten Tomatoes*, 94 percent of all reviews and 95 percent of those from top critics were positive.

19. See Dargis "Orphan's"; Lane; Turan "Life"; and Edelstein "Indian."

2009

Movies, a Nation, and New Identities

DANA POLAN

It is a perhaps inevitable and unavoidable temptation for the historian writing about any specific year to argue that his/her chosen slice of time was somehow especially meaningful and consequential: loaded with events that decisively altered the flow of time from then on. As the title of a book published in the year under consideration here would have it, *1959: The Year Everything Changed* (Kaplan). And insofar as any year, inevitably and necessarily, is the ground through which large currents of politics and culture pass and coalesce, it would be easy to make any particular year seem the one that did indeed alter everything.

Yet it would be no exaggeration to say that in the year that saw the inauguration of Barack Obama as forty-fourth president of the United States, something momentous, something unprecedented, something extraordinary had happened in the country. Power and governmentality in America had been redefined to include a new racial identity at the top. Years of racism and disenfranchisement had not been wished away, but this new presidency meant that the meaning of power in the country—who had it, who could aspire to it—had changed decisively. This seemed to be a new America, one in which diverse constituencies might begin to have more of a say and in which there might be new tolerance and new social goals for American peoples.

But even if the inauguration itself was an electrifying occurrence, it was only a punctual event in a larger history (which includes the long history of racial and ethnic struggles in America). Indeed, Obama's victory in November the previous year was probably the more spectacular happening (spectacular both in the sense simply that a black man was elected president and in the euphoric celebrations in the streets when the news came through), with the January inauguration itself coming both as a confirmation, albeit an inspiring one (here was a president who could indeed give rousing speeches redolent with signs of change), of an already anticipated hope *and* as a signal that now it was time to get down to work and to the negotiations and even, it must be said, the inevitable compromises and pull-backs of realpolitik.

Indeed, for all the change that the Obama victory heralded, there could be no absolute fresh start. On the one hand, the Bush presidency left the new administration with a complicated, even foreboding legacy: for instance, the dismal endurance of the wars in Iraq and Afghanistan; a banking and mortgage crisis that would eventuate in an international recession marked by home foreclosures, drastic rise in unemployment (and especially in length of unemployment for many Americans), budget slashing in both the public and private sector, failures of some nation's economies, and on and on; and an image crisis around America's standing in the world after all the revelations about torture, prisoner abuse, and general violation of human rights in the name of the so-called War on Terror.

Key to the ensuing right-wing assault on the Obama presidency was the role of media, including the Internet and, especially, shock-jock AM radio and right-wing TV (such as Fox News), which relentlessly went after Obama, harping on his every vacillation (even if some had been caused by the very desire to conciliate and not move too quickly in support of one faction over another) and painting him with broad strokes that ranged from the farcical (he was depicted as a traitorous socialist) to the racist. This was a battle waged over representation and public image, and if Obama's election had shown how much the politics of race were now on the agenda of America, the media assault made clear how much that politics for conservative white America was still fixated around the image of the racialized Other. It matters, then, that two of the biggest news stories of the year, ones that led to endless debate and discussion in the media, were also about the position of the charismatic black man in American life: the death of entertainer Michael Jackson in June and the budding sex scandal toward the end of the year around golfer Tiger Woods. (We might add to this list the arrest of black Harvard intellectual Henry Louis Gates in July at his home in Cambridge: here, too, was a story around race, less connected perhaps than the others to broad issues of celebrity but one that nevertheless catapulted into a major news story.)

As with the Obama presidency, these media events were very much about the publicness of racial identity and about what it might mean for black men to strive for forms of power and privilege in America: they showed that realms of entertainment and culture were also political through and through in contemporary America. For example, it is easy to see that much of the lascivious scandal-mongering in the Woods case had to do with mythologies of black male sexual voraciousness and also, perhaps, about the seeming impertinence of blacks in not keeping to their place (Woods had dared, in this view, to enter into a stereotypically white, leisured sport and there was no little degree of smugness in media coverage of his downfall). In their own way, the Jackson death and the Woods scandal were about the paths to success that had been open to blacks (often, these had indeed been limited to the sports and entertainment realms) and about the role of media both in building celebrity and in making it a fraught venture for the lives caught up in it.

If the media were thereby obsessed—to the point of morbidity—with the travails of celebrity black men, there also seemed to be a fascination with hitherto unknown, unassuming, and even common folk who proved themselves worthy of newfound celebrity by fighting the odds and showing exceptional talent: from quite different realms, two dramatic success stories that enraptured the public had to do with a commercial pilot (Chesley Sullenberger) whose plane lost power after takeoff but who saved his passengers by a daring landing on the Hudson River, thereby becoming a national hero, and with a frumpy would-be singer (Susan Boyle) who seemed at first to lack necessary glamour and stage talent only to surprise a worldwide audience with her mesmerizing performance on a TV musical competition, "Britain's Got Talent," and become an overnight global sensation.

The movies of the year played out concerns of failure of character and unexpected heroism in their own fashion. In particular, narratives of ethical downfall but also of opportunities for redemption run rampant through quite a number of films, from *Star Trek* to *The Hangover* to *The Taking of Pelham 1 2 3*. The last of these, for instance, updates the subway-train-held-hostage story of the original film (1974) to a new moral climate by having its trainman (Denzel Washington) be an ethically fallen figure who has taken a bribe and brought sin into his very household: the hostage crisis gives him a new reason for being and a chance to redeem himself in everyone's eyes (even the arch-criminal gains a new respect for him and engineers it so that his own eventual downfall is attributed to the trainman and makes him even more of a hero).

It is perhaps revealing that the newest and highly successful offering in the *Transformers* series had as its subtitle "Revenge of the Fallen"; it was all about the young hero trying to bring defeated and destroyed Transformers back into military readiness while trying to restore his own masculine image in his girlfriend's eyes. Even as many everyday Americans were facing the hard reality of economic destiny decided from afar, the movies would often mythologize an ordinary person who had every reason to pack it all in but who persevered and triumphed.

Movies and Masculinity: From
The International to *Paul Blart: Mall Cop*

Just as it is tempting to want to make any year seem the consequential one for ongoing history, it is likewise easy but risky to want to draw too close a connection between the content of a year and the content of the popular cinema of that year. Indeed, one intriguing phenomenon, so under the shadow of the recession, was the plethora of newspaper articles that tried to determine if the dire economic times were being reflected in the movies (or in attendance figures—up or down). Such journalistic musings might claim to explain something about the place of film in the culture at large, but ultimately their ubiquity makes them a symptom of the operations of film culture rather than a comment on it. In other words, they don't so much explain the movies as participate in and extend the very ambiguities that the movies represent in the fraught cultural moment. Typical is an article early in the year by Joseph Morgenstern for the *Wall Street Journal*, "When Bad Times Make Good Movies." Asking whether the recession will lead to more escapist fare, Morgenstern answers with a predictable "it's too early to tell" and offers the equally predictable hope that whatever path filmmakers choose, it will be one that leads to dramatically engaging films, no matter their tone and outlook. The point is not to criticize Morgenstern for not being more committal but to accept that he could do no better—that there is no evident way to say that the films of a moment really do speak clearly and unambiguously to the concerns of that moment.

Take, for example, a release from February, the action thriller *The International*. In an early scene, the two intrepid investigators (Clive Owen and Naomi Watts), who are trying to figure out why whistle-blowers about the shady dealings of a global bank are dying in suspicious fashion, meet with a rogue banker who clarifies the realm of super-high finance: "You control the debt," he explains, "you control everything. . . . This is the very essence of the banking industry: to make us all, whether we be nations or individuals, slaves to debt." In a year so much about banking crises—endless foreclosures and failure of subprime mortgages, escalating reverberations of Ponzi schemes, cascading failures of financial institutions, breakdown of pension funds and so on—and their worldwide rendition as a recession with devastating impact on myriad lives and institutions (for instance, the budget-tightening effects would be felt in higher education for years to come), it would be easy to imagine that *The International* is in this speech reflecting its moment in some particularly canny way.

But *The International* had long been in production before the year began, and it is only by random fate that this one film came to talk so seemingly directly of an immediate crisis. That randomness might itself be a caution against hasty assumption of cinema's direct reflecting of its times: why, if easy reflection-models work, would there have not been more films like *The International* to speak of the banking crisis? Why, conversely, did this one film not do so well at the box office if it resonated so trenchantly with its historical times? Except for films made quickly to cash in on some pressing news of the moment (as, for example, with some of the low-budget cinema of the 1950s or 1960s, which might try to exploit the salaciousness of news scandals), the scale of Hollywood film production leads generally to a situation in which the films at best capture broader cultural and social currents than reflect direct, specific events that have a discrete punctuality in time. Indeed, it is noteworthy perhaps that the rogue in *The International* offers his explanation to support an argument that the global, evil bank of the film is creating debt from unprincipled financing of military operations around the world: the bank scandal of the film (unchecked military financing) is not exactly the same one (vulnerability of mortgage networks and of personal investment programs) that troubled the world financial markets in real life in the year the film came out. Not that the film's paranoia doesn't also click with the times (after all, the period *was* one in which there were constant indications of collusion between banks and war machines), but it does so by picking up very broad, long-running motifs (banks and militarism, an issue not reducible to this year alone) and giving them quite specific narrative form in this one particular film.

If *The International* is of its time, it is so in the most general sense: it is, for instance, a film of worry at large-scale institutions, yet it is also a film that, like so many works of American popular culture across the years, invests in the mythology both that strong individuals can fight the system (Clive Owen is a fallen figure who by film's end redeems himself by not giving in to the corruption around him) and that large-scale evil institutions are only as strong as the individually strong and locatable figures who run them (so that in catching the global bank's boss after a breathless chase, Owen effectively puts an end to the bank itself). Evil is personalized, personified, and this allows for the mythologizing assumption that by catching individual criminals, the system rights itself. This narrative of personalized and individuated punishment is somewhat like a cataclysmic event of the year: namely, Ponzi schemer Bernie Madoff admitting (in March, one month after the release of *The International*) that he had indeed cheated a vast number of investors, big and small, famous and average, out of billions.

But the film's indictment of the insidiously guilty individual resembles the outrage against Madoff insofar as the movie and the judicial process here both work according to deep-set, long-running American ideologies by which the failures of the system are attributed to corrupt individuals, thereby allowing simultaneously for evildoers to be castigated while maintaining the system as such. Thus, while we find few examples of films like *The International* dealing with banking crises (let alone the real banking crisis of the moment), if we broaden our perspective and suggest that what the film more broadly is about is individualism—both the individualism of evil and the possibility of individualized goodness in an age of systemic downgrading of personal initiative, then the examples multiply.

Take, for instance, the unexpected boxoffice hit *Paul Blart: Mall Cop.* This seemingly comic film is quite cynical in its image of the bad guy, who turns out to be a SWAT team leader working both sides of the terrorist game. It thereby suggests problems with leadership at upper levels, but it is still quite typical and conventional in its tale of masculine redemption and triumph, even in a world where supposedly higher figures of law enforcement have betrayed the state and let us citizens down. Blart is a schlumpy, unlucky-at-love, seeming loser until, à la *Die Hard*, he has to defend his mall against criminal takeover, succeeds at the task, and wins a bodacious babe's love. For all its status as a silly comedy filled with pratfalls and other manifestations of physical humor (Paul suffers from narcolepsy and keeps careening over when he hasn't gotten an energy fix), *Paul Blart* taps into resonant and, in reality, often uncomic issues of the moment such as broken families, dead-end jobs, the impact of the recession on shopping trends, and the kitschification of everyday life by chain stores. It is also resonant in his mythologization of the possibilities for redemption of the ordinary guy. But, as with *The International*, *Paul Blart* is of its moment in only the broadest sense: beyond any tapping into anxieties of this one year specifically, the film is more generally about everyday fear after 9/11 and about the readiness of everyday masculinities to cope with that and everything else that is generally problematic in the air of the times.

Public Enemies: Historical Reflection on the Present

If the case of *The International* and other mythic narratives of everyday male redemption cautions us to look at the cultural resonances of narrative films at a broad rather than too historically specific level, it is intriguing to see how much contemporary concerns seep into the historical film *Public Enemies*, which purports to be a biopic about John Dillinger (Johnny Depp) and his pursuit by indefatigable FBI agent Melvin Purvis (Christian Bale) but is in many ways a direct, albeit fractured, look at governmentality under the shadow of the War on Terror. Yet even as the film taps into concerns over the ethics of government action in the fight against criminality, it offers up fraught, complex, even contradictory images that suggest no easy correlation of the film to a defined political ideology.

It's not inevitable that contemporary issues would break through the lavish reconstructions of the past in the historical film. It is, for instance, a curious accomplishment of another film of historical re-creation, the underappreciated Ang Lee film *Taking Woodstock*, that it manages to create a narrative world that seems fully of the time of the story with little or no references from today's world creeping in. (True, the film's concern with a coming out of *gay* identity might seem contemporaneous to the time of the film's production until we remember that the festival took place the same year, 1969, as the Stonewall explosion of gay pride in New York City.) But in its deliberate historicism (the attempt to re-create a time within its own terms and exclude all resonance of current issues), *Taking Woodstock* ends up seeming a curiosity indeed, a veritable exception to today's cinema's seemingly inevitable engagement with the present, even in films set in the past. If, as we saw with the case of *The International*, entertainment doesn't tend to offer overly specific reference to punctual concerns of the moment, it nonetheless resonates with broader issues of the day, and even films ostensibly about the past are enlisted into present-day questions. Some historical films flaunt anachronism and deliberately confuse past and present (for instance, *Inglourious Basterds*, set in World War II, but with a sequence choreographed to David Bowie), while others are all about how the present-day concerns creep into stories that would have seemed far from the fears of today. In the post-9/11 context, so many films, whatever their nominal subject, whatever their historical setting, end up with references to the tensions between security and insecurity and with discussion of governmentality and the proper path to justice, virtue, and personal and political morality. Thus, while it is logical that the contemporary parts of *Julie & Julia* bring up 9/11 (if only to see that tragedy as an impediment to the self-centered Julia Powell's personal development; in her job providing support for survivors of the attacks, she has to spend so much time with whiny ingrates and can't find a path to fulfillment), it was less expected that the Julia Child sections would deal so clearly with McCarthyism and thereby offer up commentary on the abuses of a "security state" in times of national urgency.

In the case of *Public Enemies*, a big-budget star vehicle, it is easy to see in its anachronistic flirtations with contemporary relevance another of the strategies by which the film tries to sell itself as hip and up to date. Certainly, one of the film's most resonant exploitations of fraught contemporary issues—the role of torture in the battle against forces of evil—is presented with little consistency or clarity of political purpose. Instead it seems to float through the film as one more motif designed to connect to the modern audience by little more than the fact that the topic of torture is in the air as a vexed, publicly debated issue.

Significantly, there are two key scenes in *Public Enemies* in which government agents set out to torture people associated with Dillinger's gang in an effort to close in on the master criminal. In one instance, Purvis himself squeezes information out of a Dillinger gang member who is dying in a hospital: the fact of imminent demise for the bad guy combined with knowledge both that one of Purvis's own men was shot down in cold blood by the gang and that this one gangster has been shown to be incorrigibly cruel seem to justify what Purvis here has to do. In contrast, in a later scene, when another government agent is beating up Dillinger's girlfriend Billie (Marion Cotillard), it is Purvis who comes to her rescue and heroically spirits her off, carrying her in his arms like some momentary knight in shining armor.

In a period where there is great divisiveness in the country about the ethics of governmental procedure in the War on Terror, *Public Enemies* hedges its bets by making torture a relativistic activity whose morality varies according to case and context. You can torture criminals but not a woman. At the same time, what isn't relativized is a heroic masculinity that is always rising to the occasion (tough when need be, tender when need be: it's all right to torture guys but gals need to be rescued) and will generally be pictured in redemptive fashion.

This politics of the heroic male who is allowed to choose when torture is an acceptable practice in the fight against evil plays into another aspect of *Public Enemies*. Even though Melvin Purvis, in his pursuit of Dillinger, is serving as an employee of the FBI, the film contrasts his personal and purposive righteous mission from that of the government agency itself, portrayed as a coldly rationalistic bureaucracy lorded over by a J. Edgar Hoover (Billy Crudup) whose only concern is coming off well in the national media. This is also a hedging of its bets on the part of the film. In a year in which divisiveness about executive power in Washington led to libertarian critiques of overbearing governmentality (but with a selective application of that critique so that libertarians could call on the very government they excoriated for its liberal leadership to be tough on criminals, terrorists, and ethnic and racial others such as illegal immigrants), *Public Enemies* has Melvin Purvis ultimately fulfilling the government's mission in the war on crime but in his own self-worthy fashion. One of director Michael Mann's central thematic preoccupations—the cat-and-mouse duel of two men, who ultimately find honor in the combat, across each side of the criminal/do-gooder divide (the definitive rendition is Mann's *Heat*, 1995)—is here made to shore up an antigovernmental parable about honorable individualism where what really matters are the bonds that men form with each other, whether as colleagues (both Purvis and Dillinger lose dear friends to the battle) or as ultimate enemies worthy of each other.

At the same time, however, it is important to recognize that even within the narrative of the film, the FBI does catch up with Dillinger and shoot him down (although ironically, it's not Purvis but one of his men who actually does the deed). For the viewer the battle is not just about good guy/bad guy but also about two movie stars going up against each other, with one clearly having all the advantage to himself: whatever the story world of *Public Enemies* is about, the film ultimately is "about" star Johnny Depp and his projection of cool seductiveness. (Christian Bale is far from the same level of stardom, and he had hurt whatever image he did have with an infamous rant on the set of *Terminator Salvation*, a film that itself did little to boost his career since it split its attention between three heroes with Bale somewhat lost in the shuffle.) In fact, in a way, the film's story and the film's own entertainment status blur since here Johnny Depp is playing on his own sexy charisma as movie star to portray a gangster with charisma. In this respect, it is noteworthy that so much of the film is devoted to Dillinger's amorous pursuit of Billie while Purvis is granted no equivalent romance: Dillinger/Depp is the figure of attractiveness—for the female lead in the film *and* for the spectator of the film—and gives the film its fundamental raison d'être.

This, more than any sort of political intent, may explain why *Public Enemies'* allegories of present-day governmentality, especially around the question of justifiable methods in the ultimate fight against forces of bad, are so contradictory: it's not that the makers of the movie had an explicit ideological project but that, quite the contrary, their interest was to sacrifice all political clarity to the seductions of charismatic entertainment. While there are always movies with a direct investment in politics (and this can happen across the spectrum from the radical to the reactionary), there are also many more whose "politics" is that of distraction from any commitment to any politics. In a sleek, star-driven entertainment like *Public Ene-*

mies, little is supposed to matter other than the pleasures of the viewing moment—the cut of a great three-piece suit, the wafting of cigarette smoke, the well-edited action sequence, the seductions of a manly grin. Torture can change from a good thing to a bad one if the latter case allows for a rousing moment of male redemption—a rousing moment of good entertainment.

From Identity Politics to Identity Products: Hannah Montana and Fast and Furious

The Obama presidency meant that new social identities would be key to any definition and debate about being a citizen participant in the project of the country. But two of the highest grossing films from the first quarter of the year well demonstrate how ethnic and racialized forms of citizenship could easily be inflected into consumer and entertainment driven modes of identity: *Fast and Furious* and *Hannah Montana: The Movie*. The films were released within a week of each other, and very quickly they shared the top of the box office but for very specific, very different, and very discernable audiences. *Fast and Furious* was a hit above all with Latino men, while *Hannah Montana* wore its merchandising appeal to young girls on its teen-fashion sleeve. If Hollywood's ultimate dream is to find the vastly appealing four-quadrant movie (industry parlance for a film that might reach young *and* old, men *and* women), and if the newest Washington dream was to speak to new racial and ethnic constituencies, *Fast and Furious* and *Hannah Montana* suggest that specifically delimited constituencies might constitute cultures and ways of (consumerist) life all their own (with little crossover from other social groups and identities) and that these constituencies might be ones that marketers *and politicians* very much had to take into account.

Obviously, *Fast and Furious* and *Hannah Montana* are not works of politics in any official sense (although the latter does have a populist theme of protest against a shopping mall that threatens to overturn folksy values in Hannah/Miley's hometown; at first, Hannah welcomes the idea of another place to shop but then her Miley side kicks in and she realizes that small-town virtues matter more). But the films' lack of political engagement is the point. Even as politicians court specific populations and even as Hollywood valorizes some movies over others (neither *Fast and Furious* nor *Hannah* were geared to garner critics' acclaims and prestige award nominations, nor do they get them), the two movies speak of forms of popularity that go under the political radar and that also remind us just how much America has become a niche nation.

In a year marked by the ascension of an African American to the presidency, neither *Hannah* nor *Fast and Furious* are about black identity in any central fashion, but neither are they bereft of moments of black representation. *Hannah*, for instance, plays into old Stepin Fetchit stereotypes of the scaredy-cat, bumbly black (the small town's black mayor is a buffoon who goes crazy with panic when a ferret climbs up his pants leg), and it also mockingly presents Hannah's black publicity manager (Vanessa Williams) as a snooty urbanite who is out of place in small-town USA. Meanwhile, *Fast and Furious* makes the key nemesis of the Latino hero Dom (Vin Diesel) be a vile, mohawk-headed black man responsible for the hero's girlfriend's dismal, violent death. Marginalizing and othering blackness, the two films hone in instead on other constituencies in America and find new power in them through new investment in them.

Both *Hannah* and *Fast and Furious* are components of franchises (the *Hannah* film is the first movie spinoff from a highly successful Disney Channel TV show and undoubtedly will have its sequels) and are all about an intense commodification that sells quite specific lifestyle accoutrements to quite specific and quite demarcated identity cultures. For all the expected differences of plot, there is also a lot that is quite the same in both movies as they use cinematic dazzle to captivate their target audiences: starting both with vehicular chases (Miley rushing in a motorized cart to a concert in which she will appear as Hannah and being pursued by a security guard; Dom racing to steal the petrol tanks from a trunk convoy) that are filmed with a frenetic editing and keyed to a vibrant music beat, the films are all about kinesis, rush, explosions (*Hannah* has a birthday cake blow up), scenes of dynamic transformation (cars that smash into bits, people who put on and off disguises), and showy and spectacular set pieces (both films have extended music-videoish sequences in which women in bathing suits or short shorts dance to pulsating beats as the editing fetishistically cuts their bodies into visually consumable, seductive close-up bits).

Further, the plots of the two films are similarly minimal in premise and development (Dom and FBI agent O'Connor [Paul Walker] infiltrate a drug dealer's smuggling ring; Hannah is brought back by her dad to the country world where she grew up as Miley so she can reconnect to authentic roots) and seem to exist in large part to enable the set pieces (car races and musical numbers). Interestingly, both films have to do with the problems of being something you're not and having then to find your true self. In *Hannah Montana*, Miley hesitates between her folksy origins and her show business identity (a hesitation encapsulated in a sequence in which she, in her two identities, has to be two places at once and keeps getting caught in a

Dynamic vehicular action: *Hannah Montana: The Movie* (Peter Chelsom, DisneyChannel). Digital frame enlargement.

revolving door, an obvious metaphor for her shifts of personality). In *Fast and Furious*, Dom hesitates between wanting to kill the drug lord for personal vengeance's sake and wanting to do the right thing, which is to bring the criminal in for prosecution by the forces of law. And Agent O'Connor hesitates between hoping to arrest Dom and wanting him to go free if he does indeed do the right thing. In all cases, the films appear to suggest that in a fast, ever shifting, ever pulsating world, there are still basic good values to uphold—authentic ones, honest ones, moral ones.

Of course, the irony of the *Hannah Montana* movie claiming that one can go back to authentic roots and throw off a corruptive consumerist surface identity is that the film is itself so much a calculated, consumerist piece of work. So, in its own way, is *Fast and Furious*: its ending, in which Agent O'Connor joins with Dom's Latino buddies to save Dom from going to prison, may hint at new coalitions of cross-ethnic friendship beyond the obfuscations of state politics, but it also builds that new friendship to generate an inevitable sequel that will be about the franchised, further adventures of Dom and O'Connor. In other words, the film needs Dom to go to jail so it can claim the authenticity of his moral choice and the sense of personal sacrifice it entails (by not killing the drug lord and instead turning him into the law, Dom knew that he himself would likely be arrested too), and it also needs him to be freed from imprisonment so the frenetic fun of the franchise can be continued.

This ending is similar to that of a film from a few years earlier, *3:10 to Yuma* (2007), where at the end, after farmer Dale Evans (Christian Bale) has been shot dead trying to get notorious criminal Ben Wade (Russell Crowe) onto a train to take him to prison, Wade kills all of his own gang and boards the train on his own in a seeming moral-epiphany recognition and acceptance of Evans's sacrifice. The film here appears to endorse ethics, commitment, authenticity. Yet it then takes all that back in the last moments when we see that Wade has actually set up to escape from the train. This is typical of many recent Hollywood films that insist on a moral moment they don't really believe in and that they opportunistically contradict for the needs of trick endings, sequels, immediate narrative impact, and so on. Movies like *Hannah Montana* and *Fast and Furious* (and, to pick up an earlier example, *Public Enemies* with its inconsistent rendition of the moral meaning of torture) want to have their cake and eat it too (an image that is apt for *Hannah*, which is so much about the privilege of endless consumption). *Hannah Montana* even admits its own interest in the balancing act of moral commitment/opportunism in its climax where Miley, having made the choice to commit to (small-town) honesty and authenticity, says goodbye to "Hannah" in front of her fans at a concert, only to be implored by a young girl to "please be Hannah, we'll keep your secret." This is both a joke on the fact that Miley has revealed her dual identity in a very public venue that means there can be no keeping of secrets and an expression of the film's conceit that one can have it all—the quiet, out-of-the-spotlight simplicity of the Miley life, the public celebrity of the Hannah life. The conceit is then given further confirmation when Hannah's black manager, who previously had been opposed to the juggling of identities, now implores Miley to put her Hannah wig back on since she'll never have a normal life otherwise. Might this not be the film's ultimate opportunistic concession to shopping mall materialism? The teen consumer, whether Hannah/Miley in the movie or the girl viewers who made this movie a big success, can buy all manner of fashion and identity-shifting add-ons while still having the right, authentic life.

Believing in Yourself: From *Hannah Montana* to *Precious*

If *Hannah Montana* luxuriates in the ironies of selling white teen lifestyle while claiming that such whiteness can have an uncommercial authenticity, we might see another film about teenage anxiety, *Precious, Based on the Novel 'Push' by Sapphire*, as *Hannah*'s racial converse. Although obviously a commodity that has to enter into a fraught business climate (especially for independent movies: *Precious* got most of its initial financing from a entrepreneurial white couple in Denver and then had to struggle up the film festival circuit until a national distributor, Lionsgate, picked it up), *Precious* is not about franchising, not about selling the dismal lifestyle portrayed in its story world. But in calling it the "converse" of *Hannah Montana* (rather than, say, its "subversion" or an anti-version of the white teen film), I mean to suggest how the two can be paired as parts, both of a larger cinematic field in which each serves its function and in which neither challenges the overall model. In fact, there are some ways in which *Precious* is not that different in visual look from the Disney offering: for an ostensibly gritty film set in rough ghetto space, *Precious* is surprisingly often a glitzy, showy film with lots of frenetic editing and frequent splashy digital effects. From the first shots of a vibrant bit of red gleaming out from the deadened gray of the inner city as slow motion pigeons fly by, *Precious* announces that it will be as much about cinematic virtuosity as a realist look at black life in America. This is a film where snowflakes drift to the ground in lyrical fashion and where it seems almost impossible for the resilient heroine (Gabourey Sidibe) to walk down the city's mean streets in anything other than poetic slow motion. True, some of the special effects are restricted to instances of fantasy (Precious imagining herself a famous star) or of horrific violence (Precious raped by her father and imagining the ceiling opening up), but this makes scenes of relative stylistic understatement mere pauses between moments of ostentatious visual display. In its own way, *Precious* is as much an experience of cinema, and what it can do in telling a story, as is *Hannah Montana*.

In its depiction of the bleak options (or "alternatives," as the promise of one-on-one schooling is described to her) that face the inner-city black teen, *Precious* complements *Hannah Montana* as its mirroring inverse (there's even a scene where Precious imagines herself in a mirror as a well-off, snappy young white woman). Hannah has family, food, fame. Precious is abused by her family, steals food to appease her hunger, and can only dream in fantasy sequences of a fame that will never be hers (in one sequence, she visualizes dancing in a show with a Latin lover; from his erotic nibbling at her ear, the film cuts to a ghetto dog licking her after she's been knocked down by sexually predatory bullies).

It is tempting to read *Precious* as one more example of the pathologizing victimization of African American people—as did Ishmael Reed, who, in a controversial *New York Times* op-ed piece, excoriated the film's fatalistic view of black possibility and suggested in no ambiguous terms that a large degree of interest in the film came from a white-centered liberalism that claimed to support black causes but ultimately needed blacks to be figured helpless victims in order to do so (Reed). In this respect, it may matter that Ms. Rain (Paula Patton), the schoolteacher who stands by Precious and goes the extra yard to get her out of her hellish situation, is a light-skinned African American with a glamorous look that (to white audiences) would not signal ghettoness but, quite the contrary, a bourgeois sense of educated contentment (she's also hip and lesbian—which for the film sort of means the same thing). If the film first presents the front desk at the alternative school as a bureaucratic hurdle in danger of daunting Precious from her quest for personal betterment, entrance into Ms. Rains's classroom is figured unironically as a transcendental experience with a glowing golden sheen as Precious is beckoned in. Despite its own avowed investment in black identity, Precious plays into an ideologically charged color hierarchy in which lightness is associated with privilege and darkness is pathologized. It makes sense, then, that Precious's fantasies of potential redemption revolve often around Latino lovers since, like Ms. Rain who is figured as less ghetto black than Precious, they represent a step up in privilege and success with the American dream.[1]

Toward the end of the film, when Precious's mother (Mo'Nique) reveals all the failings of will and control that let her let Precious's father abuse Precious, it is easy to feel that Precious's case is so particular and so aberrant and exceptional that this is not the "black condition" but just the situation of this one woman. The film piles on the problems for Precious (she has a Down's syndrome first child, she is obese, she has had an inadequate education, she has HIV) to such a degree that the story really becomes just hers (not for nothing is the title her proper name). Just as The International offered the manageable fantasy of the individually responsible and identifiable evil banker as a way of personalizing monetary crisis, so does Precious individualize and thereby psychologize Precious's story. One understands why Oprah Winfrey so defended the film since, like other uplifting Oprah-promoted fictions, it is about the ostensible need for the individual to take control of his/her destiny. Ultimately, though, it can only be about that by personalizing the source of Precious's problems (the evil here is not the black condition but her father and even more her mother) and by downplaying the systemic blockages to progress for African American people. In this moral universe, if institutions at first are seen as bureaucratic, they ultimately turn out to be beneficent: teachers will go all out to help you, nurses will devote lots of time to you, welfare workers will take your case to heart. It's up to you to take all that support and make something of yourself.

■■■■■■■ *The Hurt Locker* and *Avatar*:
Multiculturalism in Another Dimension

As noted, politics during Obama's first year in office was centrally about media politics, and the multiple voices that debated (sometimes violently) the place of new identities in today's America. The Obama White House may have been up to date by using communication formats such as Twitter, websites, and old-style television to get its message out, but it was countered as frequently by other constellations of media; in one of the most reported occurrences, numerous parents in conservative areas refused to let their children come to school on the day Obama was broadcasting a (relatively benign, as it ultimately transpired) speech about education.

But it's an open question, then, whether popular cinema could serve as political media in the same way as these more immediate communication forms and speak to present issues in the same manner. Beyond the fact that length of production means that few films are even made fast enough to speak to or about their times, there is the more specific, historically rooted question of whether or not cinema by the end of the first decade of the twenty-first century was still maintaining its place as a key mode of American popular culture. In a complicated, overloaded media landscape, were the movies to be anything but one signal among others, or did they (still) have priority as the cultural form that most trenchantly captured its times, in however broad a fashion?

True, by the end of the year, Hollywood had enjoyed its highest box office ever. But several facts and factors help us keep that seeming success in perspective. For instance, American movies made about $29.9 billion over the course of the year, but in the same period video games scored $19.7 billion, suggesting that this latter mode of user-driven visual entertainment had become very much a consequential rival player on the media landscape. And, in any case, no small part of the enhanced movie revenues was due to rising ticket prices as well as to the disproportionate success of a very few films. Of these, the most successful—and it was a success beyond all predictions, beyond all precedent box office for other films—was Twentieth Century–Fox's *Avatar*, which also benefited from increased ticket prices at those cinemas that showed the film in 3D (or, even more lucratively, in 3D and IMAX).

The movies were fighting a desperate battle to hold onto entertainment dollars: some tried to adopt a pared down visual style that would work well when sold as DVDs or to TV broadcast (for example, the romantic comedy *The Proposal* or the hugely successful bromantic comedy *The Hangover*, which tried to hedge its media crossover potential by using TV actors such as Ed Helms from cable's "The Daily Show" in key roles). Some tried to make newer media the source of their subject matter and their look (for instance, *Paranormal Activity*, shot for a mere pittance and ending up a gigantic success, which adopted the conceit that the whole film was actually found footage from home video recording). Some tried to outfox journalistic media at their own game of topicality by honing in as best they could on current events: thus, a certain degree of critical acclaim went to the Iraq War film *The Hurt Locker*, which used hand-held camera, extreme close-up, and a general jitteriness to suggest an in-your-face immediacy. To be sure, one perhaps shouldn't overestimate the extent to which *The Hurt Locker* serves as an investigation of the politics of the war in Iraq. The film borrows various conventions of the combat film from over the years—for example, the hotshot who doesn't really work with the team and often endangers the mission—and is as much a comment on the war film genre as it is on any real war, such as the one it purports to be about (for example, it uses the hotshot convention to upend it; he turns out to be the best at his job rather than the one who screws things up). Unlike many war films, *The Hurt Locker* takes us inside the lives of people from the local culture, both civilians and enemy combatants (although the central encounter of the hotshot and a young Iraqi also plays on the war movie convention of the young waif befriended, often at first begrudgingly, by the G.I.), but it still often treats these others as inscrutable, voiceless (or voicing an incomprehensible foreign tongue), without logic or background explanation to their actions—a sheer irrationality that the American soldier frustratingly butts up against. Like many war films (for example, *Full Metal Jacket* [1987]), *The Hurt Locker* is not really about explaining military conflict except to say that it does something to American masculinity and that this (rather than, say, war's political causes or the concerns of indigenous populations) is what best merits dramatization.

In any case, whether *The Hurt Locker* really is an "Iraq War film" or just one more war film about American masculinity, the strategy of centering its story in a topical world didn't seem to work: over the course of the year, *The Hurt Locker* didn't do that well in ticket sales (it was much more a critic's succès d'estime than a financial hit), and many film market diagnosticians read it as one confirmation that audiences didn't want to see the current war onscreen. When in the last quarter of the year the film started being touted as a dark-horse favorite for Oscar nominations, pundits then noted that, if it were to win Best Picture, it would be the lowest-grossing honoree in modern Oscar history.

The Clash of Civilizations: *The Hurt Locker* (Kathryn Bigelow, Summit Entertainment). Digital frame enlargement.

Avatar also was an explosion-laden war movie (and it was debated as such: did its condemnation of voracious mercenaries out to despoil primitive cultures make it anti-American even as it became the most financially successful film in America ever?). It has its own ambiguities about the rendition of war in a moment where real wars were being waged by real Americans and with real casualties on both sides. On the one hand, more than, say, *The Hurt Locker*, *Avatar* does offer a picture of the indigenous people whose lands the Americans are on as they wage war. Much of the film, indeed, is from within the world of the other (to the extent of inventing a language for them). On the other hand, this is a world far removed from resemblance to ours (and the melodramatic voracious capitalists, scene-chomping marine commanders, and psycho mercenaries all enable the viewer to not see the forces of war here as in any way systemically similar to our own real-world U.S. military).

In its own way, like other films of the year, *Avatar* hedges its bets by yoking together seemingly incompatible impulses. On the one hand, the film claims to deeply respect its natives but then must picture them as creatures pretty much helpless before the onslaught of modernity. Like, say, the *Matrix* trilogy (especially *Matrix Revolution* [2003] with its scene of natives swaying mystically to a rhythmic beat, a scene replayed in *Avatar*), *Avatar* portrays its insurgents as a rag-tag group of amateurs who need a white cyber-hero to come from other worlds to organize them into an effective fighting force. Natives have value, virtue, and moral right, but they have no agency.

Technological Pastoralism: *Avatar* (James Cameron, Twentieth Century–Fox). Digital frame enlargement.

On the other hand, the film valorizes the purity of nature over the overbearing inauthenticity of machines and the crass capitalist interests behind them, but it itself is a work concocted at tremendous expense and extensive scientific research-and-development that could have only come about through corporate support and through intense investment in machines and technology. *Hannah Montana* at least explicitly admits and accepts a similar paradox when it has Hannah's manager declaring that without her entertainment identity, Miley won't have a life but that with it, she can be both authentic and performative. The film is cynically aware that it is yoking conflicting value systems together, whereas *Avatar* doesn't seem to fully admit the irony of its parable of the dangerous "machine in the garden" being produced by the biggest entertainment machine ever.

Or perhaps the film does make that admission by means of the 3D glasses the spectators wear. The glasses certainly immerse us in a fictional world and help to make a fantastical place seem all so possible. But the glasses are never just about creating a reality effect for an imagined world: they are also about their own ability to make that world seem to exist, and the viewer probably never forgets that performative dimension to the glasses. In other words, that is, the glasses simultaneously need to make us believe that we are in a fantastic world while requiring us to marvel knowingly at the very gadgetry that is making that belief happen. *Avatar* wants viewers to feel deeply for an imaginary world made to seem authentic, not just in the sense that we believe in its existence but that we also believe in its virtuousness and feel for the terrible things that threaten it. Furthermore, it also wants us to marvel at the very technology that is delivering the images to us. In its own way, this is no less an opportunistic commercial calculation than the double ending of *Fast and Furious,* where we're supposed to admire Dom for giving himself up but we're also supposed to cheer the fact that his buddies will set him free and enable more installments to the franchise. In like fashion, *Avatar* holds out its moments of morality, authenticity, and virtuousness for the audience to sympathize with, but it envelops those in a larger framework where all that ultimately matters is the sheer effectiveness of a machinery of entertainment.

For all its bigness of budget and ambitiousness of story (the allusion-rich parable of man-versus-nature), *Avatar*'s recourse to 3D harkened back to the 1950s in cinema history when a number of low-budget films were shot in three-dimensional format in a desperate attempt to enable movies to compete with television. No doubt many of today's viewers don't have that historical reference when they watch *Avatar,* but it is nonetheless the case that whatever else *Avatar* is "about" (its themes, its message), it is also about an explicit experience of cinema, one that is in many ways also about the experience of the history of cinema. Beyond the 3D, for instance, *Avatar* is also about all the white-man-who-journeys-to-a-primitive-culture-and-ultimately-prefers-it-to-his-own films that preceded it: critics endlessly compared it to, for example, *Dances with Wolves* (1990), and there's a strong sense in which, like the Indiana Jones films that derive from cliffhanger serials, *Avatar* is very much a postmodern film that reprocesses the genre films that have preceded it. (In this respect, more than *Dances with Wolves,* it is the MGM Tarzan films from the 1930s that seem to me to form the resonant background to *Avatar.* Like Tarzan/Lord Greystoke, *Avatar*'s Jake Sully [Sam Worthington] is, for instance, able to summon all the creatures of the forest to come to his aid in the battle against the bad guys. Such a lineage for the film would indeed bring *Avatar* closer to the history of lowbrow popular cinema, just as the serial heritage for the Indiana Jones film does.)

The 3D technology for *Avatar* may have seemed to many to be a vast improvement over the headache-inducing glasses of the 1950s (although some viewers still found there to be that flattening of surfaces that had characterized the supposed three-dimensionality of 1950s 3D). It was, nevertheless, a gimmick, something added to the narrative experience to appear to give it extra punch. As confirmation, other studios soon would be retro-fitting spectacle films shot in 2D to the 3D format to jump on the bandwagon as if the technique were fairly malleable and not logically integrated with narrative. Significantly, though, while all of Hollywood was abuzz with how *Avatar* had revived the box office and revitalized Holly-wood storytelling magic, its success would turn out to be elusive for some other 3D or 3D-reformatted films. As significant, when *Avatar* eventually came to DVD (the following year), that version also did incredibly well (to the extent that it gave new gasps of energy to the dying DVD market), sug-gesting that viewers didn't just need the theatrical 3D experience as incen-tive to spend money on the film.

In this respect, what might have been the most consequential event of the year for the business future of the movies might not have seemed at first glance to directly have anything to do with film at all: namely, the FCC-mandated switchover of commercial television to digital standards. The switchover was not just about television—not, for instance, just about improving image quality on the home screen, even if that was touted as one of its strongest benefits—but moved the commercial movie–image indus-tries a major step closer to enabling that dream of media convergence after which they had long been questing. Digital television gave greater possibil-ity for home computers to be linked to the television set, but for our pur-poses it also provided a new and stronger, more tempting home platform for film distribution. True, the boxoffice bump from *Avatar*'s 3D and IMAX theatrical presentations confirmed that audiences would still invest in the-atergoing as special occasion, and the unexpected success of some smaller films that wouldn't have seemed to need theatrical presentation to get their entertainment across (for example, *Paul Blart* or *The Hangover*—seemingly perfect cable or DVD rental movies) suggested that even casual moviegoing was far from dead. But the digital switchover did promise new ways to bring movies more quickly into the home. By the end of the year, for instance, industry journals were talking about how digital television could make it tempting for video-on-demand presentation of movies to intensify as a distribution practice. By this year, the DVD business had gone essen-tially flat (with exceptions, like *Avatar*'s gigantic DVD sales the following year, being just that: exceptions), and video-on-demand was shaping up to be the preferred mode for high revenue–generating film distribution on television. Digital television sets facilitated the streaming of demanded video, and studios began pushing for ways to reduce the window (the amount of time) between theatrical release of a film and its video-on-demand exhibition. (By early the following year, indeed, an important FCC decision allowed just that and brought the process of cinema/television convergence to a pivotal point.)

In this respect, in a central way again *Avatar* may represent another hedging of Hollywood's bets. The most expensive movie ever produced, it is so much about an irreducible experience of cinema as an in-the-theater event. But it is also about the ways in which digitalization prepares for the fickle move of movies across multiple platforms. (Significantly, there was even talk about how high-definition digital television could contribute to the development of 3D viewing technologies for the home.) Media industry figures had long been speaking of theatrically exhibited movies as the "loco-motive" that exists to pull along other viewing formats in its stead. By the end of the first decade of the twenty-first century, the procession was moving faster and more furiously than ever before.

NOTE

1. In a trenchant profile in the *New Yorker* of *Precious* executive co-producer Tyler Perry, Hilton Als notes how often Perry's own films present dark-skinned women as bearing an authentic connection to inner-city life that others don't have: the paradox, Als argues, is that Perry's women are criticized when they forget their roots (as happens, for example, when they become professional working women and try to rise up through careerist self-reliance), but that they can (and should) in fact better themselves through romance with a light-skinned, sometimes Latino, man (Als).

2 0 0 0 – 2 0 0 9

Select Academy Awards

2000

Best Picture: *Gladiator*, DreamWorks SKG

Best Actor: Russell Crowe in *Gladiator*, DreamWorks SKG

Best Actress: Julia Roberts in *Erin Brockovich*, Universal

Best Supporting Actor: Benicio Del Toro in *Traffic*, USA Films

Best Supporting Actress: Marcia Gay Harden in *Pollock*, Sony Pictures Classics

Best Director: *Traffic*, Steven Soderbergh, USA Films

Best Original Screenplay: Cameron Crowe, *Almost Famous*, Columbia

Best Adapted Screenplay: Stephen Gaghan, *Traffic*, USA Films

Best Cinematography: Peter Pau, *Crouching Tiger, Hidden Dragon*, Sony Pictures Classics

Best Film Editing: Stephen Mirrione, *Traffic*, USA Films

Best Music (Original Score): Tan Dun, *Crouching Tiger, Hidden Dragon*, Sony Pictures Classics

Best Music (Song): Bob Dylan, "Things Have Changed," *Wonder Boys*, Paramount

2001

Best Picture: *A Beautiful Mind*, Universal

Best Actor: Denzel Washington in *Training Day*, Warner Bros.

Best Actress: Halle Berry in *Monster's Ball*, Lionsgate

Best Supporting Actor: Jim Broadbent in *Iris*, Miramax

Best Supporting Actress: Jennifer Connelly in *A Beautiful Mind*, Universal

Best Director: Ron Howard, *A Beautiful Mind*, Universal

Best Original Screenplay: Julian Fellowes, *Gosford Park*, USA Films

Best Adapted Screenplay: Akiva Goldsman, *A Beautiful Mind*, Universal Pictures

Best Cinematography: Andrew Lesnie, *The Lord of the Rings: The Fellowship of the Ring*, New Line Cinema

Best Film Editing: Pietro Scalia, *Black Hawk Down*, Columbia

Best Music (Original Score): Howard Shore, *The Lord of the Rings: The Fellowship of the Ring*, New Line Cinema

Best Music (Song): Randy Newman, "If I Didn't Have You," *Monsters, Inc.*, Pixar

Best Animated Feature Film: Aron Warner, *Shrek*, DreamWorks SKG

■ 2002

Best Picture: *Chicago*, Miramax

Best Actor: Adrien Brody in *The Pianist*, Focus Features

Best Actress: Nicole Kidman in *The Hours*, Miramax

Best Supporting Actor: Chris Cooper in *Adaptation*, Columbia

Best Supporting Actress: Catherine Zeta-Jones in *Chicago*, Miramax

Best Director: Roman Polanski, *The Pianist*, Focus Features

Best Original Screenplay: Pedro Almodóvar, *Talk to Her*, Sony Pictures Classics

Best Adapted Screenplay: Ronald Harwood, *The Pianist*, Focus Features

Best Cinematography: Conrad L. Hall, *Road to Perdition*, DreamWorks SKG

Best Film Editing: Martin Walsh, *Chicago*, Miramax

Best Music (Original Score): Elliot Goldenthal, *Frida*, Miramax

Best Music (Song): Eminem, "Lose Yourself," *8 Mile*, Universal

Best Animated Feature Film: Hayao Myazaki ,*Spirited Away*, Studio Ghibli/Nippon Television Network

■ 2003

Best Picture: *The Lord of the Rings: The Return of the King*, New Line Cinema

Best Actor: Sean Penn in *Mystic River*, Warner Bros.

Best Actress: Charlize Theron in *Monster*, Newmarket

Best Supporting Actor: Tim Robbins in *Mystic River*, Warner Bros.

Best Supporting Actress: Renée Zellweger in *Cold Mountain*, Miramax

Best Director: Peter Jackson, *The Lord of the Rings: The Return of the King*, New Line Cinema

Best Original Screenplay: Sofia Coppola, *Lost in Translation*, Focus Features

Best Adapted Screenplay: Fran Walsh, Philippa Boyens, and Peter Jackson, *The Lord of the Rings: The Return of the King*, New Line Cinema

Best Cinematography: Russell Boyd, *Master and Commander: The Far Side of the World*, Twentieth Century–Fox

Best Film Editing: Jamie Selkirk, *The Lord of the Rings: The Return of the King*, New Line Cinema

Best Music (Original Score): Howard Shore, *The Lord of the Rings: The Return of the King*, New Line Cinema

Best Music (Song): Fran Walsh and Howard Shore and Annie Lennox, "Into the West," *The Lord of the Rings: The Return of the King*, New Line Cinema

Best Animated Feature Film: Andrew Stanton, *Finding Nemo*, Walt Disney/Pixar

2004

Best Picture: *Million Dollar Baby*, Warner Bros.

Best Actor: Jamie Foxx in *Ray*, Universal

Best Actress: Hilary Swank in *Million Dollar Baby*, Warner Bros.

Best Supporting Actor: Morgan Freeman in *Million Dollar Baby*, Warner Bros.

Best Supporting Actress: Cate Blanchett in *The Aviator*, Miramax

Best Director: Clint Eastwood, *Million Dollar Baby*, Warner Bros.

Best Original Screenplay: Charlie Kauffman, *Eternal Sunshine of the Spotless Mind*, Focus

Best Adapted Screenplay: Alexander Payne and Jim Taylor, *Sideways*, Fox Searchlight

Best Cinematography: Robert Richardson, *The Aviator*, Miramax

Best Film Editing: Thelma Schoonmaker, *The Aviator*, Miramax

Best Music (Original Score): Jan A.P. Kaczmarek, *Finding Neverland*, Miramax

Best Music (Song): Jorge Drexler, "Al Otro Lado del Río," *The Motorcycle Diaries*, Focus Features

Best Animated Feature Film: Brad Bird, *The Incredibles*, Walt Disney/Pixar

2005

Best Picture: *Crash*, Lionsgate

Best Actor: Philip Seymour Hoffman in *Capote*, MGM

Best Actress: Reese Witherspoon in *Walk the Line*, Twentieth Century–Fox

Best Supporting Actor: George Clooney in *Syriana*, Warner Bros.

Best Supporting Actress: Rachel Weisz in *The Constant Gardener*, Focus Features

Best Director: Ang Lee, *Brokeback Mountain*, Focus Features

Best Original Screenplay: Paul Haggis and Bobby Moresco, *Crash*, Lionsgate

Best Adapted Screenplay: Larry McMurtry and Diana Ossana, *Brokeback Mountain*, Focus Features

Best Cinematography: Dion Beebe, *Memoirs of a Geisha*, Columbia

Best Film Editing: Hughes Winborne, *Crash*, Lionsgate

Best Music (Original Score): Gustavo Santaolalla, *Brokeback Mountain*, Focus Features

Best Music (Song): Jordan Houston, Cedric Coleman, and Paul Beauregard, "It's Hard Out Here for a Pimp," *Hustle & Flow*, Paramount

Best Animated Feature Film: Nick Park and Steve Box, *Wallace & Gromit in The Curse of the Were-Rabbit*, DreamWorks SKG

2006

Best Picture: *The Departed*, Warner Bros.

Best Actor: Forest Whitaker in *The Last King of Scotland*, Fox Searchlight

Best Actress: Helen Mirren in *The Queen*, Miramax

Best Supporting Actor: Alan Arkin in *Little Miss Sunshine*, Fox Searchlight

Best Supporting Actress: Jennifer Hudson in *Dreamgirls*, Paramount

Best Director: Martin Scorsese, *The Departed*, Warner Bros.

Best Original Screenplay: Michael Arndt, *Little Miss Sunshine*, Fox Searchlight

Best Adapted Screenplay: William Monahan, *The Departed*, Warner Bros.

Best Cinematography: Guillermo Navarro, *Pan's Labyrinth*, Picturehouse

Best Film Editing: Thelma Schoonmaker, *The Departed*, Warner Bros.

Best Music (Original Score): Gustavo Santaolalla, *Babel*, Paramount Vantage

Best Music (Song): Melissa Etheridge, "I Need to Wake Up," *An Inconvenient Truth*, Paramount Vantage

Best Animated Feature Film: George Miller, *Happy Feet*, Warner Bros.

2007

Best Picture: *No Country for Old Men*, Miramax

Best Actor: Daniel Day-Lewis in *There Will Be Blood*, Paramount Vantage

Best Actress: Marion Cotillard in *La Vie en Rose*, Picturehouse Entertainment

Best Supporting Actor: Javier Bardem in *No Country for Old Men*, Miramax

Best Supporting Actress: Tilda Swinton in *Michael Clayton*, Warner Bros.

Best Director: Joel Coen and Ethan Coen, *No Country for Old Men*, Miramax

Best Original Screenplay: Diablo Cody, *Juno*, Fox Searchlight

Best Adapted Screenplay: Joel Coen and Ethan Coen, *No Country for Old Men*, Miramax

Best Cinematography: Robert Elswi, *There Will Be Blood*, Paramount Vantage

Best Film Editing: Christopher Rouse, *The Bourne Ultimatum*, Universal

Best Music (Original Score): Dario Marianelli, *Atonement*, Focus

Best Music (Song): Glen Hansard and Marketa Irglova, "Falling Slowly," *Once*, Fox Searchlight

Best Animated Feature Film: Brad Bird, *Ratatouille*, Walt Disney/Pixar

2008

Best Picture: *Slumdog Millionaire*, Fox Searchlight

Best Actor: Sean Penn in *Milk*, Focus Features

Best Actress: Kate Winslet in *The Reader*, The Weinstein Company

Best Supporting Actor: Heath Ledger in *The Dark Knight*, Warner Bros.

Best Supporting Actress: Penélope Cruz in *Vicky Cristina Barcelona*, The Weinstein Company

Best Director: Danny Boyle, *Slumdog Millionaire*, Fox Searchlight

Best Original Screenplay: Dustin Lance Black, *Milk*, Focus Features

Best Adapted Screenplay: Simon Beaufoy, *Slumdog Millionaire*, Fox Searchlight

Best Cinematography: Anthony Dod Mantle, *Slumdog Millionaire*, Fox Searchlight

Best Film Editing: Chris Dickens, *Slumdog Millionaire*, Fox Searchlight

Best Music (Original Score): A. R. Rahman, *Slumdog Millionaire*, Fox Searchlight

Best Original Song: A. R. Rahman and Gulzar, "Jai Ho," *Slumdog Millionaire*, Fox Searchlight

Best Animated Feature Film: Andrew Stanton, *WALL-E*, Walt Disney/Pixar

2009

Best Picture: *The Hurt Locker*, Summit Entertainment

Best Actor: Jeff Bridges in *Crazy Heart*, Fox Searchlight

Best Actress: Sandra Bullock in *The Blind Side*, Warner Bros.

Best Supporting Actor: Christoph Waltz in *Inglourious Basterds*, The Weinstein Company

Best Supporting Actress: Mo'Nique in *Precious: Based on the Novel 'Push' by Sapphire*, Lionsgate

Best Director: Kathryn Bigelow, *The Hurt Locker*, Summit Entertainment

Best Adapted Screenplay: Geoffrey Fletcher, *Precious: Based on the Novel 'Push' by Sapphire*, Lionsgate

Best Original Screenplay: Mark Boal, *The Hurt Locker*, Summit Entertainment

Best Cinematography: Mauro Fiore, *Avatar*, Twentieth Century–Fox

Best Film Editing: Bob Murawski and Chris Innis, *The Hurt Locker*, Summit Entertainment

Best Music (Original Score): Michael Giacchino, *Up*, Walt Disney/Pixar

Best Music (Song): Ryan Bingham and T-Bone Burnett, "The Weary Kind," *Crazy Heart*, Fox Searchlight

Best Animated Feature Film: Peter Docter, *Up*, Walt Disney/Pixar

WORKS CITED
AND CONSULTED

Abagnale, Frank, with Stan Redding. *Catch Me If You Can: The True Story of a Real Fake*. New York: Broadway Books, 2000.

Adalian, Josef. "Shell-Shocked Showbiz." *Variety* 17–23 Sept. 2001: 1, 36.

———. "Showbiz Frozen." *Variety* 17–23 Sept. 2001: 36.

"Afghan Conflict Prompts Uzbek-American Engagement." *Institute for War and Peace Reporting*. iwpr.net/report-news/afghan-conflict-prompts-uzbek-american-engagement19 Oct. 2009. Accessed 5 Jan. 2010.

"Alfred Angelo and Disney to Debut Their First Disney Princess-Inspired Bridal Gown Collection." eon.businesswire.com/news/eon/20100928005662/en/wedding-dresses/gown/disney28 Sept. 2010. Accessed 3 Oct. 2010.

Als, Hilton. "Mama's Gun: The World of Tyler Perry." *New Yorker* 26 April 2010: 69–72.

Altman, Rick. *Film/Genre*. London: British Film Institute, 1999.

Anhedonia from the planet earth. "Bridget Jones Goes beyond the Edge of Reason into Sheer Stupidity and Boredom." IMDb.com 17 Nov. 2004. Accessed 31 May 2011.

Ansen, David. "Eye of the Beholder." *Newsweek* (Pacific ed.) 16 Aug. 2005: 53.

Argy, Stephanies. "Rags to Riches." *American Cinematographer* (Dec. 2008).

Ayres, Chris, Alexi Mostrous, and Tim Teeman. "Oscars for *Slumdog Millionaire*—the Film That Nearly Went Straight to DVD." *Times (London)* 24 Feb. 2009.

Balio, Tino. *Grand Design: Hollywood as a Modern Business Enterprise, 1930–1939*. Berkeley: U of California P, 1993.

Baron, Rebecca. "The Idea of Still." Interview by Janet Sarbanes. *Still Moving: Between Cinema and Photography*. Ed. Karen Beckman and Jean Ma. Durham, N.C.: Duke UP, 2008. 119–33.

Baughan, Nikki. "Is It Too Soon?" *Film Review* 1 July 2006: 52–60.

Bing, Jonathan, and Cathy Dunkley. "Kiddy Litter Rules H'wood." *Variety* 7–13 Jan. 2002: 1, 38, 69.

Bingham, Dennis. *Whose Lives Are They Anyway? The Biopic as Contemporary Film Genre*. New Brunswick, N.J.: Rutgers UP, 2010.

Booth, William. "Alexander the Actual." *Washington Post* 22 Nov.2004: C1+.

Bordwell, David. *The Way Hollywood Tells It: Story and Style in Modern Movies*. Berkeley: U of California P, 2006.

Bowles, Scott. "2003 Blockbusters." *USA Today* 6 Jan. 2004: D5.

Bradshaw, Peter. "Turning Japanese." *Guardian* 23 Feb. 2007: 12.

Braun, Liz. "Sliding over the Edge; There Is Absolutely No Reason to Bridget Jones Sequel." *Toronto Sun* 21 Nov. 2004: E2.

Broder, John M., and James Risen. "Contractor Deaths in Iraq Soar to Record." *New York Times* 9 May 2007.

Brody, Richard. "Best of the Decade." *New Yorker* 30 Nov. 2009.

Brook, Tom. "US Critics Take Aim at Pearl Harbor." *BBC News* 13 July 2009.

Brooks, Xan. "For One Moment It Was Possible to Dream That the Ending Would Be Different." *Guardian* 27 May 2006: 31–33.

Brown, Megan. "Somehow We All Survived: The Ideology of the U.S. Backlash against Risk Management." *South Atlantic Quarterly* 107:2 (2008): 287–307.

Buckland, Warren. *Directed by Steven Spielberg: Poetics of the Contemporary Hollywood Blockbuster.* New York: Continuum, 2006.

Chandra, Mridu. "In Conversation: Jehane Noujaim." *Brooklyn Rail: Critical Perspectives on Arts, Politics, and Culture.* www.brooklynrail.org/2004/06/film/jehaneJune 2004. Accessed 1 May 2011.

Chang, Justin. "The Dark Knight." *Variety* 6 July 2008.

———. "Films of the Decade." *Los Angeles Film Critics Association.* www.lafca.net. Accessed 6 June 2009.

Chocano, Carina. "Alfie? Naah, He's Carrie Bradshaw." *Los Angeles Times* 5 Nov. 2004: E1.

———. "'Bridget Jones' Is the Reigning Queen in the Court of Chickdom." *Los Angeles Times* 12 Nov. 2004: E1.

Chomsky, Noam. *Failed States: The Abuse of Power and the Assault on Democracy.* New York: Henry Holt, 2007.

"Cinderella Castle." www.wdwinfo.com. Accessed 15 Oct. 2010.

Cohan, Steven. *Masked Men: Masculinity and the Movies in the Fifties.* Bloomington: Indiana UP, 1997.

Collins, Max Allen. *The Road to Perdition.* New York: Simon & Schuster, 1998.

Corner, John. *Television Form and Public Address.* London: Arnold, 1995.

Corrigan, Timothy. *A Cinema without Walls: Movies and Culture after Vietnam.* New Brunswick, N.J.: Rutgers UP, 1991.

Coyne, Michael. *Hollywood Goes to Washington: American Politics on Screen.* London: Reaktion, 2008.

Crary, Jonathan. *Suspensions of Perception: Attention, Spectacle, and Modern Culture.* Cambridge, Mass.: MIT Press, 1999.

Currid-Halkett, Elizabeth. *Starstruck: The Business of Celebrity.* New York: Faber and Faber, 2010.

Custen, George F. *Bio/Pics: How Hollywood Constructed Public History.* New Brunswick, N.J.: Rutgers UP, 1992.

Dalton, Stephen. "Braced for Critical Impact." *Times (London)* 16 Sept. 2006: 10.

Dao, James. "Carrier Turns Theater for Premiere of 'Pearl Harbor.'" *New York Times* 25 May 2001: A4.

Dargis, Manohla. "Just Try to Stop 'Bourne.'" *Los Angeles Times* 23 July 2004: E1.

———. "Orphan's Lifeline Out of Hell Could Be a Gameshow in Mumbai." *New York Times* 12 Nov. 2008: E2.

———. "Showdown in Gotham Town." *New York Times* 18 July 2008: E4.

Debord, Guy. *The Society of the Spectacle.* Detroit: Black & Red, 1983.

Denby, David. "Angry People." *New Yorker* 81:11 (2005): 110–11.

———. "Past Shock." *New Yorker* 21 July 2008: 53.

———. "Unsafe." *New Yorker* 5 May 2008: 43.

"Diablo Cody." *Yahoo! Movies.* movies.yahoo.com. Accessed 13 Nov. 2010.

DiGiacomo, Frank. "The Lost Tycoons." *Vanity Fair* March 2009.

Diorio, Carl. "Mouse atop Summer B.O." *Variety* 8–14 Sept. 2003: 12.

Doane, Mary Ann. "Pathos and Pathology: The Cinema of Todd Haynes." *Camera Obscura* 57 (2004): 1–21.

Doyle, Sady. "It's All about Bromance." *Guardian* 15 July 2009.

Drake, Philip, and Michael Higgins. "I'm a Celebrity, Get Me into Politics: The Political Celebrity and the Celebrity Politician." *Framing Celebrity: New Directions in Celebrity Culture.* Ed. Su Holmes and Sean Redmond. New York: Routledge, 2006.

Dyer, Richard. *Stars: New Edition.* London: British Film Institute, Palgrave Macmillan, 1999.

Ebert, Roger. "Black Hawk Down." *Chicago Sun-Times* 18 Jan. 2002.

———. "Freddy Got Fingered." *Chicago Sun-Times* 20 April 2001.

———. "Lara Croft: Tomb Raider." *Chicago Sun-Times* 15 June 2001.

Edelstein, David. "Hulk B-a-a-a-a-d: Ang Lee's Green Monster Never Comes to Life." Salon.com. Accessed 19 June 2003.

———. "Indian Love Song." *New York.* 16 Nov. 2008.

Eller, Claudia. "Risky Quest for Treasure." *Los Angeles Times* 21 April 2008.

Elsaesser, Thomas. "The Mind-Game Film." *Puzzle Films: Contemporary Storytelling in Contemporary Cinema.* Ed. Warren Buckland. Malden, Mass.: Wiley-Blackwell, 2009. 13–41.

Everett, Anna. "'Spike, Don't Mess Malcolm Up': Courting Controversy and Control in *Malcolm X.*" *The Spike Lee Reader.* Ed. Paula Masood. Philadelphia: Temple UP, 2008. 91–114.

Farocki, Harun, and Kaja Silverman. *Speaking about Godard.* New York: New York UP, 1998.

Ferris, Suzanne, and Mallory Young. "Introduction Chick Flicks and Chick Culture." *Chick Flicks: Contemporary Women at the Movies.* Ed. Suzanne Ferris and Mallory Young. New York: Routledge, 2008. 1–25

Figgis, Mike. "Into the Abstract." *Sight and Sound* 17:3 (2007): 18–19.

Fleming, Michael. "'Hobbit' Back on Track as Twin Bill." *Variety* 18 Dec. 2007.

Galloway, Stephen. "Film Finance." *Hollywood Reporter* 11 April 2006.

Garrett, Roberta. *Postmodern Chick Flicks: The Return of the Woman's Film.* Basingstoke: Palgrave Macmillan, 2007.

Gates, Henry Louis Jr. *The Signifying Monkey: A Theory of African American Literary Criticism.* Oxford: Oxford UP, 1988.

Gill, Mark. "Yes, the Sky Really Is Falling." *Variety* 15 June 2006.

Glanz, James. "Billions in Oil Missing in Iraq, U.S. Study Says." *New York Times.* 12 May 2007.

Gleason, Carmen L. "Tourists Visit Pentagon Crash Site as Anniversary Approaches." www.defense.gov/news/newsarticle.aspx?id=47359 8 Sept. 2007. Accessed 1 Aug. 2010.

Goldstein, Patrick. "Warners' Films: Movie Overboard!" *Los Angeles Times* 12 Aug. 2008.

Goss, Jacqueline. "Artist's Statement." www.jacquelinegoss.com/bio.html. Accessed 12 Nov. 2009.

Gourevitch, Philip, and Errol Morris. *Standard Operating Procedure: A War Story.* New York: Penguin, 2008.

Graser, Marc. "Attacks Force Rejig of Vidgame Elements." *Variety* 24–30 Sept. 2001: 7.

Greengrass, Paul. "The Treatment." *Written By* 11:2 (2007): 32–33.

Gunning, Tom. "What's the Point of an Index? Or, Faking Photographs." *Still Moving: Between Cinema and Photography.* Ed. Karen Beckman and Jean Ma. Durham, N.C.: Duke UP, 2008. 23–40.

Halbginger, D. M. "Master of 'Rings' to Tackle 'Hobbit.'" *Variety* 19 Dec. 2007.

Hart, Steven. "Who's Sauron—bin Laden or Bush?" Salon.com/entertainment/feature/2004/02/28/lord 28 Feb. 2004. Accessed 30 May 2010.

Hassan, Robert, and Ronald E. Purser, eds. *Time and Temporality in the Network Society.* Stanford, Calif.: Stanford Business Books, 2007.

Hau, Louis. "New Line, Warner Bros. to Merge Operations." Forbes.com 28 Feb. 2008. Accessed 2 Feb. 2010.

Havill, Adrian. *The Spy Who Stayed Out in the Cold: The Secret Life of FBI Double Agent Robert Hanssen*. New York: St. Martin's, 2002.

Hayes, D., and D. McNary. "New Line in Warner's Corner." *Variety* 28 Feb. 2008.

———. "Picturehouse, WIP to Close Shop." *Variety* 8 May 2008.

Hewitt, Chris. "UA93: The Full Story behind the Year's Most Important Film." *Empire* 205 (2006): 96–100.

Heywood, Leslie, and Jennifer Drake. "We Learn America like a Script: Activism in the Third Wave; or, Enough Phantoms of Nothing." *Third Wave Agenda: Being Feminist, Doing Feminism*. Ed. Leslie Heywood and Jennifer Drake. Minneapolis: U of Minnesota P, 1997. 40–54.

Hiscock, John. "Diablo Cody: 'I Feel More Naked Writing Than I Did as a Stripper.'" *Telegraph* 2 Feb. 2008.

Hoberman, J. "The Lord of the Rings: The Return of the King." *Village Voice* 12–23 Dec. 2003: C62.

———. "Meet the Depressed." *Village Voice* 23 Oct. 2001.

———. "Unquiet Americans." *Sight and Sound* 16:10 (2006): 20–23.

Hofmann, Katja. "Does My Gun Look Big in This?" *Sight and Sound* 12:3 (2002): 10–11.

Holben, Jay. "Lords of Illusion." *American Cinematographer* 87:11 (2006): 64–72, 74–75.

Holmes, Su, and Sean Redmond, eds. *Framing Celebrity: New Directions in Celebrity Culture*. New York: Routledge, 2006.

Horn, Geoffrey. "The Katrina Disaster." *The World Almanac and Book of Facts 2006*. New York: World Almanac Books, 2006. 5–6.

Hoskins. Andrew. *Televising War: From Vietnam to Iraq*. New York: Continuum, 2004.

Iggulden, Conn, and Hall Iggulden. *The Dangerous Book for Boys*. New York: William Morrow, 2007.

"Iraqi Families Sue Blackwater in U.S. Court." www.cnn.com/us 11 Oct. 2007. Accessed 13 Nov. 2010.

James, Nick. "The Best Intentions." *Sight and Sound* 12:9 (2002): 3.

———. "Own Goals All Round." *Sight and Sound* 11:2 (2001): 3.

———. "To Be or Not to Be." *Sight and Sound* 12:9 (2002): 14–17.

Jayson, Sharon. "Is This the Next Baby Boom?" *USA Today* 17 July 2008.

Jenkins, Henry. *Convergence Culture: Where Old and New Media Collide*. New York: New York UP, 2006.

"Juno." *The Numbers*. www.the-numbers.com/movies/2007/juno.php. Accessed 13 Nov. 2010.

Kahana, Jonathan. *Intelligence Work: The Politics of American Documentary*. New York: Columbia UP, 2008.

Kaplan, Fred. *1959: The Year Everything Changed*. Hoboken, N.J.: John Wiley & Sons, 2009.

Kelly, Kate. "Defying the Odds, Hedge Funds Bet Billions on Movies." *Wall Street Journal* 29 April 2006.

Kerbel, Matthew R. *If It Bleeds, It Leads: An Anatomy of Television News*. Boulder, Colo.: Westview, 2000.

Kerley, David, and Ki Mae Heussner. "First Photos of Fallen Soldier Ends 18-Year Ban." abcnews.go.com/us 6 Apr. 2009. Accessed 13 Nov. 2010.

Kilborn, Richard. *Staging the Real: Factual TV Programming in the Age of "Big Brother."* Manchester: Manchester UP, 2003.

Klavan, Andrew. "What Bush and Batman Have in Common."*Wall Street Journal* 25 July 2008.

Kracauer, Siegfried. "Basic Concepts." *Film Theory and Criticism*. Ed. Leo Braudy and Marshall Cohen. New York: Oxford UP, 1999.

"LA Critics Name Mulholland Dr. Film of the Decade." *Screen Daily* 12 Jan. 2010.

Landy, Marcia. "'America under Attack': Pearl Harbor, 9/11, and History in the Media." *Film and Television after 9/11*. Ed. Wheeler Winston Dixon. Carbondale: Southern Illinois UP, 2004.

Lane, Anthony. "Hard Times." *New Yorker* 24 Nov. 2008.

LaSalle, Mick. "Drama Crashes through Barriers Already Down." *San Francisco Chronicle* 5 June 2005.

Lauzen, Martha. "2005 Celluloid Ceiling Report." www.films42.com/feature/lauzen-2005 .asp.Accessed 11 Dec. 2009.

Leblanc, Michael. "Melancholic Arrangements: Music, Queer Melodrama, and the Seeds of Transformation in *The Hours*." *Camera Obscura* 61 (2006): 104–45.

Lethem, Jonathan. "Art of Darkness." *New York Times* 21 Sept. 2008.

Lynch, David. *Lynch on Lynch*. Ed. Chris Rodley. London: Faber & Faber, 2005.

Lyons, Charles. "Disney Preps PR Blitzkrieg." *Variety* 30 Apr.–6 May 2001:1, 87.

———. "Family Pics Get a Fix." *Variety* 7–13 Jan. 2002: 69.

McCarthy, Todd. "Cloverfield." *Variety* 16 Jan. 2008.

———. "Spy Pic's Bourne to Be Wild." *Variety* 26 July–1 Aug. 2004: 54, 63.

———. "Ten Years Later, the 'Kids' Are Definitely Not Alright." *Variety* 30 Jan.–2 Feb. 2005: 3, 71.

———. "This 'Hawk' Is All War." *Variety* 9 Dec. 2001: 31, 35.

McClintock, Pamela. "Legendary Soups Up Pic Presence." *Variety* 30 Oct. 2005.

McNary, Dave. "Fests Test Their Traction." *Variety* 7–13 Jan. 2002: 6.

———. "Guillermo del Toro to Direct 'Hobbit.'" *Variety* 24 Apr. 2008.

Mellencamp, Patricia. *A Fine Romance: Five Ages of Film Feminism*. Philadelphia: Temple UP, 1995.

Miller, D. A. "On the Universality of *Brokeback Mountain*." *Film Quarterly* 60:3 (Spring 2007): 50–60.

"Moore Defends Incendiary Film." www.msnbc.msn.com. 18 June 2004.

Morgenstern, Joe. "An Incredible Soulless 'Hulk.'" *Wall Street Journal* 20 June 2003: W1.

———. "When Bad Times Make Good Movies." *Wall Street Journal* 9 Jan. 2009: W1, W6.

Motion Picture Association of America. "The Cost of Movie Piracy: An Analysis Prepared by LEK for the Motion Picture Association." www.archive.org/stream/MpaaPiracyReort/ LeksummarympaRevised_djvu.txt.

Accessed 11 Dec. 2009.

Naremore, James. *More Than Night: Film Noir in Its Contexts*. Berkeley: U of California P, 1998.

North, Dan. *Performing Illusions: Cinema, Special Effects and the Virtual Actor*. New York: Wallflower, 2008.

O'Sullivan, Mike. "New Focus on Celebrity Impacts Mainstream Journalism." *Voice of America News*. www.voanews.com/english/news/ 11 Feb. 2004. Accessed 11 Feb. 2010.

"Pearl Harbor: Reliving History." *BBC News* 22 May 2001.

Peters, Jenny. "Paul Haggis and Robert Moresco 'Crash.'" *Variety* 3 Feb. 2006: A1.

"Presidential Approval Ratings—George W. Bush." Gallup.com. Accessed 13 Nov. 2010.

Proulx, Annie. "Blood on the Red Carpet." *Guardian* 11 March 2001.

Puig, Claudia. "'Bourne Supremacy' Has a License to Thrill." *USA Today* 23 July 2004: 1E.

Rafael, George. "Gosford Park." *Cineaste* 27 (2002): 30–31.

Rafferty, Terrence. "Indiana Jones and the Savior of a Lost Art." *New York Times* 4 May 2008.

Ray, Robert. *A Certain Tendency of the Hollywood Cinema, 1930–1980*. Princeton, N.J.: Princeton UP, 1985.

Rea, Steven. "Law's Englishman-in-NY Turn Has a Hollow Center." *Philadelphia Inquirer* 5 Nov. 2004: W4.

Reed, Ishmael. "Fade to White." *New York Times* 5 Feb. 2010: A25.

Rich, B. Ruby. "Documentary Disciplines: An Introduction." *Cinema Journal* 46:1 (2006): 108–15.

Rich, Frank. "The Jerry Bruckheimer Whitehouse." *New York Times* 11 May 2003.

Richter, Hans. *The Struggle for the Film: Towards a Socially Responsible Cinema*. Ed. Jürgen Römhild. New York: St. Martin's, 1986.

Ricks, Thomas E. *Fiasco: The American Military Adventure in Iraq*. New York: Penguin, 2006.

Robb, David. *Operation Hollywood: How the Pentagon Shapes and Censors the Movies*. Amherst, N.Y.: Prometheus, 2004.

Romney, Jonathan. "Family Album." *Sight and Sound* 12:6 (2002): 12–15.

Ross, Alex. "The Ring and the Rings: A Critic at Large." *New Yorker* 22 Dec. 2003: 161.

Rothenberg, Michael. *Traumatic Realism: The Demands of Holocaust Realism*. Minneapolis: U of Minnesota P, 2000.

Rothkopf, Joshua. "The Tony Top Fifty Movies of the Decade." *New York Time Out*. 1 June 2011.

Ryan, Tim. "'Pearl' of a Prem." *Variety* 28 May–3 June 2001: 67.

Safrath, Bernadette A. "How Improvements in Technology Have Affected the Entertainment Industry: Writers and Actors Fight for Compensation." *Touro Law Review* 6:1 (2010): 115–43.

Sarris, Andrew. "Ang Lee's Angst-Ridden *Hulk*: The Not-So-Jolly Green Giant." *New York Observer* 6 June 2003.

———. "Shrek and Drek? Well, Not Quite." *New York Observer* 10 June 2001.

Schatz, Tom. "New Hollywood, New Millennium." *Film Theory and Contemporary Hollywood Movies*. Ed. Warren Buckland. London: Routledge, 2009. 19–46.

Sconce, Jeffrey. "Smart Cinema." *Contemporary American Cinema*. Ed. Linda Ruth Williams and Michael Hammond. New York: McGraw-Hill, 2006. 429–31.

Scott, A. O. "At the Movies, It Was the Year of 'Yes, But. . . .'" *New York Times* 28 Dec. 2003.

———. "How Many Superheroes Does It Take to Tire a Genre?" *New York Times* 24 July 2008.

———. "Pearl Harbor: War Is Hell, but Very Pretty." *New York Time* 25 May 2001.

———. "Portrait of Genius, Painted in Music." *New York Times* 29 Oct. 2004.

Sedgwick, Eve. *Between Men: English Literature and Male Homosocial Desire*. New York: Columbia UP, 1985.

Sidious, Darth. "Quality!" IMDb.com 23 Dec. 2001. Accessed 31 March 2011.

Stacey, Jackie. "Feminine Fascinations: Forms of Identification in Star-Audience Relations." *Stardom: Industry of Desire*. Ed. Christine Gledhill. New York: Routledge, 1991, 1998.

Stein, Rob. "Teen Birth Rate Rises in U.S., Reversing a 14-Year Decline." *Washington Post* 6 Dec. 2007.

Stewart, James B. *Disneywar*. New York: Simon & Schuster, 2005.

Suskind, Ron. "Faith, Certainty, and the Presidency of George W. Bush." *New York Times Magazine*. 17 Oct. 2004.

Swanson, Tim. "Studios Slip Slo-mo." *Variety* 24 Sept. 2001: 1, 84.

Szpilman, Wladyslaw. *The Pianist*. New York: Picador/St. Martin's, 2000.

Thompson, A. C. "Katrina's Hidden Race War." *Nation* 2 May 2009.

Thompson, Anne. "Dark Knight Review: Nolan Talks Sequel Inflation." *Variety* 6 July 2008.

———. "Diablo Cody Strikes a Pose." *Variety* 7 Nov. 2007.

Thompson, David, and Paul Thomas Anderson. *Altman on Altman*. London: Faber & Faber, 2006.

Thomson, Desson. "'Alfie': Only a Pretty Face." *Washington Post* 5 Nov. 2004: T35.

"A Timeline of the Iraq War." Center for American Progress Action Fund. Thinkprogress.org. Accessed 13 Nov. 2010.

Tollman, Vera. "Foreign Affairs: The Video Work *How to Fix the World*, by Jacqueline Goss." www.springerin.at/dyn/heft_text.php?textid=1627&lang=en. Accessed 11 Dec. 2009.

Travers, Peter. "*The Return of the King/The Lord of the Rings* (Full Trilogy)." *Rolling Stone* 940:22 (2004): 76.

Turan, Kenneth. "Life Is the Answer." *Los Angeles Times* 12 Nov. 2008.

———. "A Wing and a Player." *Los Angeles Times* 17 Dec. 2004: E1+.

Turner, Graeme. *Understanding Celebrity*. Thousand Oaks, Calif.: Sage Publications, 2004.

Ullman, Harlan K., and James P. Wade. *Shock and Awe: Achieving Rapid Dominance*. Washington, D.C.: National Defense University, 1996.

Usborne, David. "How Stone Won Over the Right." *Independent* 29 July 2006: 32–33.

Vercammen, Paul. "Fall Movies Undergo Changes." edition.cnn.com/2001/US/09/26/rec.fall.movies/index.htm126 Sept. 2001. Accessed 3 Dec. 2008.

Vineberg, Steve. "Frodo Finish." *Christian Century* 121:1 (2004): 41.

Walker, Rebecca. *To Be Real: Telling the Truth and the Changing Face of Feminism*. New York: Anchor, 1995.

Walker, Tim. "King of Bromance: Judd Apatow." *Independent* 19 Aug. 2009.

Wapshott, Nicholas. "*United 93*." *Sunday Telegraph* 9 Apr. 2006: 29.

Warner, Marina. *Phantasmagoria: Spirit Visions, Metaphors, and Media into the Twenty-first Century*. Oxford: Oxford UP, 2006.

Wasko, Janet. *How Hollywood Works*. London: Sage, 2003.

White, Jennifer. "Whitman Authorized Editions for Girls." *Vintage Series Books for Girls . . . and a Few for Boys*. www.series-books.com. Accessed 30 Dec. 2009.

Williams, Sally. "*United 93*." *Daily Telegraph Magazine* 5 May 2006: 40–41, 43–44.

Willis, Susan. *A Primer for Daily Life*. New York: Routledge, 1991.

Winter, Jessica. "An Officer and a Gentlewoman." *Village Voice* 27 Nov. 2001.

Wyatt, Justin. *High Concept: Movies and Marketing in Hollywood*. Austin: U of Texas P, 1994.

CONTRIBUTORS

NORA ALTER is a professor at Temple University, where she is the chair of the FMA department. She is author of *Vietnam Protest Theatre: The Television War on Stage*, *Projecting History: Non-Fiction German Film*, and *Chris Marker*.

KAREN BECKMAN is a professor of cinema studies in the department of the History of Art at the University of Pennsylvania. Her publications include *Vanishing Women: Magic, Film and Feminism*, *Crash: Cinema and the Politics of Speed and Stasis*, *Still Moving: Between Cinema and Photography* (co-edited with Jean Ma), and *Picture This! Writing with Photography* (co-edited with Liliane Weissberg, forthcoming).

TIMOTHY CORRIGAN is a professor of cinema studies, English, and the history of art at the University of Pennsylvania. His recent books include *The Essay Film: From Montaigne, After Marker*, *Critical Visions in Film Theory: Classic and Contemporary Readings* (co-edited with Patricia White and Meta Mazaj), and *Film and Literature: An Introduction and Reader*.

ANNA EVERETT is a professor of film and media studies at the University of California, Santa Barbara. Along with numerous essays, she has published *Returning the Gaze: A Genealogy of Black Film Criticism, 1909–1949*. A founding editor of the journal *Screening Noir: A Journal of Film, Video and New Media Culture*, she is currently at work on projects entitled "Digital Diaspora: A Race for Cyberspace" and "Inside the Dark Museum: An Anthology of Black Film Criticism, 1909–1959."

NIGEL MORRIS is principal lecturer in media theory and programme leader for BA Film and Television at the University of Lincoln, UK. His publications include *The Cinema of Steven Spielberg: Empire of Light*; his current research explores media representations of science and technology.

DANA POLAN is a professor of cinema studies at New York University. He is the author of eight books including, most recently, *Julia Child's The French Chef*.

BOB REHAK is an assistant professor in film and media studies at Swarthmore College. He has published essays in the journals *Film Criticism* and *Information, Communication, and Society* as well as in the edited collections *The Video Game Theory Reader*, *Videogame/Player/Text*, and *The Cybercultures Reader*.

THOMAS SCHATZ is a professor of film and media studies at the University of Texas at Austin. He is the author of several books on American film, including *Hollywood Genres, The Genius of the System: Hollywood Filmmaking in the Studio Era*, and *Boom and Bust: American Cinema in the 1940s*, and he has edited many others. He is currently writing a book-length study of conglomerate-era Hollywood.

DINA SMITH is an associate professor of English at Drake University, where she teaches a variety of courses in cultural theory. She has published essays on Audrey Hepburn, the Guggenheim Museum, and mobile homes.

LINDA RUTH WILLIAMS is a professor of film in the Department of English at the University of Southampton, UK. She is the author and editor of, among other books, *The Erotic Thriller in Contemporary Cinema* and *Contemporary American Cinema* (co-edited with Michael Hammond), as well as numerous articles on feminism, sexuality, censorship, and contemporary culture. She is now writing a book on childhood and Steven Spielberg.

SHARON WILLIS is a professor of art history and visual and cultural studies at the University of Rochester. Her books include *Marguerite Duras: Writing on the Body, Male Trouble* (co-edited with Constance Penley), and *High Contrast: Race and Gender in Contemporary Cinema*. Her current project is entitled "Islands in the Sun: The Civil Rights Movement and Its Legacies in Film, 1949–2003."

INDEX